Count Me Out

Selected Writings of Filmmaker Bob Quinn

Edited by Toner Quinn

Published by
Boluisce Press
An imprint dedicated to culture and ideas
From the publishers of *The Journal of Music*
An Spidéal, Co. Galway, Ireland
www.journalofmusic.com

ISBN 978-1-7395774-2-1

Cover design: Laura Rooney
Cover: Bob and Robert Quinn, Cinegael, 1976 (Photo: Jimmy Murp
Printed by CPI

The Journal of Music is supported by the Arts Council/An Chomha
Ealaíon.

The publication of this book was made possible through the gene
support of the following:

Acadamh na hOllscolaíochta Gaeilge, Ollscoil na Gaillimhe,
An Cheathrú Rua, Conamara
Grattan Healy
Telegael
TG4
Bill Whelan

Do Saise, Samir, Katie, Jamie, Cal, Jacob, Leo, Ruby, Oliver agus Oisín

Contents

Introduction

These days, my father and I meet once a week. From Leitir Péic in Conamara I drive the half-hour west along Cois Fharraige and through the moon-like landscape of Bóthar Loch an Iolra to the townland of Tuairín, where Bob's dwelling is almost entirely hidden from thirty years of tree-planting. He is now 89 and there are always practical things to discuss, but we are rarely in the mood. Instead, we continue on to the village of An Cheathrú Rua where in the early evening we have our choice of seats in An Chistin pub and we settle down to talk about what matters – writing, thinking, ideas, music, the world.

It has always been like this. My father is known as a filmmaker, photographer and writer, but beneath these pursuits is a relentless inquiry. That is why his artistic work is so polymathic, from the anarchic *Caoineadh Airt Uí Laoire* to the first Irish-language feature film *Poitín* to the intellectual explosion that is *Atlantean*. 'A low threshold of boredom,' is his bald explanation, but there is more at play of course.

I have heard many different versions of my father's public story, but the bones of it are true: in 1969, he walked out of employment with RTÉ as a protest against commercialism, published a damning critique of the broadcaster, made a controversial appearance on the *Late Late Show*, and then took refuge with my mother Helen and their young baby in the Conamara Gaeltacht. After three years of trialing a number of careers, from writing television columns for the *Western People* to selling toffee apples to creating political batiks, Bob returned to making films as a result of the Gaeltacht Civil Rights Movement, set up a company named Cinegael, and he and my mother opened a small cinema. Over the next number of years, Cinegael produced a series of radical works that changed the course of Irish film.

But Bob's cultural effect reached beyond that. Throughout the 70s, 80s and 90s he was also an outspoken and often ferocious critic of the broadcasting and film establishment, insisting that filmmaking was an art first and not simply an industry. In this, as in many endeavours, he was sailing against the wind. But there were always other ways to challenge the consensus. In 1987, he and a number of Irish-language activists set up a pirate television station in Conamara that eventually led to the founding of the channel TG4. The impact on the Gaeltacht and the language was profound. He also railed against consumerism and the impact of television advertising on society, and in one chat-show appearance emptied a black sack of domestic refuse out at the presenter's feet. In 1995, in a twist worthy of Hollywood, the Minister for Arts, Culture and the Gaeltacht, Michael D. Higgins, appointed Bob to the RTÉ Authority. Twenty-six years after he walked out of the broadcaster he was back – and with no lessening of his reforming views on Irish broadcasting. A one-line postcard from a friend captured the moment: 'The lunatics have taken over the asylum.'

Bob set about proposing his reforming agenda in RTÉ – banning advertising towards children, regionalisation of the service, clear lines between editorial content and advertising, encouraging new talent, and more independence for programme-makers – but his ideas soon hit organisational thinking. Without serving the full term, he resigned and published his controversial book *Maverick*, blowing the whistle on how RTÉ worked on the inside. 'RTÉ was out of control,' he wrote. He was not thanked. On RTÉ radio he was accused of being 'disloyal' and his thinking was dismissed as naive and impractical. Angry but not surprised, Bob returned to Conamara, continued planting trees, producing films, writing books, and photographing life around him.

There is a cultural lesson in what happened next. In the summer of 2023, twenty-two years after *Maverick*, RTÉ became engulfed in another crisis because of the very issues that Bob had been trying to address, and suddenly his thinking and solutions became mainstream. I asked him what he thought of the fact that the ideas he proposed two decades ago were now being discussed on daytime radio. 'Of course,' he said.

Ever since I was young, I was conscious of being 'Bob Quinn's son'. He seemed to attract both curiosity and regard – the man who made *Poitín*, who heard a connection between Conamara sean-nós and North African music, who suspended his membership of the RTÉ Authority every Christmas in protest against advertising towards children, who spoke his mind, refused to fit in and made things difficult – this applied at home as much as in his work. One morning at secondary school, the Vice Principal sidled up to me: 'Have you read that book yet?' he demanded. It turned out he was referring to *Smokey Hollow*, Bob's fictionalised memoir that had just been announced in the papers.

I didn't always know what my father was doing. After my parents separated, my siblings and I lived in Bray, near Dublin, and Bob returned to Conamara, where the family had previously lived from 1970 to 1980. Henceforth, for every school holiday – summer, Halloween, Christmas and Easter – we would travel west to Galway on the three-hour train to live another life for weeks or months at a time in the Gaeltacht with Bob, Miriam and our two new younger brothers. It was a house where artists would arrive unannounced and stay for days, dinner conversation was bracing, music was played into the night, and every morning I would be woken by the sound of Bob's tapping on the typewriter, or later a computer, downstairs.

'I have to invent my reality every day,' he would tell me. It was true. Unlike other fathers, he didn't seem to have a job, but he never stopped working. He lived in an old factory by a lake and his office was at the end of the house with my attic bedroom above it, so his work patterns were always known to me.

The day would begin in the kitchen with black coffee, pipe smoke, collecting the post and reading the *Irish Times*, and then – in a mini eruption – the paper would be folded and cast down on the table. 'Half-nine and not a child in the house washed!' he would pronounce, then disappear down to the office.

The working day would be punctuated by an ink-jet printer screaming as it tried to work through whatever script, book or finance-raising correspondence he was working on. While printer paper fell to the floor, he would march up the corridor for a lettuce sandwich, or walk around the house with his hands behind his back, thinking, pausing to foot the turf or shake his head and pick up a child's bike left rusting in the rain, then remind us to hang up our togs and towel from the beach, and return to the office.

When he wasn't working, there were events to attend or matters to be seen to: one of my teenage memories is travelling at night through South Conamara with Bob, checking every pub's television for the signal from the Irish-language pirate television station. On other occasions it might be an exhibition in Clifden, a screening in Derry, or a Gaeltacht community occasion that needed support. But while everyone sat dutifully and listened to whatever was taking place, Bob would wander around the action and take photographs. The camera was his freedom. He refused to sit and conform, regardless of what was taking place or who was there, clinging to his creative approach no matter what was happening.

And people seemed to love him for it. They stopped him on the street to engage in conversation about his *Atlantean* theory; when we screened *Budawanny* together one summer in Galway, the audience would come around to the projectionist's box afterwards and tell him how affecting the film was; the phone would ring and it would be Mike Scott from the Waterboys or Bono from U2. Everyone wanted to talk to this man, who didn't seem to care what he said or who he was talking to.

When I was 23, Bob told me he was going to India with his camera. I invited myself and my fiddle along and we were joined by his close friend, Denis 'Dinno' Ryan. Beginning in Goa, we journeyed down the west coast by train to Kochi and Kerala and then back up again to Mumbai. Each evening, we would drink, smoke and discuss this extraordinary Indian culture, drawing comparisons with our own music and history, trying and failing to understand.

But it was on that trip that I learnt to talk to Bob, and he learnt to talk to me, and that is why we still enjoy a good conversation. When we meet in An Chistin, we go back and forward discussing the madness of the world, but generally agree on Bob's philosophy, which he draws from Antonio Gramsci: *pessimism of the intellect, optimism of the will*, which basically means that, while ultimately doing anything about anything may be futile, you have to be doing something.

An rud a bhíonn sa chú bíonn sé sa choileán – whatever is in the hound is in the pup. In one such pub conversation, I suggested to Bob that we put together a collection of his writing. I was conscious of the young artists and thinkers who still make their way to his door, who look to him for perspective in the confusing place that is the world today. A book of his writing would at least provide one insight: how to achieve the impossible, with very little, and when everyone says you are wrong.

This collection, dating from the 1960s to the 2020s, provides some indication of the range of topics that have occupied him over seven decades of artistic, activist and intellectual work. The essays and articles document his exploits in film and broadcasting, his travels and campaigning, his love for Conamara, and include some startling experiences too. They capture something of his extraordinary life, and will, I am sure, start many new conversations.

Toner Quinn
Leitir Péic, An Spidéal
Nollaig 2024

Part I

Conamara Revolution
Réabhlóid Chonamara

A Letter to RTÉ
(Sit Down and Be Counted, 1969)

Clare Island
Wednesday, 14th May 1969

Dear Friends and Colleagues,

Over the past couple of years, it will have become apparent to the more perceptive among you that RTÉ (henceforth to be known as the Factory) has been developing along certain regrettable but inevitable lines.

These tendencies towards a large, impersonal technocracy have been justified on the grounds of efficiency, the same grounds on which the wholesale exploitation of the resources of this country by our speculative leaders is based. In this sense, the Factory is fulfilling one of its functions, i.e. the reflecting of the country as a whole. This of course is ignoring one of its other, equally important functions, the educational one. It is also ignoring the fact that one has not only the duty of reporting fairly what is happening, but if the situation is serious enough, of intervening personally, not as an organisation man, but as a man.

The Factory, as we are all aware, has grown into a large organisation. Organisations are not run by people. They are run by the systems which people invent to avoid the business of thinking. Eventually the people become functionaries of the systems, in some cases, happy functionaries, in most cases, vaguely dissatisfied employees. The liberal conservative would describe the latter category as an expression of the human condition. This is not only rubbish, but dangerous rubbish. The human condition is defined by man; the degrees of its comfort or discomfort are the direct responsibility of man.

What can one person do?

When confronted by a monolith which proposes to eat you, even in the nicest possible manner, you must do something. The worst thing to do is to allow the monolith to define the terms of the battle. Ignore its pleas for logic, because it uses logic to obscure the truth; ignore its calls for reasonableness, the assumptions and premises of which are entirely questionable; query its sacred cows, its gods and its liturgies, its systems, its impeccable phrases imported from the respectable corruption of business management. Ignore above all its offers of a comfortable place in the technocratic womb; its bribes of security, status and free burial service.

Having ignored all of these expressions you will find yourself out of a job. And you can't afford this because you have a mortgage, an overdraft, a hire-purchase agreement and a realisation that you were never free. So you will not follow the advice in the preceding paragraph. That is when the organisation laughs.

What all this amounts to is that you can do absolutely nothing. You are completely trapped. You must now enter a period of despair, in which you will fulfil your functions in a perfect mechanical, unthinking, organisational manner. And this is all that is required by the system of organisation in which you work. And that is why the organisation decays and becomes a bloated and swelling corpse, feeding the increasing number of parasites but incapable of directing itself because there is no life, no human spirit to quicken it.

This I suggest is the situation in which the Factory finds itself. This despite the efforts of bright young men in advertising agencies to string gaudy beads round the neck of the corpse, the vile body, in an effort to persuade the people of this country that their property is still working on their behalf. It is not. It is simply a vehicle for the frustrated fantasies of ad-men, the megalomania of insane technocrats and the sanctification of the acts of a conservative government. If one looks closely at those lines, one will see evidence of the greatest sell-out ever perpetrated on a nation – by the nation itself, through its sons.

And what do I propose to do about it? Mine is a personal philosophy of responsible irresponsibility. It attempts to counter the organisation's pseudo-philosophy of irresponsible responsibility. If you follow me. I propose to get a boat and sail off, Charlie-Bubbles-like, into the setting sun. All contributions will be tolerated, and appreciated if they're in the form of moral support.

Yours sincerely,
Bob Quinn

Count Me Out: The Cultural Evolution of a Television Producer
(Sit Down and Be Counted, 1969)

Following Bob's departure from RTÉ, producers Lelia Doolan and
Jack Dowling also resigned and published the book Sit Down and Be
Counted: The Cultural Evolution of a Television Station, *which*
included the following chapter by Bob.

Statistics
'Those Platonists are a curse,' he said,
'God's fire upon the wane,
A diagram hung there instead,
More women born than men.'
– W.B. Yeats

… for the world, which seems
to lie before us like a land of dreams,
So various, so beautiful, so new,
Hath really neither joy, nor love, nor light,
Nor certitude, nor peace, nor help for pain;
And we are here as on a darkling plain
Swept with confused alarms of struggle and flight,
Where ignorant armies clash by night.
– from 'Dover Beach' by Matthew Arnold

B ob Quinn first showed signs of 'instability' at the age of twenty-
one. In the bleak year of 1957 he left the pensionable womb of
the Civil Service to tour the world.

Intending to make his fortune, he got as far as working on a farm
in Bavaria. There he learned some earthy phrases.

In the following four years before he joined the embryo RTÉ,
he engaged in seventeen different occupations. He became proficient
at two: pub pianist and bus conductor. In addition he had been a
commercial traveller, English teacher, travel courier, freelance

journalist and, not least, washer of Coca-Cola bottles. When occasion offered he involved himself in the theatre.

His social background had been 'improving working-class'. He had a mystique of this class which was, perhaps, pardonable. If allowed, he would tend to talk rather vaguely about the essential worth and dignity of the individual person. Even to those people who had not the ability or the desire to conform to middle-class standards, he attributed a meaning which transcended their social status. Any ordinary man could think as imaginatively or even as metaphysically as any theologian or philosopher. At least their conclusions, he felt, were equally worthy of respect.

Burdened with these simple ideas he joined Radio Telefís Éireann as a trainee studio operator in 1961.

He was one of thirty young men, drawn from many occupations, selected as the raw material from which the operational staff of the new service was to be moulded. Everybody had their own fantasy about this new, complicated world of television. A common one was that television was simply an extension of show business; another held that it was a sort of parlour game. There was also a powerful view that it was going to 'educate' the nations.

Quinn's particular fantasy was a combination of all three. Television was a place where theatrical people could get a regular salary for trying out ideas that hadn't worked in the theatre; balancing this was the view that television was a vehicle for cosy discussions about fashion, flying ducks on the wall, plastic fruit arrangements and holidays in a place called 'Barthelona'.

Whatever their separate fantasies may have been, many of the young men felt a lack of fulfilment and started doing 'nixers'. These were part-time jobs like private recordings, freelance filming, wiring houses, etc. There was even one excellent chimney sweep. Quinn's outlet was writing ponderous satire for the press and occasional radio writing.

Two years after he joined the service he was offered three jobs: Programme Assistant in radio, trainee continuity announcer in radio, and Producer-Director in television. The glamour of this last appointment claimed him.

Now his unresolved adolescent idealism came to the fore. He had a chance to articulate the views and attitudes of the Silent Majority. This, he thought, was the great mass of intelligent working-class people who were just waiting for the chance to speak. He aimed to give them their long-denied opportunity.

There gradually dawned on him a realisation of what his producer colleagues had long known: television talent in a country of this size is in short supply. Put a witty, even brilliant, docker in a studio and he shrivels up into his Sunday suit. Some of Quinn's colleagues were equally frustrated by this discovery; but they were aiming higher. They were looking for Sammy Davis in Ballyferriter.

In the course of producing shows like the *Late Late Show*, *Club Céilí*, *Open House*, *Ailliliú*, etc., this depressing fact was borne in on him, that the studio atmosphere had a lot to do with this striking-dumb effect. He tried Outside Broadcasts, where at least the participants were comfortingly near their own environment. But again the oppressive paraphernalia of television cameras and lights ultimately inhibited the very people he had hoped would be encouraged to speak.

Meanwhile he was learning other and harder facts of life, this time about politics. While organising the original *Open House* forum programme, he discovered that not he, the producer, but the party whips were to choose the participants. When, in his innocence, he mildly objected to this, his views were dismissed as melodramatic.

In another, the first *Ailliliú* with Seán Ó Riada, he associated the United Irishmen's charter, the UN Declaration of Human Rights and the first Selma march with a photograph of Jim Larkin. It was conveyed to him that the basic philosophy underlying this association of ideas was not approved.

However, being an apolitical animal, he was concerned with other things: such as how he might help the real owners of the national television service to use it themselves. He still had the apparently quaint idea that the docker should have his say.

Quite by chance he made a film. It was about new methods of kindergarten education and, because children are invariably box-office material, it was well received. Quinn was assigned to *Discovery*, a documentary film series.

Film was a godsend. A 16mm film camera is less obtrusive and consequently less inhibiting than the electronic television camera. Physically, it is smaller and its lightness means that a dexterous operator can use angles and capture moments that would require hours of preparation for the electronic camera. At this stage RTÉ seemed to be unaware of the existence of equally flexible electronic equipment.

However, Quinn learned that the film camera did not dominate the environment as much as the television cameras. Not that it was a passive recorder of 'magic moments'. It created its own version of reality. But at least it didn't frighten the life out of performers. If used with a certain kind of humility towards the subject it could, at least as well as words, imaginatively evoke the essence of that subject. And if the camera appeared to lie, it was because its director was lying.

Quinn, then, had a most flexible instrument of expression. It allowed him to escape the studio strait-jacket. It was, also, a more personal medium. In the studio, any personal contact a director might build up with a performer ran the risk of being bludgeoned by three cameras, third-degree lights and the deathly spell of a countdown. Using film in, say, the performer's home, the director and crew entered into an intimate relationship with him.

There was a grave danger here of course: it was much more difficult to preserve that distance so apparently necessary for 'professional' objectivity. Quinn found it impossible not to get involved in his subject. This became a problem when he was expected to churn out a half-hour documentary film for *Discovery* every fortnight.

After a number of films he decided that justice could not be done, at least by him, to a serious subject under such limitations. In 1964 he requested a transfer to the gentle pastures of religious programmes. The consensus was that he must be out of his mind. The prevailing attitude to religious programmes considered this area to be a sort of limbo to which erring producers were sent for their sins.

His desire coincided with a request for his services by the Religious Adviser, Romuald Dodd, OP.

Fr Dodd was, and is, a man of wide humanity. He gave Quinn his trust and a freedom to make programmes which was unequalled in any other area of the station. As a direct result of this intelligent use of authority, Quinn's subsequent work was considered good enough to represent RTÉ internationally on at least six occasions. Quinn noted with surprise that when a position of Head of the Religious Department was created in January last, Fr Dodd was ignored.

Apart from directing the studio Mass, *Horizon* discussions, *Word in Action* and *Outlook*, his main work was in documentary films. In his first effort for the department – a series of films on *The Psychological Development of the Normal Child* – he made a discovery. Discussions with a psychologist, Francis Forde, OMI, and a scriptwriter, Jack Dowling, introduced him to the relationship between subjectivity and objectivity. Given the distinct possibility of his having misinterpreted these men, he understood it thus:

A child of three years sees a bus coming towards him. To the child, that tiny dot moving in the distance is actually growing into an immense and noisy monster. The bus literally grows, and not in any adult's metaphorical sense. The child is believing its eyes. As the bus departs it actually grows smaller. To the child, that is the simple truth of the matter. Every other visual thing has the same quality. Even the child's parents are small at one end of the room, large when they move up close. Only the child has the good sense to stay the same size! In order to survive in this chaos, to reduce objects and people to the same consistency as himself, the child is eventually forced to perform a rational act.

Stated crudely, he forms a mental 'picture', then an abstract concept which he calls 'bus'. This bus stays the same size because his intellect abstracts a consistent idea from the welter of changing sense-impressions.

In this way the child has started to organise his world into a manageable system. As he develops this capacity he will realise that each time he meets an object he need not go through the laborious process of correlating his sense-impressions and forming his own concept. There is a short cut. There are people around to supply him with these concepts. He discovers one of the functions of his community.

He is, of course, forced to qualify to a large extent what his eyes and ears, his individual and subjective senses, tell him. There is thus a tension set up between what he subjectively knows and what he objectively learns to know. The child is, in part, learning not to believe his eyes. But the reward is survival.

The only difficulty about this arrangement is that what he objectively learns (even this secondhand information) comes through these same 'deceitful' eyes and ears. Further to compound the awkwardness is the fact that the people from whom the child learns must be similarly handicapped.

Quinn, strangely, derived some personal reassurance from this phenomenon. He had often had grave reservations about the validity of his personal opinions. This new knowledge gave him some confidence. However, he decided to ignore for the moment its social implications. He resolved to find out what kind of perceptual disability could cause a child to think and say 'The Emperor has no clothes'.

In collaboration with a fine audiologist, Mother Mary Nicholas, OP, and the scriptwriter, Jack Dowling, he produced a film called *The Silent World*. This was a study of deafness and its implications. It is still used in the training of teachers of the deaf.

In this study of the deaf, what was emphasised again to Quinn was the fact that all the information that is the basis of our ideas, comes through our senses. This was not to say that we understand things by means of our senses. It simply meant that before we understand anything, we have to receive it sensibly. This was a revelation to somebody who had been led to believe that the ultimate truths were conveyed to us by a mysterious system of communication called Revelation. The latter consisted, in his mind, of an image of the Holy Ghost cutting a hole in one's head, so to speak, and pouring truth into it. Long afterwards he was introduced to the difficult notion of the truth contained in metaphor and analogy, but at this stage he had no access to such ideas. The only hole in the head which Quinn could see was the earhole.

This was an introduction to the process by which we learn. There was also the problem of expression.

If you can't hear words, he learned, you can't speak. If you can't speak you can't express yourself verbally or musically. And if you can't express yourself you are locked into a silent, 'atomic' and individualistic world. Quinn saw evidence of the amazing extent to which verbal and visual interplay between human beings is realised. They derived their personalities from others. Without this mutually creative interplay people would remain vegetable or, at best, animal. What price then the blossoming of the Human Spirit?

He saw the deaf as a dramatic symbol of the predicament in which the majority of people could find themselves individually and collectively if, as he thought, they did not have access to the media of group expression. If most people were regarded as the 'great unwashed', or the 'masses', incapable of grasping the finer points of human aesthetics, they were surely in the same quandary as the deaf. And the deaf were regarded traditionally as gesticulating dummies. They obviously couldn't speak in their own defence.

However, in Mother Nicholas' clinics, Quinn saw the dumb open their lips and speak!

He saw children who had hitherto been taught a primitive set of signs – the 'dummy sign-language' – actually communicating with words. He saw how they grasped complex ideas, impossible to master with signs. He actually saw them experiencing the aesthetic pleasures of music. They literally 'felt' the music by means of its vibrations on relatively simple equipment.

Human beings, up to now considered inadequate, could be introduced to dimensions of human exhilaration and imagination previously considered totally beyond them. Applying this to the 'mass' of people, Quinn realised their eminent educability. There seemed to him to be some sort of parallel between the work of the speech therapist he had met, and the professional business in which he was involved.

He realised now that the problem of educating people was not fundamentally one of educability. It was a question of: who is considered worth educating? It comes down to the esteem in which the human person is held.

He continued to make religious and social programmes, among which was *Why Don't They Shoot People?*, the second of two films about disabled persons.

In another, he examined the mental processes of a poet in the consumer society. In this society, the presence of a God was intuited rather than evidenced. The title of the film was *Missing, Believed Dead.*

A film called *The Island* considered, perhaps somewhat romantically, the worship patterns and attitudes of an isolated community. In *Many Hands Make Life Work*, the principle of co-operation was examined as a means of restoring rural confidence in the small farmer and one's neighbour, as the basis for community building and economic salvation.

By this time his original concern for the 'Silent Majority' had become an 'obsession' with the underdog, the socially deprived, the have-not and the deviant. The 'norm', as advertised on telly, he decided, did not exist.

Quinn next turned to the subject of autism. This was a form of mental illness considered at the time to be peculiar to the children of intelligent middle-class parents. Its more dramatic symptoms were absolute withdrawal from human relationships and an obsession with the manipulable world of objects. It was suggested that the seeds of this condition were latent in everybody.

A further film attempted to describe the tensions of living in a corporation housing estate. It was called *The Flowerpot Society*, which indicated the problem of young people transplanted from organic communities in central urban parishes like City Quay to the fresh air of Finglas, Co. Dublin. It mentioned that the last thing considered worth erecting was a community centre. In an effort to describe the personal costs of a worthy, but shabbily carried out, social plan it featured housewives attending a local psychiatric clinic. One of these interviews, in which the lady was visually and vocally well disguised, constituted the climax of the film. It was excised before transmission, without Quinn's knowledge or consent, by well-meaning authorities in RTÉ.

One of the images retained by Quinn from his preparations for this film was a housewife watching television with her five children. They were attentively watching commercials for the affluent society. He wondered at the time if it was seriously held that that woman could or should aspire to the goodies so tantalisingly held out to herself and her children. A psychiatrist he had consulted in connection with this film introduced him to the concept of 'cognitive dissonance'. He used it to describe the pathological tension set up in that woman's mind by the discrepancy between the way 'normal' people were expected to live and her personal experience of what she could expect.

Like many of his countrymen, Quinn at this point was slightly confused. None of the tendencies he had noted fitted peacefully into the traditional concepts of community and society. Television was obviously contributing to the situation in no small way; so rather than go ahead blindly 'getting on with the job', he decided to declare a personal inquest. Principally he wished to acquire a frame of reference with which to study the 'Consumer Society' towards which we were heading. He also wished to see if it worked for others. He decided to go to the source.

In September 1967 he was given generously subsidised leave of absence and spent the winter in a university in Nova Scotia, Canada. There he attended courses in sociology and read voraciously.

In the course of his studies he was impressed most by:

1. Role Theory – The 'I'm only doing my job' syndrome.
2. The effect of institutionalism on good ideas. (He particularly noticed the assessment of the fate of charisma and personal integrity in different kinds of organisations. It helped him to understand the condition of Christianity as well as the secular world.)
3. The discrepancies between manifest and latent function in enterprises.
4. The relationship between culture and personality.
5. Anthropological descriptions of 'primitive' verses 'civilised' cultures.

As was his habit he tried to relate all this to the reality around him. Canada was described as the second richest country on earth. In the 1961 census it was established that the wages of 47.9 per cent of the labour force were below the officially defined poverty level. They had, apparently, learned how to create wealth but the technique of distributing it evaded them.

Canada was also described as a 'cultural mosaic'. In 1965 *The Vertical Mosaic* by John Porter was published. It detailed precisely how the power complexes, interlocking directorships and corporate monopolies made, not only individual aspirations, but even the concept of 'private' enterprise appear as simple lip-service to an ideological strait-jacket. It also gave figures showing the control, through outright ownership as well as in blocks of shares, that the United States exercised on the Canadian economy.

As far as the respect for ethnic and cultural idiosyncrasies implied in the 'cultural mosaic' idea was concerned, Quinn saw the French in Quebec so enraged with the situation that they were on the verge of civil war with the federal government.

In the same predicament, but reacting differently, were the Indians. The Micmacs were a tribe Quinn visited often. In their school (state-run) there was not a shred of evidence to indicate to the children that they had a group identity quite different to the white man's. They knew nothing of their history and their language was not a formal school subject. After school they watched the television cavalry making mincemeat of their television ancestors. This was on the same programme that carried endless commercials and other items that urged them: 'You have no existence as a separate group. Forget your identity, jump into the melting pot and become white, clean homogeneous consumers like the rest of us'. The Micmacs, however, seemed to find this difficult. The average life expectancy for a male Indian was 33; for a female, 36. They had developed the habit of making their own moonshine and drinking themselves to death.

Quinn decided he would inspect the other half of this continent. With a Dominican priest, he drove to New York, across to Chicago, down to New Mexico, westwards to California, up the West Coast and returned across the 4,000 miles of Canada. They spent three months and 12,000 miles driving, looking and listening.

They discussed and argued all the way on the various aspects of the culture they were experiencing.

They noted that New York had the highest proportion of walking schizophrenics in the world. The Manhattan Survey of 1965 indicated that four-fifths of the population of that part of the metropolis was emotionally disturbed. They experienced the four-hour physical and mental strain of driving across rush-hour Chicago. They noted how the auto-freeway 'Howard Johnson Eatery' motel complex made it difficult to actually encounter the land or its people. It sealed off from the casual observer the 10 million people who lived in squalor, the many others living in poverty. They remembered the President's Council of Economic Advisers assessment: 33 to 35 million Americans were 'living at or below the boundaries of poverty in 1962 – nearly one-fifth of our nation'. America seemed to have the same problem as Canada: how do you share wealth? But one rarely saw evidence of this state of affairs. It was all camouflaged in a plastic efficiency that tended to whisk them from one chromium environment to another. It was a smooth, comfortable non-existence.

At the end, both agreed that it was all very worrying and casual imitators would best be wary. Quinn had walked through Harlem, Berkeley, Albuquerque and Seattle; he had listened to cold discussions by police chiefs on the latest in anti-riot weapons; he had spoken to the people on whom these weapons would be used. He had previously, in theory, learned about the cultural arrogance and egocentricity that enabled the richest country in the world to rationalise its destruction of one of the smallest countries in Asia. Now it was preparing to act similarly on its own citizens. He didn't wonder, then, at the despair of a journalist who said to him in a bar in San Francisco: 'The Great Experiment has failed'.

Quinn returned to Ireland in August 1968 to resume his work with RTÉ. He noticed that a certain apathy had settled on the station. He also noticed the flowering of business terminology, the increased emphasis on systems-analytic descriptions of 'problems', the obsession everybody had with costings. The station had all the verbal trappings of a factory, as well as the alienation of the employees of such an enterprise.

He noticed, with a sharpened sensibility to such things, the Americanism of the service's output, both sound and television. This was especially noticeable on radio, possibly because it had always been evident on television. The crudely inserted commercial jingles produced a remarkably accurate impersonation of the many brash, small-town radio stations he had heard in the US. There seemed little indication that it was the sound of an Irish broadcasting service. The occasional interpolations in Irish seemed to him to have all the authenticity of Bing Crosby singing 'Top o' the Morning'.

The main midday news bulletin was so patently and unsuccessfully an attempt to simulate the synthetic excitement of America that he felt the Head of News would have done better to have employed actors rather than misuse the talents of excellent journalists. He noticed that the majority of European Continental news reports were spoken by Americans. It seemed to him obvious that English-speaking Continentals might have had a better insight into the workings of their own internal affairs. On enquiry in the newsroom he was told that a better and more economic service was provided by American agencies.

Quinn was to start work on a new series which was to be orientated to home-making. It was natural that he should think the social, cultural and economic contexts in which people make their homes to be relevant. This series would have been the natural successor to *Home Truths*, as no other programme in the schedules covered this area.

However, the Programme Controller of television made it quite clear that this programme must discuss nothing more complex than do-it-yourself gardening, home-making, etc. It was to avoid controversial topics of consumer interest. He recommended the Irish Countrywomen's Association as a valuable source of material, which indeed it was.

Quinn felt that if we were aiming at a full-blooded consumer society in the American style, and RTÉ was actively, through commercials and canned films, endorsing this, the least it might do was to provide a consumer advisory service. This could play a valuable part in educating our viewing public into the intricacies of such a society, with open discussion of possible pitfalls. This was of course assuming that the public had voluntarily decided to become such a society. However, he learned that there was to be no place for these wider considerations in the proposed programme.

Assessing his impression of the television organisation, Quinn decided that it had moved into a new phase, far removed from the fairly open atmosphere in which he had worked before. It appeared now to see its function as a passer-on of policies and decisions formulated somewhere 'up there', rather than an investigator and commentator on the texture of Irish life. Quinn was happy neither about the latter nor about the sort of society RTÉ was permitting and assisting in bringing about. He decided to withdraw his formal professional support from the organisation rather than acquiesce in a process which he did not like. He resigned his stall status, indicating clearly that he would be available in the future on a freelance basis, to do work he felt moved to do. He left on quite amicable terms, at no time having expressed his disquiet in terms of personalities.

He then bought an old car and drove to Iran and back. He experienced the way of life, or culture, of eight different peoples and was able to compare their richness with the sterility of our adoptive one.

Returning in January 1969 he offered his services to RTÉ and was given a contract. He was assigned to produce a history series for schools. This was to be done in conjunction with the Department of Education who finance and who largely control the operation of *Telefís Scoile.*

Through reading and conversations with the experts he eventually grasped an idea of the nature of history, particularly its subjective nature. Any historical account is intended by somebody to make somebody else think something. Value-free history is impossible.

Hitherto, he knew that Irish history had been taught as a series of woeful anecdotes showing how we had suffered under British imperialism. This was because we were a small country struggling to preserve our identity and sense of nationhood. Very properly, the new line for schools was to play down the emotional aspects of our history and to concentrate on the texture of Irish life in the past. At that time Quinn saw nothing sinister about this, although he did find it remarkable to be told that, really, the Famine wasn't the major catastrophe we had been led to believe; anyway, its worst effects were felt mainly in the West. The Pale was relatively healthy. Further, the viciousness of the landlords had been greatly exaggerated. They weren't all bad; nor was life in the Empire too bad either.

Since then Quinn has often speculated on the possible reasons for such a *volte face*. He thinks it is probably a coincidence that our revolutionary past might be a bit of an embarrassment to a country which now openly aligns itself with the counter-revolutionary countries of the Western World.

However, he proceeded with the task of organising an educational series. This was the point at which he met The Organisation, whose formal orientation was towards efficiency and which was openly applying the techniques of business management to broadcasting.

He requested film facilities informally, was asked to put it in writing, did so and waited. After a fortnight he contacted, in the appropriate department, the people who had asked for the early requisition of facilities. They could not allocate facilities yet. They were awaiting a decision from above. Quinn noted that bureaucracy was making inroads and thought it paradoxical that this was happening in the name of systematisation.

Quinn started to apply the principles of education, on which he was actually working, to the social phenomenon of television itself.

He was aware that we in Ireland were emerging from the stagnation of a traditional academic concept of education. This formal, functional process had often obscured the true nature of the educative process. A person is educated by everything that enters his mind, captures his attention and retains his interest. Everything that entertains, educates. If it is entertaining, television will educate. If it is entertaining, the worst canned rubbish or the most insidious commercial will educate and form the mind of the viewer. In an environment increasingly influenced by television, it seemed likely that few would escape this mind-forming effect.

Quinn considered the sort of consumer mind, the absorption in trivia, that would be the result of viewing RTÉ over a long period. It could do little damage to those who already thought superficially or those who could afford other forms of entertainment. There were some who do not fall into these categories: the Irish communities in the West; the lower-income urban groups; the many people who have not the desire or, perhaps, the means, to achieve immediately the form of affluence presented as desirable on RTÉ. Quinn speculated that when a voice as authoritative as the national broadcasting service urged on its viewers a particular way of life, it was likely to be believed. The viewer's subjective assessment of his own aspirations would be rather shamefacedly repressed. If this happened often and to enough people it would surely result in a national state of cognitive dissonance; we would rapidly approach the stage where all of the people would be fooled all of the time.

Quinn considered other aspects of the broadcasting situation. He was familiar with the conventional wisdom, the 'common sense' rationalisations that made discussion of the problem difficult. By pretending that audiences were unappreciative, that there was no 'television talent' in the country, that engineers were unimaginative, producers unreliable; by advertisers pretending that they financed the service completely, by bureaucrats pretending that new forms of accounting were the answer; by all of these and many more, everybody was excusing the bad programmes and avoiding the necessity for considering the effect of the service on the community. Everybody was simply getting on with the job. This was a reasonable reaction because the problem was so complex it made the mind boggle.

Quinn tried very hard to ignore it, to persuade himself that somebody somewhere was sorting it all out. He failed.

Quinn was one of many people whose concern had been to keep the television organisation human. He had seen the efforts (and supported them when possible) of people like Jim Plunkett Kelly, Jack Dowling, Lelia Doolan, Aindrias Ó Gallchóir and many others, to keep the system sensitive to the needs of the programme makers. Despite major eruptions like the *7 Days* affair, when staff protested a management decision to mute the current affairs programme, he felt that a condition of progressive atrophy had seized the station. He felt that the main barrier to the making of good programmes was the commercial strait-jacketing of schedules. The frustrations always experienced in making programmes had intensified and were a logical outcome of trying to work within a programme schedule dictated by a commercial framework.

This framework appeared to be the only aspect of the problem, the only given premise, that was not considered open to change. Quinn sounded out some of his colleagues on the possibility of forming an internal group to study the effect of commercial advertising. The reaction was a wry: 'And accept Government control? Where would the money come from? Don't be daft!' Quinn had personally decided that the social costs of continuing the present commercial broadcasting set-up were probably infinitely greater than any loss in revenue.

He remembered reading a book called *The Politics of Experience*, by R.D. Laing. In it the psychiatrist author suggested that in this age of 'senescent capitalism ... Can we do more than sing our sad and bitter songs of disillusion and defeat?'

So what could he do? What could anybody do who wasn't good at sad and bitter songs? Shut oneself in a comfortable £2,500 p.a. job and make 'safe' programmes? The alternative was to publicly draw attention to one's misgivings and show that, at least, one could personally withdraw unquestioning support from the process. There was really no choice. He just counted himself out.

The RTÉ Supermarket
(Western People, 20 February 1971)

After the publication of Sit Down and Be Counted, *Bob made a contentious appearance on the* Late Late Show *with Lelia Doolan and Jack Dowling. At the time he was living in London. He subsequently moved back to Ireland, settled in the West, and began contributing to magazines and newspapers.*

'A self-opinionated, bombastic swine ... a rudderless intellectual drop-out who can't see the wood for the trees'. These are some of the names I was publicly called after my one and only appearance on RTÉ fifteen months ago. You can imagine how nervous I am, then, at further commenting on our national broadcasting service. However, at the risk of being bombastic again I have to say that I am in a unique position to comment on RTÉ. Beside the fact that it was my spiritual home for eight years, my bias towards it is, unlike most critics, crystal clear. I can't pull the wool over your eyes. For anyone who has been dead or interned for the past couple of years it might be as well to spell out this bias:

I regard radio and TV as potentially the most magnificent instruments of social communication; they are the means by which we might understand each other, at long range. Therefore, our present use of these instruments as soap-vending machines I regard as a very obscene expression of man's inhumanity to man. RTÉ's constitutional claim to be educative, informative and entertaining can only be supported by someone who has the misfortune to be both deaf and blind. Instead of social communication, RTÉ provides one-way communication – a monologue of advice to consumers during which we sit down, watch, listen and are counted!

After nearly ten years of it we must accept this situation and no longer pretend it is otherwise.

It was no accident that this country's drive towards economic expansion coincided with the initiatives to set up Telefís. If you manufacture something you have to persuade people to buy it. If you want a consumer economy you must create a climate of acceptability. Telefís was as much a part of the First Programme as T.K. Whitaker.

We can ignore, as the Government of the time did, the fact that the original TV Commission recommended a non-commercial service. The Commission was as naive as the rest of us in thinking that TV could be preserved from the claws of political and commercial speculators.

It was decided that RTÉ would be (as an English Lord described commercial broadcasting) 'a licence to print money.' Money for whom is a question beyond the scope of this piece. Ask Seán Lemass.

However, now let us, as the whizzkids say, face it.

For the best part of last week I lay on my back in Galway Regional and tried to do precisely that. Each day I listened to Radio Éireann from 8am until 5.30pm. Then I watched Telefís until closedown.

Was I nauseated? Was I irritated? Did I put my foot through the screen? Did I throw my transistor in the spittoon? I did not. I lay there and was massaged by the great mindless mediocrity of it all. It was chewing gum for my eyes and my mind. It did not disturb me: the perfect place for the patient.

Now if this country were a gigantic hospital and we were all bored, mildly distressed inmates, RTÉ would be providing a very useful service: something to distract us from our predicament – nothing to unsettle us. In fact, to reverse this delightful idea, if RTÉ is considered to be fulfilling a useful function then we must be all patients in a gigantic hospital. You can see why they called me bombastic.

But how else can you accept Liam Nolan's fantasy that the entire population consists of pious old babushkas; Larry Gogan's assumption that there are no adults in the country – only fifteen-year-old showband followers; Frank Hall's pre-scripted notion that all inhabitants outside the Pale are illiterate County Councillors; Gay Byrne and Valerie McGovern's smooth implication that between 5.30pm and 6.30pm all the children of the nation are cherished equally in a traffic jam at Ballsbridge?

I busied myself in hospital by inventing a popularity poll among our radio and TV personalities. It consisted of awarding an Indecent Exposure Trophy to the person who presented the most programmes. Guess who won? A staff employee? Mike Murphy? Charles Mitchel? Brendan O'Reilly? You're miles away. With a top score of twelve programmes per week, plus what sounded like a hundred commercial voiceovers, Larry Gogan won hands down.

Now the funny thing I noticed was that ten of Larry's twelve programmes were not made by RTÉ at all. They were the products of advertising agencies. It struck me as a little odd that somebody who, in the vast majority of his work, is not employed by RTÉ, is not responsible to RTÉ or to any producer in RTÉ – that he should be the one whose personality and ideas we are most exposed to on RTÉ.

In fairness I should add that with ten programmes – half of them commercial – the runner-up was Gay Byrne. If the rules of the competition had allowed husbands and wives to join forces, Kathleen's two sponsored programmes would have ensured a draw between Gay and Larry.

To sum up these idle convalescent musings: RTÉ is quite nice in spots – as when the *Late Late* is stimulating (a tribute to the sheer insurance man's professionalism of Gabriel – he says so himself); the service is temporarily satisfying when Liam Nolan does not interrupt an interview by somebody else; it is transiently superb when it features Alastair Sim in *Misleading Cases*; but in my perhaps apocalyptic view the overall impact of RTÉ in toto is in the selling racket. Communal aerials are a symptom; the station's real business is in the selling of a way of life, the plastic consumer way of life. RTÉ's message is: *buy*

And what, as Quinnsworth founder Pat Quinn might say, is wrong with that? Radio and TV are good business. Yes, ladies! There is absolutely nothing wrong with it – as long as we realise it, RTÉ admits it and stops expecting us to pay for a licence.

The staff of RTÉ admitted it a long time ago – about May 1969 in fact. If I am to believe my friends in Montrose and Henry Street, most of them are now openly devoting their talents to obtaining jobs in the managerial hierarchy of the Organisation. Like the small farmer of the West, the job of TV or radio producer has achieved an all-time low in status.

Agreed, some people are ignoring the general mess and bravely plodding away at making good package-deal programmes like *Amuigh Faoin Spéir* or *Radharc*. There are even a few mavericks within the stations who refuse to accept the situation. They produce a magazine called *Feedback*, which Dónall Ó Móráin, Chairman of RTÉ, has admitted to reading in order to find out what is going on.

People in the East of this country are quite happy with RTÉ. They simply ignore it and watch BBC or ITV – as was discovered in a census of Ballymun viewers a little while ago: little more than fifteen per cent watched the home station!

But in the West, if we want to watch television or listen to radio, we're stuck with RTÉ. But then, do even we watch it? In the hospital last week, in a ward of four men I was the only viewer. Where were the rest? Very sensibly they had formed a card school. RTÉ could not compete with Twenty-Fives!

Maybe there's hope for us yet.

Saor-Raidió Éireann?
(*The Irish Times, 6 January 1971*)

In 1970, the Irish Government announced that an Irish-language radio service would be established. In this article, Bob interviews people in the Gaeltacht about the initiative.

In Tigh Mhóráin, a pub in the Connemara Gaeltacht, the news on television was in Irish. The barman approached me. He is a native speaker. 'What's that all about?' he asked. I explained that the item in question was about internment and inquired why he could not understand his own first language. 'Ah, they use words and accents I never heard before,' he said.

This is not to slight the Gaelicised newsreaders on RTÉ. A lady in Loch Con Aortha told me that her favourite newsreader in Irish is now Charles Mitchel. Up to quite recently his vocabulary was limited to '*Oíche mhaith agaibh*'.

Nor is the anecdote to introduce another laboured discussion on our native tongue – although mention of the proposed Gaeltacht Radio Service appears to stimulate only this dreary topic. In fact, despite the widespread assumption that the proposed radio is another 'revival' gambit, the achievement owes little to conventional language-movement tactics. The plan announced by Minister George Colley is the fruit of a movement whose relations with official revivalism can best be described as cool.

But insofar as the language is involved – and obviously it is – the significance of the barman's reaction is this: Gaeltacht language is idiomatic and grows from a way of life; the RTÉ or Dublin equivalent is 'book Irish' – a valuable intellectual exercise which nevertheless is seen to be of little immediate relevance to the needs of the Kerry, Galway and Donegal Gaeltachts. In this lies a pointer to the thinking behind the successful demands for a Gaeltacht Radio. The nature of 'Irish' activity outside these areas is almost exclusively cerebral; in the Gaeltachtaí it is integrated with a socio-economic lifestyle. To enable the latter wholeness to bear witness to itself in a twentieth century manner would seem to be the hoped-for function of the proposed service.

How have people whom Alasdair Micawber (as he is referred to here) describes as 'human debris … in their rock-bound ghettoes' attained the sophistication to ask for and get a service which seems aeons from the dole and the summer visitor? Might one suspect the workings of adventurers, pressure groups, agitators, a visionary band? The answer is, simply, yes – and choose your epithet carefully; the Apostles were considered subversive. The provision of a radio service for the Gaeltachtaí is largely the result of comprehensive agitation over a two-year period by a small number of people, most of them associated with Gluaiseacht Cearta Sibhialta.

There are two points here to be clarified: First, the activists did not operate in a social vacuum. Unlike 'Maoists', they are all of the Gaeltachtaí. Further, the people whom they represent do not appear to be the numb creatures they are occasionally painted as. Their reaction to the Bogside drama testifies to this. In Carna, for instance, over £300 was collected and its value in goods delivered personally by a local shopkeeper to the besieged. This is significant because the first practical headline for using a pirate radio as a means to achieving the real thing came from Radio Free Derry. From this emerged Saor-Raidió Chonamara and thence the stimulus to have an official station developed. It is possible that the Gaeltacht people saw an affinity between the Bogside ghetto and their own situation.

The second point is this: unlike popular activists' boasts, the Gaeltacht agitators would not claim to have beaten the radio service out of the Establishment. On the contrary, they all testify to the fact that both RTÉ (whose draft plan Mr Colley adopted) and Government circles seemed favourably disposed to the idea from the start. One gets the distinct impression that they are all a little taken aback at the promptness with which their suggestions/demands were met.

To ask some of the non-militant people about the service is initially disappointing – especially if you are mad about media. However, when one realises that not everybody is a McLuhanatic and reduces the pace to an intelligible level, the interest emerges.

In the Connemara Gaeltacht the poor self-image first shows: 'we'd have to get experts down from Dublin to run it' and 'Who'd leave a good job in the city to come down here?' are typical. When it is pointed out that Saor-Raidió Chonamara was put on the air entirely by non-Dublin people, interest revives.

Strangely, the attitude of Donegal Gaeltacht dwellers appears to be the opposite. A recent meeting of Coiste Troda na Gaeltachta in Bunbeg wanted assurances that the station would not be run by people 'from the South'. I understand the meeting broke up in disorder.

A mechanic in Rosmuc found the idea intriguing, though his first impressions were that the service would be a mass purveyor of sean-nós singing and *scéalaíocht*. Certainly his (and most other people's) ideas of an Irish radio service are derived from material traditionally provided by Radio Éireann. This material he did not find particularly attractive even though it is, presumably, directed at him, a native of the Gaeltacht. In fairness, he did say that he made a point of listening to an Irish programme every morning – from Cork. He also gave the opinion that the novelty of the service would persuade himself and his fellows (young men) to listen until the station went off the air at night. Then they would tune in to Radio Luxembourg as usual.

Very few go round madly debating the topic. In the pub I mentioned earlier, initiating a conversation on the matter was a delicate operation. But once begun, it flowed freely. What would they like to hear on the radio? All agreed that ideas about bringing a microphone into a pub to capture scintillating gems of conversation would be doomed. 'All they'd talk about is cattle and the weather. Pub talk, that's all – the same as you'd get in England or America.' The barman said there was one thing he'd like to hear on the air: 'The doings of this Parish Council. They're meeting down there all the time and we only hear secondhand what they're deciding.' The Parish Council is a recent innovation here and is, itself, an exercise in democracy. That the radio could be seen as a possible instrument of extending this democracy was interesting.

In south Connemara a grocer said: 'What is it? Wouldn't the quarter million be better used on roads or houses?' I found myself with the invidious task of pointing to the commercial advertising uses to which broadcasting can be put. This aspect is greeted with enthusiasm. (In fact, the grapevine says that the RTÉ powers are not in favour of it being a commercial service.)

A publican's son, educated in Dublin, said it wouldn't make any difference to life in the area. 'Still,' he added, 'if it's going, we might as well have it.'

For those who fear subversion under every twisted bed, the attitude of the secretary of the recent successful Oireachtas na nGael and prominent member of Cearta Sibhialta, Pádraic Ó Concheanainn, would be reassuring. He sees the radio service simply as one of many necessary services for a community which has been deprived of everything except handouts. He did not couch his point of view in ideological language, unless one considers 'uniting the geographically scattered people of the fíor-Gaeltachtaí' as such. 'Their own radio service will give them confidence,' he said.

The publican who housed the last edition of the pirate/pilot radio and who appears to be rare among the businessmen of Connemara in his approval of Cearta Sibhialta's activities, is of a similar mind: 'It might persuade the young people that there's more than rocks in Connemara.'

A schoolteacher voiced a majority view when he said it was difficult to pronounce judgment on the proposed service before anything concrete existed. His wife ventured: 'It all depends on who is in charge' and named Pádraic Ó Raghallaigh of RTÉ as a man who would have the sensitivity to run such a delicate affair.

In the still tight-knit communities of the Gaeltacht, approval for a project often depends thus on the personalities involved. It is natural in a society that is not yet object-oriented, but this is not conducive to speculation in the abstract on a future physical format of the radio service.

A group of 14-year-old schoolgirls had heard of the new radio. One said she would like a job in it and they all said it should be located in their own parish.

Which leads to one point that does appear to provoke a strong reaction among the people involved: the location of the proposed stations. In the Connemara area, Carraroe has been designated by the planners. This peninsula, some miles off the main Galway road, would have appealed to an urban planner (and possibly a politician) because there is a relatively dense population there. It also has an incipient industrial estate and happens to be the favoured working-place of Dubliners seeking the summer sun. The station is to be located in the south and in west Connemara. Carraroe is in the south. A Rosmuc man, on the next peninsula, might easily view a station in the former area in the same light as he now considers Henry Street.

Those who ventured a thoughtful opinion on this subject said that a neutral and more central site, say in Camus, would have been more judicious.

If the foregoing gives the impression that little soul-searching has been, or is being given to actual broadcasting concepts, it may be because of the suddenness of Dublin's decision to grant the technological boon. It is not more than two years since the possibility of a Gaeltacht radio service was first mentioned (*en passant*, in this paper, by Deasún Fennell). Realistically, one would expect such a major initiative to require a longer gestation period.

However, the idea was enthusiastically grasped by Cearta Sibhialta and built into its own ambitious programme. A journalist member, Seosamh Ó Cuaig, wrote a piece in *Inniu*, inviting technical help from those interested. This led to a young Cork graduate, Mícheál Ó hÉalaithe, joining forces with Connemara man, Seosamh Ó Tuairisg, to lay the technical foundation for Saor-Raidió Chonamara which went on the air at Easter last year. It was a quite daring step, because contact with RTÉ had already shown that organisation's willingness to organise a full service for the Gaeltachtaí. Fortunately, the pioneers' action did not prejudice the matter as, in September last, Mr Colley was able to announce definite plans for an official network.

This unusually easy compliance with their aims probably accounts for the reserved manner with which Cearta Sibhialta received the announcement. As one member said: 'We'll wait and make sure it's not just another electioneering gimmick.'

Raidió Pobail
(Comhar, May 1971)

In this essay from the Irish-language journal Comhar, *Bob discusses his concerns regarding the influence of commercialism and RTÉ management on the proposed new radio service for the Gaeltacht, and also provides his own ideas on the venture.*

Ó cheart is éard atá i seirbhís raidió ná pobail ag comhrá le chéile. Is iomaí bealach atá ann le leas a bhaint aisti: dallamullóg intinne a chur ar dhaoine; bolscaireacht pholaitíochta; fógraíocht a dhéanamh ar ar an tomhaltachas nó siamsaíocht a choinneáil le héisteoirí éighníomhacha. Ach go bunúsach cuireann sé barr biseach teicneolaíoch ar an *social grapevine*.

Ó tharla gur rud úrnua é is ar an mbonn idéalach seo ba chóir Raidió na Gaeltachta a thógáil. De réir a chéile maolóidh cora crua an tsaoil an aidhm ach is cuma sin; níor cheart feacadh orlach ón móraidhm ghlan le linn na pleanála.

Tá roinnt mhaith samplaí de sheirbhísí raidió pobail ann cheana féin.

Ar an gcéad dul síos, féach ar na Stáit Aontaithe; tá níos mó forbartha déanta thall ansin ar an raidió pobail ná mar atá ag aon tír eile. Is beag mionbhaile nach bhfuil stáisiún raidió ann, is é á á rith ar cheadúnas stáit agus i bhformhór na gcásanna é faoi cheannas fhear gnó, fear gaimbín. Forbairt phragmatach atá déanta acu; airgead a rialaíonn an tseirbhís agus cothaíonn sé sin gaol níos láidre idir an lucht éisteachta agus luach na n-earraí san ollmhargadh. Tríd is tríd is lábánta, lodartha, suarach an tseirbhís í. Ní hé go ndúirt bean liom go ndúirt bean léi é seo ar chor ar bith; chonaic agus chuala mé féin é.

Mar fhreagra sóisialach ar an stáisiún bradach Radio Caroline a thosaigh an Bhreatain ag bunú seirbhísí áitiúla. Is ar éigean a d'éirigh leis an mBBC a scór stáisiún áitiúla a stopadh ó lomaithris phopúil a dhéanamh ar Radio Caroline. Anois, ar ndóigh, tá cead pleanála tugtha ag na Tóraithe d'fhir ghnó suas le 70 stáisiún tráchtála áitiúil a chur ar bun. Tá na Sasanaigh ag leanacht sampla na Meiriceánach.

Is fiú a lua ag an bpointe seo go bhfuiltear ag tabhairt cúl de bheagán le fógraíocht teilifíse. De bharr taighde a rinneadh sna Stáit níltear chomh cinnte anois, agus a bhí, go ndéantar mórán brabaigh as fógraíocht chostasach teilifíse. Is mó ná ariamh an t-airgead atá á infheistiú sa tseirbhís raidió. Tuigtear anois go bhfuil an raidió tábhachtach agus tairbheach.

Dá mba rud é go leanfadh Raidió na Gaeltachta sampla na Breataine agus Mheiriceá ní bheadh ann ach mar a bhíonn Radio Éireann idir 1in agus 3in (i lámha na bhfógróirí) agus bheadh Bill Fuller i gceannas air. D'fhéadfadh sé go dtarlódh sé. Má tá smacht ag Eamonn Andrews ar an *Catholic Standard* céard a stopfadh Fuller ó bheith ina cheannasaí ar Raidió Gaeltachta? Ní bheadh stró ar bith ar Dolly McMahon fógraíocht a dhéanamh do Theach Furbo i nGaeilge bhinn bhlasta. Má cheapann tú gur seafóid é seo smaoinigh ar phointe a luaigh mé in alt liom sa *Western People* le gairid: gurb é Larry Gogan an duine is minice a chloistear ar an tSeirbhís Náisiúnta Craolacháin cé nach bhfuil sé ar fhoireann RTÉ ar chor ar bith agus, dá bhrí sin, nach bhfuil sé freagrach do phobal na hÉireann.

Ach seans nach ndéanfar baileabhair chomh mór sin de Raidió na Gaeltachta. Bheadh faitíos ar na húdaráis go bpléascfaí san aer é. Sin an chúis is mó b'fhéidir nach bhfuil sé i ndán don tseirbhís Ghaelach a bheith ina lagaithris ar Radio bocht, tnáite, clóite Éireann. Ina cheann sin tá cumhacht mhorálta agus pholaitiúil ag an dream a throid ar son na seirbhíse nua.

Na daoine seo a bhunaigh Saor-Raidió Chonamara, féadfaidh siad dhá bhrí a bhaint as flaithiúlacht Cholley dar luach £¼ milliún.

(1) gur seift é lena mbéal a dhúnadh; gléas teicniúil a thabhairt dóibh a chuirfeadh ar a gcumas a nguth a ardú tuilleadh agus gurbh amhlaidh a dhúnfadh sin a mbéal sa deireadh;

(2) Ar an taobh eile, b'fhiú a bheith dóchasach; gurb amhlaidh atá na húdaráis ag éirí tuisceanach agus gur cúis áthais dóibh cabhrú le beart a dhéanamh sa nGaeltacht féin.

Cé go bhfuil cáil na ciniciúlachta orm, bheinn dóchasach gurb é cúis a (2) atá fíor.

Dúirt mé ar ball gurb ionann seirbhís raidió agus pobail ag comhrá le chéile. Bíonn fáilte roimh strainséirí freisin, ar ndóigh, agus roimh chúléisteoirí.

Is strainséir mé féin anseo i Ros Muc, ach mura bhfuil dul amú orm níl muintir na Gaeltachta sásta go bhfuil RTÉ ag comhlíonadh a ndualgas ar an mbealach atá mínithe agam. Méadaíodh a míshástacht tar éis dóibh blaiseadh a fháil de Shaor-Raidió Chonamara mar ní hamháin gur eiseamláir maith a bhí sa Saor-Raidió den chaoi ar cheart raidió pobail a bheith, ach 'sén chaoi go ndearna sé smidiríní de mhistíc seo na 'proifisiúntachta' atá ag plúchadh na simplíochta atá ina bunchloch ag seirbhís raidió ar bith.

Tá airgead geallta ag na húdaráis anois chun seirbhís raidió a bhunú sa nGaeltacht. Abraimis go bhfuil siad thar a bheith dáiríre faoin scéal. Faoi láthair is í an bhainistíocht thionsclaíoch an chloch is mó ar pháidrín na n-údarás céanna agus iad ag leagan amach saol na hÉireann. Ní bhaineann sé seo le cúrsaí tionsclaíochta amháin; féach RTÉ mar shampla: is é prionsabal an tsochair agus an dochair a riarann é, prionsabail an line management agus an fhiontair phríobháidigh. Caolseans go n-athródh siad a bport sa gcás seo – rud a d'fhágfadh Raidió na Gaeltachta ag brath ar na prionsabail chéanna.

Nuair is mian le fear Gaeltachta a ghnó féin a thosú is iondúil gur comhlacht de chuid an stáit (Gaeltarra) a dhéanann meas ar fhiúntas an togra agus má shásaítear iad, tugann siad deontas fial dó. Ba thogra thar a bheith tábhachtach é Saor-Raidió Chonamara agus shílfeá go ndéarfadh na húdaráis an rud loighciúil: 'a chairde, chruthaigh sibh gur dream cumasach sibh. Rinne sibh an beart seo as bhur stuaim féin ar bheagán airgid. Ní bheidh sibh gan airgead níos mó; seo chugaibh £¼ milliún agus coinnígí suas an dea-obair.'

Táthar ann a déarfadh nach bhfuil an mianach, an dúthracht ná an tseasmhacht i muintir na Gaeltachta leanacht orthu, ach níl ansin ach deargamaidí. Bhréagnaigh an Saor-Raidió an tuairim go bhfuil sé de nós traidisiúnta againn beag a dhéanamh dínn féin.

Ach de bhrí go bhfuil cúrsaí cumhachta agus polaitíochta mar atá, níor chualathas smid ó na húdaráis. Ceannródaithe a bhí i lucht an tSaor-Raidió ach níorbh fhiú leis na húdaráis aird a thabhairt orthu. Ina áit sin thosaigh na cora crua a luaigh mé ar ball á sníomh féin thart ar gheallúint an rialtais agus á cúngú dá réir.

Tá sé soiléir anois gurb é RTÉ a rithfidh an tseirbhís nua. Tá RTÉ, mar a d'admhaigh Seán Lemass, ina ghéag de pholasaí an rialtais.

Nuair a chuimhníonn tú ceart air, nach aisteach gurb í an eagraíocht a rinne an oiread sin faillí ar mhuintir na Gaeltachta gur thogair siad Saor-Raidió a bhunú, a bheidh i gceannas ar an tseirbhís nua.

Bíodh sin mar atá, caithfear féachaint céard is féidir a dhéanamh laistigh de na teorainneacha atá á leagan síos ag na húdaráis.

Rud suntasach, mar shampla, is ea an leas atá á bhaint as an teileafón i gcúrsaí craolacháin le blianta beaga anuas. Teach ar bith a bhfuil teileafón ann, d'fhéadfá a rá gurb ionann é agus stiúideo a bheith ann. Cuirtear ar chumas an compere fanacht ina shuí i stiúideo oifigiúil agus tá deis ag an lucht éisteachta páirt ghníomhach a ghlacadh sa gclár; an clár a dhéanamh go hiomlán iad féin beagnach. Níl an oiread sin teileafón sa nGaeltacht ach tá na hallaí damhsa sách fairsing ann. Seachas dul i gcostas le trí mhórstiúideo faoi mar atá beartaithe, nár chiallmhaire i bhfad trí cinn bheaga a thógáil agus fuílleach an airgid a chaitheamh ag feistiú micreafón agus gléasanna méadaithe fuaime sna hallaí seo? D'fhéadfadh lucht Oifig an Phoist iad a cheangal go héasca leis an stiúideo láir agus ar an gcaoi sin bheadh deis ag an bpobal trí chéile lámh a bheith acu sna cláracha gan a gceantar féin a fhágáil.

Níl an moladh sin chomh haisteach agus a cheapfá; bhain Teilifís Éireann an-leas as teicníc den chineál céanna agus iad ag déanamh cláracha feirme roinnt blianta ó shin.

An t-aon bhac amháin a bheadh ar an moladh ná go bhfuil dearcadh áirithe fíorchoitianta sna seirbhísí craolacháin go dtí seo, sé sin nach bhfuil sa raidió ná sa teilifís ach gléasanna le cur ar chumas réimse faoi leith daoine 'gairmiúla' a dtuairimí a bhrú ar thréad 'caorach'.

Ní shásódh tada iad seo ach stiúideo mór feiceálach a léireodh a dtábhacht féin. Agus, ar ndóigh, ní dhéanfadh sé cúis go deo cuireadh a thabhairt d'Easpag na Gaillimhe seirbhís raidió a oscailt i gcarbhán nó i seomra os cionn tábhairne.

Ceann de na ceisteanna is tábhachtaí atá le socrú is ea cé a bheidh ag obair sa stáisiún nua.

Arís is é mo bharúil go gcuirfidh na húdaráis an fhealsúnacht a mhínigh mé ar ball i bhfeidhm, sin cur chuige na mbainisteoirí tionsclaíocha. Tá an-seans go deo ann go dtoghfar fear atá in ann a chruthú go bhfuil sé fíoréifeachtach ag déanamh ispíní ina cheannasaí ar an tseirbhís. Má chinntíonn sé go leanfar ag craoladh de réir sceidil áirithe, beidh leis. Ní hé fiúntas an ábhair chraolta a bheas tábhachtach.

B'fhéidir go bhfuil mé róghéar ach maithigí dom é mar go bhfaca mé le mo shúile féin an mhísc atá déanta ag an eagraíocht a bheidh ag rith na seirbhíse. I ndáiríre bheinn dóchasach faoi Raidió na Gaeltachta. In ainneoin na laincisí a chuirfear air, beidh buntáiste amháin aige nach bhfuil ag Radio bocht tnáite Éireann; beidh sé ag freastal ar phobal faoi leith, ní ar an dream sin atá imithe ar seachrán agus a léiríonn a 'n-indibhidiúlacht' i gcanúint Lár-Atlantaigh an Bhéarla. Chomh luath is a bheidh deis acu, cloisfear glór mhuintir na Gaeltachta agus ardóidh sé leis go gcaithe siad díobh seanchuing na craoltóireachta. Cá bhfios nach é Raidió na Gaeltachta a leigheasfaidh na galair iomadúla atá ar RTÉ!

The Landlord Who Passed Back a Handsel Pound
(The Irish Press, 7 May 1971)

After twelve months living in rural areas and my first winter away from the city lights I have not yet run screaming back to Dublin. In fact, I'm beginning to like it here. There's a lot to be said for waking up on a spring morning and seeing the blue sea on one side of the bedroom and the Twelve Bens on the other.

But it's not just the touristic Conamara scenery. Nor is it the exotic dimension which the language gives to the place. I would venture that the most attractive part of the Gaeltacht is the mode of living – as exemplified, say, by the landlord.

Recently he visited us from Dublin. I gave him a month's rent (£10) and he felt the occasion should be celebrated. After a couple of hours in the local hostelry I ran out of cash. He called me into the gents and insisted on handing me back £2 of the rent. Then he went up to the baby (a well-known pub-crawler) and handselled it with another £1. It wasn't that he thought we were hard up. Money was simply not an end in itself for him.

We had already experienced this with our previous landlady. She made a bad first impression by striking a price for her cottage and then saying she had made a mistake and required double the amount. But all she was doing was testing the market; anybody who came to live in Conamara in the depths of winter must be a rich eccentric.

When I indicated that we were no such thing she was quite happy with the original sum – again, £10 per month! When we were leaving she returned three pounds to us – 'for luck'.

In the first week of our residence a couple of neighbours called and welcomed us to the area with a head of cabbage and a bottle of poitín. It was the first of innumerable gifts – spuds, drinks, turf and eggs. For weeks afterwards the landlady supplied us with fresh milk and eggs. When we left she presented a hand-knitted cap to the child. People who are so patently generous must be fairly content. Why, then, has there been so much agitation in the Gaeltacht recently?

I live a few hundred yards from Pearse's cottage in Rosmuc. Recently I saw a line of twenty cars pulling up outside it. The crowd entered, paid homage to the shrine of free, Gaelic and revolutionary Ireland and drove away, probably to Galway and Dublin. They ignored a pretty cottage in which live a couple with eight children, the eldest fourteen. This cottage has neither running water, electricity or gas. The husband is on the dole. They are thinking of getting gas for cooking and illumination. Why not electricity? Because the grant for private enterprise gas is much bigger than nationalised electricity.

Further up the road a family of five live in a caravan. They have been there all winter.

Further again is my nearest neighbour. A bachelor, he lives in a tiny caravan. He was on the dole up to a fortnight ago. Now he has one cow, a small vegetable patch and few sheep to live on until November when the dole returns.

Then there is us. We live in a fine house beside the main road, surrounded by freshwater lakes. But we have no running water. A piped supply has been promised for a long time. But Galway County Council moves slowly.

It also tends to look after the part of the county, the East, where most of the rates originate. Which seems reasonable, if one ignores the fact that a lot of its funds come from a central Government account.

Helly and I were judges at a beauty contest in the school recently. It wasn't the flesh parade type of contest. Fourteen girls, picked at random at the céilí, answered questions to establish their personality, sense of fashion, civic-mindedness, talent and deportment. The main point that emerged was that most of them would be willing to stay at home if they could earn even £8 per week. As it was, they all anticipated having to emigrate. There is no work for them in this parish.

Things like this have spurred on the young people of the Gaeltacht to form themselves into a Civil Rights Movement (Gluaiseacht Cearta Sibhialta na Gaeltachta) which has recently been causing a shindig.

I imagine the shade of Pearse is looking out approvingly from its cottage down the road.

The Dole as Fuse
(This Week, 7 May 1971)

In 1971, the Irish Government announced that the dole would be cut for single men under 50 living in rural areas. In this article, Bob writes about the response from Gluaiseacht Cearta Sibhialta na Gaeltachta.

'A s of now there are at least 800 potential revolutionaries in the Connemara Gaeltacht alone,' commented a member of the Civil Rights group to me on the day the dole was withdrawn. You could have arms crises, credibility gaps, split Ard Fheiseanna and the people would just shrug their shoulders. But stop the dole and you had them thinking.

Gluaiseacht Cearta Sibhialta have held three meetings in Connemara to discuss publicly what can be done. The first thing they have decided is to extend their dole campaign to all rural areas. This means the Gaeltacht taking an initiative on a national scale, a significant development in an ever-growing movement that is only two years old.

The sort of statistic that gives Cearta Sibhialta its dynamic is the following: in 1946, sixty-three infants were baptised in Gorumna and Lettermullan. Today, of those twenty-five-year-olds, fifty-two are in England, eight in America and three remain in Ireland. In late '69 members of Cearta Sibhialta painted out the English versions of road signs in Connemara. Kevin Boland wrote to one of the members saying that he was taking steps to arrange for all-Irish signs. Last week the original signs were being restored to the bilingual state. On Thursday the signs were uprooted and broken. Cearta Sibhialta have not at the time of writing taken credit for this act, which means that the message has reached a broader-based and non-passive audience.

One of Cearta Sibhialta's most recent acts was to declare war on Comhairle na Gaeilge, the Government advisory body. The latter suggested that the Gaeltachtaí be given the same whizz-kid treatment as Shannon Free Airport. The Civil Righters reject any suggestion that outsiders be brought in to make the Gaeltachtaí 'viable.' This attitude – which includes an equal condemnation of Dublin Gaelgeoirí's well-meaning ideas – has caused some concern in such circles. Bodies like Conradh na Gaeilge feel that the Gaeltacht agitators are throwing them out in the Galltacht cold – which is precisely Cearta Sibhialta's openly expressed wish.

A Gaeltacht authority is the aim. Sick of fifty years of Dublin mismanagement of their affairs, the militants will settle for nothing less than complete self-determination. Their two-year campaign has already achieved a number of things: the promise of a Gaeltacht radio service; the serious consideration by Colley of their own plan for a Local Authority; the stealing by their candidate, Peadar Mac an Iomaire, of 1,500 first preferences in the '69 General Election – this is strong Fianna Fáil territory; the organisation of a tremendously successful Oireachtas na nGael in competition with the Dublin version; the successful defiance of the Broadcasting Act with a pirate radio last year.

The recent Dún Chaoin march was a sort of climax. It co-ordinated the efforts of all Gaeltachtaí in an assault on Dublin and the offices of Roinn na Gaeltachta. With four marchers arrested, cries of police brutality, an emotional *Irish Times* leader and a *Féach* programme exclusively devoted to it – some say with questionable emphasis – the movement is now in line with conventional protests.

Which might be a problem if it were not for the unconventionality and vigour of Connemara men. The withdrawal of the dole might have been a one-day exploitable wonder by opposition parties. To Cearta Sibhialta it might just be the fuse which the Gaeltacht bomb needs. There will be fireworks in Galway within the next three weeks.

Conamara Revolution
(New Hibernia Review, Winter 2014)

This essay from the New Hibernia Review, *the journal of the Center for Irish Studies at the University of St Thomas in Minnesota, was published in 2014 and contains Bob's reflections on his first four years in Conamara.*

On a dark November night in 1970 I finally arrived in Conamara with a wife, a baby, an old VW van, and the reality of life on the dole. Motherhouse RTÉ had been abandoned and I was jobless again. In the year since cutting the RTÉ umbilical chord, I had been a dishwasher in a fancy restaurant in Hampstead, London, cleaning up after the likes of Peter Cook and the Duke of Bedford. While there, the BBC offered me a job making documentary films. Such was my arrogance that I wrote a polite answer saying I would rather snag turnips in Mayo than engage with film again. I was going to be a writer!

But before I began raking in the royalties, I returned to Ireland, got married, and worked as a trawlerman in Killybegs on a boat called the *Donegal* that rarely seemed to go out fishing. Either our skipper was ill or the boat needed repairs. In three months, I earned thirty pounds.

One day I steered our home – the old Volkswagen van in which we were living – toward the Employment Exchange (otherwise known as the dole office), miles away in Carndonagh. Seeking directions, I explained to a passer-by that I wanted to register for any jobs that might be available. 'I don't think there's many go there for that,' was his dubious response. He was right, and I returned to the fishing industry.

It was strange that I should end up in Conamara. I was as ignorant of the place as any other east-coast urbanite. My default 'nationality' was Dublin. I felt I needed to leave Ireland again, but could think of nowhere amenable to my butterfly propensities. Instead, I became an interior emigré, accompanied by my patient wife Helen and our baby, Robert. Physically we emigrated to *an tír aneoil*, that unknown country, Conamara. The writer Desmond Fennell, who lived in the area, had written to tell me that any man willing to work could survive in Conamara. He did not mention that there were few jobs in 1970 and that most men were on the dole.

When, years before in 1959, I had first visited Conamara on the pillion of a motorbike, I did not even know that the people spoke Irish. All I recall of the trip is going up to a small cottage near Salruck (where Wittgenstein had briefly lived) on a sweltering summer's day and asking to buy some food and water for a bunch of us improvident youth hostellers swimming on a nearby beach. A handsome woman with two children clinging to her skirt handed me an untouched Gateaux cake and refused to accept payment. That made a memorable impression though I felt a little bad about the kids.

The next visit was when I brought the RTÉ stringer cameraman in Galway, the Breton Yann Guiomard, to shoot scenes for a musical insert in a studio programme I was directing. I even remember the song: 'Maidin i mBéarra', otherwise known as 'Danny Boy'. It was sung by Gráinne Yeats and acted by a beautiful model named Dolly Sheridan whom I was trying, unsuccessfully, to seduce – her excuse for resisting me was that she had 'coward's legs', an alibi she admitted getting from Spike Milligan's novel *Puckoon*. When we got back to the station and hurriedly began to edit the shots together for a live programme the editor called my attention to a donkey in the scene. The brute not only boasted a monstrous head, sickening cry, and ears like errant wings, but also a proud erection. The donkey's exuberance meant a hasty abbreviation of imagery for the musical item.

The day we arrived in 1970, an 'anti-Oireachtas' was taking place in Ros Muc. Seán Ó Riada and Cór Chúil Aodha, the famous choir that he had founded, were singing Mass in a large tent. This was both a celebratory protest against the Dublin hegemony of the Irish language and my introduction to language politics in Ireland.

Not long after the idea of Conamara claimed us, our little family went on a shopping expedition to Galway City. In a pub there I met a retired bus driver who had professional experience of the famous Conamara bus. He had dentures smiling whitely and a curiosity about my new place of residence. He had once had a minor accident involving a child running through a gate and into his halted bus. No one was around. He had to search for a neighbour. When the court case arrived, a dozen people turned up claiming to be eyewitnesses to his reckless driving. The bus driver smilingly advised me: 'Never trust a Conamara man.' For years to come, I would continue to hear slanders about Conamara.

Urban visitors, friends of mine, would often comment on their nervousness in visiting the local pubs. They felt as threatened, they said, as if they were aliens. You were dressed in city clothes, I explained. The drinkers had to make sure you were not 'gaugers' from the social security office. (The same wariness applied in other rural areas: on a large building site in Donegal all the labourers were known to be on the rural dole. These workers could smell a gauger a mile off and they vanished as soon as one came over the horizon. However, the local social welfare officer showed enterprise. He sent a pretty female clerk out to the site on a bicycle, armed with nothing more than a miniskirt and a book of raffle tickets. She got the name and address of every worker on the site and they were matched with names on the unemployment register. That ended the dole fraud.) By contrast, during the Celtic Tiger years a taxi driver in Dublin told me that he was paid by developers to drive full-time building workers to sign on and collect the dole once a week, to facilitate the building boom of the time. This practice was hardly mentioned, let alone made the subject of an exposé, in our national media. No such questions were asked of the metropolis.

In 1971 I had an article published in the *Irish Times* titled 'The Doleman Cometh'. In what I thought were unmistakably ironic terms, it praised the social welfare system and that rural subsidy, the dole, which enabled strong, unemployed men to gather around the corners of their villages, entertaining tourists, providing photo opportunities, and engaging in quaint chat. Tourist interests, I suggested, should recognise the high amenity value of such men and get four-square behind the principle of the dole.

My irony was a mistake. Where servants of a one-party state are concerned, never use irony. A week later, a man from Galway City dressed in a suit and tie came to my rented home in Ros Muc asking questions about my income from such writing. Having abandoned an urban career as a TV producer, I was on the dole, supporting a wife and child on six pounds and fifteen shillings a week, trying to supplement this with sporadic articles and stories. Because I proudly overestimated my earnings to be about two pounds a week from such writing, the man from Galway immediately docked that sum from my dole. I would term that man a professional urbanite – doing his permanent, pensionable job, and interested in how lesser beings survive only to the extent of suspicion that they are getting away with something. And there are echoes of that attitude in government as I write.

With my rent money of two pounds a week thus confiscated by the state, I applied for a job as a night telephonist in the Andrews Street telephone exchange in Dublin. It was a dreary refuge for misfits, writers, poets, and now, an ex-TV producer. Shackled by headphones, plugs, and switchboards, we were supervised to make sure we did not eavesdrop on private phone conversations. The poet Michael Hartnett was a fellow prisoner. The only excitement during that period of incarceration was in early February 1972, when we were released from our headphones and wires to march to a service in Westland Row church. The intent was that once there, we were to light candles for the souls of the thirteen protestors murdered by the British army in Derry the previous Sunday. In fact most of us slipped away like truant schoolboys and joined the protesting thousands outside the British Embassy in Merrion Square. We witnessed and applauded as the unprotected building was burned down by young activists, unimpeded by the state agencies who regarded the action as a useful letting off of steam.

I endured the nightly prison of the telephone exchange for six months, then had a brief spell as a sub-editor with the *Irish Times*, and even tried teaching film without the necessary methodology: those who can't, teach; those who can, make films. I fled back to the freedom of Conamara.

The same summer that I moved back, a close relative of mine on holiday in Conamara fulminated about the laziness of the natives. He, a city man born and bred, could not get anybody to fix a minor problem in his temporarily rented house. I explained that summer was the only time of year when my neighbours could actually earn something from the seasonal backbreaking work of fishing and turf-cutting. His trivial inconvenience was not their top priority. He remained unconvinced. Coincidentally, many years later, his son brought his bicycle on a one-day visit to the Aran Islands. The bicycle got a puncture. Now, renting bicycles for the short summer season is a small industry on Inishmore. The young man simply could not understand why it was impossible to borrow a pump and swore he would never go near the place again, at least not with his bike.

The neglect of Conamara, when I finally settled there, reminded me of Dublin in the 1950s: Fianna Fáil, Fine Gael and the Catholic Church ruled comfortably over unemployment and emigration. Party loyalists proclaimed their allegiance by shouting their votes in the polling booth rather than writing them in secret. It was less of a vote than a proclamation of faith in those three powerful groups that controlled society. The majority political parties and the church enshrined what Frantz Fanon referred to as 'the national bourgeoisie'. No matter what happened – come dungeon, fire or sword – the post-revolutionary middle class always retains its status and control. Fanon was writing in the context of the Algerian revolution and 'the wretched of the earth', but the cap fitted a lot of places.

I felt immediately at home. It was like confronting the black hole of my past with the hope of somehow redeeming it. Luckily my arrival coincided with a new air of optimism, thanks to the emergence of an educated breed of young people native to the place. Up to this it had been well-meaning urban Gaeilgeoirs who had tried to 'save the Gaeltacht' and they had failed utterly – hence, the anti-Dublin Oireachtas in Ros Muc. Now, it was the people themselves rising from their knees and saying 'no more'. In 1969 Irish speakers in Conamara had already set up a pirate radio station and three years later would be awarded a local radio station to keep them quiet. I hitched a lift on their optimism and allowed myself to be persuaded to add my rusty technical talent to the cause. Henceforth all of my filmmaking activities would be devoted to raising Conamara's profile above the romanticism of urbanites. I had placed myself literally outside the Pale.

There was one snag. I still did not enjoy making films.

Filmmaking had previously consumed me to the point of overlooking the practical exigencies of life such as making a home and a livelihood. Like everyone my age in the 1960s, I was intent on changing the world. But the activity had always drained me. On the first morning of a shoot I would feel nervous and nauseous, and curse myself for ever taking up such a career. I had abandoned it as a pointless waste of ideas, money and energy. However, in Conamara there was a new purpose to start again. Here was a chance to demystify the medium, to democratise and decentralise its applications. Unlike modern students of media, I never wanted to make films for their own sake. I wanted to use the medium as originally intended: for propaganda purposes. Filming was as painful as ever but seemed more useful now.

It was a brilliant young Conamara man named Seosamh Ó Cuaig, locally known as Josie Cooke, who induced me to pick up the tools of the trade again. Endlessly and subtly he spoke of 'his people' as if they were a separate nation. He made analogies between their condition ('we aboriginals') and that of the native North American Indians. In Jean Genet fashion, he identified with what he called the 'criminal elements', those who drank to excess and who brawled at the drop of a hat – although Seosamh himself was the gentlest of men. His *dúchas*, or sense of tradition, was so deep that he suggested if he slept downstairs in our rented house his grand-uncle's ghost would appear to him. He was certainly, to contrive an acrobatic phrase, trusting and sharing his imagination with us blow-ins. The part that was true was that his grand-uncle, Colm Ó Gaora, had been an Irish freedom fighter and writer who had died in this house.

Seosamh's energy and imagination had a touch of desperation, but were boundless and quite refreshing to me. I think we agreed on the ultimate futility of all human aims and causes, but he reminded me of the utter necessity of having some aim. It was Gramsci's philosophy. Instead of a depressed fatalism, Seosamh revived in me a stimulating and optimistic attitude to life.

His analogy to an Indian reservation even resonated with my experience of the beaten-down members of such a tribe, the Micmacs, whom I had got to know in Nova Scotia, where I studied sociology for a sabbatical year. The minimal life expectancy of the Micmacs was a national disgrace.

A superb orator, Ó Cuaig spoke as incisively in English (which he did not learn until he was nine years of age) as he did in Irish. He reminded me that the over-centralisation of the Irish media in Dublin, especially television, was a debilitating force in our lives. I was eventually persuaded that the Gaeltacht needed to create its own new self-image, as in moving pictures.

But before reinventing the wheel, our small family had to survive. My resourceful wife Helen developed the idea of making toffee apples and selling them in the market in Galway. That lasted a very short while. It is embarrassing to think that we could be described as early 'entrepreneurs' – the breed who, having recently destroyed the Irish economy, are still offered as the only class capable of restoring us to solvency. I wish them luck.

I also experimented with silk-screen and batik techniques, and even sold some interpretations of the Book of Kells; a neighbour tells me that he still has my batik portraits of Seán Ó Riada and Máirtín Ó Cadhain. Later, I developed a line of original designs on silk-screened t-shirts for summer colleges. Helen was the inspiration and salesperson. Our front room was crisscrossed with lines of string on which the t-shirts hung to dry. All went well until I made a mistake in calculating the chemicals involved and had to redo fifty shirts for

Coláiste na bhFiann in Ros Muc. That broke the bank, and my artistic career was over for a while.

Next, at Seosamh's request, I wrote a James-Bond-type thriller which he proposed to translate into Irish, and thereby get a publishing grant. His only stipulation was that there should be a death on every second page. I fulfilled this commission in a violent fortnight and the manuscript languished in the boot of Seosamh's car for many months until it was finally lost. I then tried my hand at radio: I sat down and wrote a radio play called *The Image*, about a female god living in Argentina. I submitted it to RTÉ radio who not only accepted it but allowed me to cast and direct it – another example of the hand that you once bit still feeding you.

Seosamh and I drew up a St Patrick's Day demand for saving the Gaeltacht. Our manifesto included nationalising the seaweed and putting a jukebox in every pub. Finally I capitulated to his persuasion and agreed to start making films again.

Ironically, one of my last jobs when employed by RTÉ was to persuade Seán Ó Riada to reappear on their screens. He had sworn never again to collaborate with the national broadcaster after his music was allegedly trivialised by a staff producer, Louis Lentin, whose dramatic flair could not resist contextualising the set with old images of simian 'Oirishmen' taken from *Punch* magazine. After the insult, Ó Riada had relocated in high dudgeon to the Gaeltacht of West Cork.

My courtship of the reluctant composer involved several hours drinking whiskey with him down in the Mill, a pub near his home in the Múscraí Gaeltacht. We adjourned to his house, where he sat at the piano and sketched out two entire programmes. My subsequent hangover was not in vain: Ó Riada, Seán Ó Sé and Ceoltóirí Chualann performed wonderfully.

Alas, videotape was recyclable. RTÉ had to wipe the videotapes of the two fine shows we planned in his living room. The sixties were optimistic, but money was scarce; we could always make more programmes later, because nobody thought they were going to die and certainly not Ó Riada.

The relevant point is that the pioneering Ó Riada had already thought of making films in his adopted Gaeltacht and asked me to join him in the enterprise. I reluctantly declined: I was not yet sufficiently disenchanted with my job in RTÉ. How was I to know that I would end up making films in the Conamara Gaeltacht? Here, they call it *rothaí móra an tsaoil*: the big wheels of life.

Thus, the truth is that Seosamh Ó Cuaig, the late Toni Cristofides (a mathematics lecturer in UCG), and myself were not original in aspiring to invent a Gaeltacht film industry. Ó Riada was always ahead of the posse. In 1973, we three each subscribed a borrowed thousand pounds, which sum was matched by Gaeltarra Éireann (the predecessor of Údarás na Gaeltachta) to buy film equipment and set up Cinegael. In Irish, 'cine' means 'a people' and Gael is self-explanatory. The title was more Seosamh's than mine.

We solved the problem of film versus video by acquiring both a 16mm film camera and a small video set-up, the video equipment bought from a cute Northerner named Armstrong. His living room in Ranelagh in Dublin was piled high with Akai equipment imported from Japan and sold at large increments. I got to know this room well from my frequent and desperate drives to Dublin to have the overburdened, amateur, quarter-inch black-and-white equipment repaired or replaced. Each machine had its unique helicon-scanned function. No machine was identical to the next, and so material shot on one machine could not be seen on another. Mr Armstrong couldn't be bothered, or was not technically equipped, to repair our equipment. He simply supplied replacement parts. Years later I contacted Akai in Japan, seeking similar equipment in order to view some of those tapes. The manufacturers had not preserved a single working example of the crude toy. Today, anyone with an internet connection can see pictures from Jupiter, but those tapes – many of them of great archival interest – languish largely unseen in my shed.

We ran a closed-circuit community television service. Although our showings in pubs and community halls throughout Conamara – as well as Tír Chonaill and Gaeltacht Mhúscraí – were received enthusiastically, I, being inclined to pessimism, remember showing a videotape on a TV set in the lounge of Tigh Chualáin, a pub in Indreabhán. The tape featured the delightful children of the local people talking, singing, dancing and so forth. The sparse audience that turned up for our showing was not encouraging; I wandered into the crowded bar section to find the parents enjoying a British comedy, *Some Mothers Do 'Ave 'Em*, on RTÉ.

Gradually the video equipment died from natural causes. I fell back on my film camera, with which I made short pieces like *Fág an Bealach*, the story of a language summer school, and *Oireachtas na nGael*. Appropriately, I then rented an old factory originally constructed by the Congested Districts Board, and, with the help of the filmmaker Joe Comerford, converted it into a shabby cinema. On the partition beside the projector I pinned the quotation from Antonio Gramsci: 'Pessimism of the intellect – optimism of the will.' There we showed our small local videotape scenes, along with James Bond films and Bruce Lee's *Enter the Dragon*. My neighbours much preferred the latter to O'Flaherty's *Man of Aran*.

Gluaiseacht Chearta Sibhialta na Gaeltachta, the Gaeltacht Civil Rights Movement, had a talent for bold gestures. I filmed Ó Cuaig and Cristofides painting over the English-language signposts in Conamara and submitted the footage to the RTÉ newsroom; RTÉ declined the item, but later accepted pretty pictures of dolphins. Ó Cuaig also suggested barricading Spiddal bridge so that urban Gaeilgeoirí could not enter the Gaeltacht. We even had a stimulating encounter in Dublin with the journalist Nell McCafferty, whom we tried to persuade to play Big Maggie in John B. Keane's play of that name. Seosamh declared he would translate it into Gaeilge and Nell laughed at us. Some years later she introduced a film of mine in Liberty Hall. I briefed her on its contents, which featured Amazonian women driving males to tears. Nell quoted this to the audience and said, 'I understand this film is about ballbusters. All I can say is, to paraphrase John Wayne, a woman's got to do what a woman's got to do.'

Through all of this activity I gained first-hand experience of surviving in Conamara, as well as a working knowledge of the Irish language. It should not be considered unjust that, after my forty years living in the friendly and tribal society which is Conamara, I am still a blow-in. It suits me fine, being an endorsement of my long-felt inability to fit in anywhere: 'the gap', as James Plunkett put it, 'in the circle of my friends.' My good friend Martin Duffy put it another way. One night he said to me, 'Bob, for you the world exists merely as "I" and "Not I".' Martin was referring to Samuel Beckett's play *Not I*, which features a single, spot-lit talking mouth. One synopsis says of the piece that 'The mouth utters at a ferocious pace a logorrhoea of fragmented, jumbled sentences.'

Any cap that fits I will wear, like sackcloth and ashes. *Mar a chéile muid*: we are all in the same frail barque.

Caoineadh Airt Uí Laoire
(*Cassandra Voices, October 2019*)

An extract from an unpublished memoir, parts of which were later serialised in the online publication Cassandra Voices *edited by Frank Armstrong. This essay tells the story of the making of the 1975 film* Caoineadh Airt Uí Laoire *as well as related background on the North.*

In August of 1969 I was driving across Ireland with the late Bearnard Ó Riain, the older brother of a good friend of mine, the late Dinno Ryan. Most of my old friends are now 'late'.

We were going to join others on a mountain-walking weekend. Bearnard had participated in the nineteen-fifties IRA campaign in the North of Ireland, was captured and interned in the Curragh. He could not stand being locked up and he signed a statement renouncing his involvement in the IRA and undertaking to leave Ireland. He had gone to Africa, married an English girl named Carol, had two children and spent the next ten years there. The marriage had broken up and he was now back in Ireland to gather his resources.

I switched on the car radio to get the news and we heard that the North had exploded again, that Orangemen were burning Nationalists out of their homes in Belfast. He turned to me with a look that said: 'I have to go up there'. I knew he needed some distraction from his domestic circumstance. I also suspected he needed to exorcise his old guilt at signing himself out of the IRA and I turned the car northwards.

We arrived in Derry as the Rossville flats siege was ending. On the roof of the flats we met Bernadette Devlin. Bearnard asked her if we could help in any way. 'You could help to clear up this mess,' she said and we started clearing away the broken bottles and stones, remnants of Molotov cocktails.

We found a bed for the night on the floor of RTÉ reporter Seán Duignan's City Hotel bedroom. Word came that there had also been serious trouble in Dungiven. Seán was excited, predicting a civil war.

The following morning we drove to Dungiven, which was now peaceful, recovering from a night of violence. It was all very anti-climactical. I later wrote an article that the *Evening Press* published with the title: 'Trouble will always be where I am not.'

The same applied to Belfast. The only sign that there had been trouble on Bombay Street was a lone figure whose bald head I recognised from newspaper photos as belonging to Joe Cahill. He was keeping guard with some kind of rifle.

Bearnard and I acted like tourists and strolled up the ravaged street. Encountering some suspicious young men of whose allegiance we could not be sure we prudently claimed to be Canadian journalists. Our years of travelling had smoothed the rough edges of our Dublin accents so that we could pass ourselves off as harmless.

The following morning we investigated a burnt-out factory on, I think, the Falls Road. Someone shouted 'sniper' and everybody dived for cover. I could not take it seriously and simply lined myself up behind a lamppost. If there actually was a sniper in the factory building, I reasoned, he would need to be a very good shot and at worst I could only be winged.

But there were no shots. I was beginning to think the whole situation was quite exaggerated by journalists. Later that day we witnessed the first contingent of British soldiers taking up positions on the Falls Road and being applauded by the grateful citizens. What struck me was the nervousness of the lieutenant in charge and the gaucheness, the mystified expressions of the soldiers under his command.

How were they – or we – to know that we were witnessing the beginnings of a Nationalist revolt and an occupation and vicious war that would dominate our island for the next thirty years?

The above mentioned Bearnard lived in Johannesburg. He had written a most interesting memoir of his dramatic life. It opens with the scene of a drunken man kicking a woman lying in the gutter. To his horror, the writer realises that the woman is his wife and he himself is the violent drunk. Bearnard's book is quite unlike my fanciful reminiscences. It is that unique object: a well-written, honest memoir. No publisher in Ireland was interested in it.

It would be five years before I again braved the North of Ireland, next time as the guest of 'Official' Sinn Féin.

By 1974 I was entrenched in a cottage in Baile na hAbhann, Conamara, where TG4 would be built over a score years later.

A softly spoken man named Eamonn Smullen called one day. He had the idea of making a film on the subject of the epic poem, 'Caoineadh Airt Uí Laoire'. It had been a favourite of mine in school.

He could even offer some money to make it.

I jumped at the chance. It took me six months to research, write and direct the film with an amateur cast entirely from the area. It took a few more months to edit and finish it. Essentially it was a tragic love story.

The (true) context was a hopeless one-man protest against the Penal Laws imposed by the English in the eighteenth century. Joe Comerford and myself were the only crew with film experience, Joe on camera, myself on sound. My wife Helen was the indispensable production support.

When the film was finished, my neighbours – including the cast of the film – were a little bewildered by my quite unconscious use of Brechtian alienation techniques. This was a pragmatic solution to the problem of using an all-amateur cast. I needed to creep up on and defuse audience prejudices against both amateurs and the Irish language.

I did this by using authentic native speakers rather than urban Gaeilgeoirí and scripted it accordingly as an amateur rehearsal with roughly dramatic re-enactments. It worked very well because it offended the proper targets. When it was shown at the Savoy cinema in the Cork Film Festival, actors Niall Tóibín and Donal McCann happened to be seated behind me. At the end Niall tapped me on the shoulder and whispered: 'Quinn, yer a clever hoor.'

That was as fine a compliment as I could get and certainly took the sting out of the *Irish Times'* Fergus Linehan describing the film as 'formless as the Connemara rocks.'

Dermot Breen, Director of the Festival, was delighted to be offered the film – the only other Irish entry besides my friend Louis Marcus' fine Waterford Glass job.

Naturally I thought my baby was a work celebrating the genius of Conamara but, considering the pleasant expectations of film audiences, Louis' beautiful cinematography won.

Later, Dermot Breen who was double-jobbing as Irish Film Censor, demanded cuts to certain mild profanities in my English subtitles, e.g. 'shit' and 'Jesus'. I refused and he confined the film to viewers over sixteen years. The Dublin premiere was launched by Siobhán McKenna in the Drumcondra Grand cinema in 1975 while I was having a quiet little breakdown.

It also seemed a good idea to show it at the first night of our little 'cinema' in Carraroe. Although I was entirely to blame for the film the titles included a credit for the 'Education Department of Sinn Féin' of which Eamonn Smullen was director and who had provided the £6,000 towards its making.

The war in the North was in full swing; Sinn Féin was split into 'Provos' and 'Stickies'. I had no interest in either group, nor in the subtleties of North/South politics. All I saw was an opportunity to make a film about my favourite poem in Irish, which is still a landmark in Irish literary history.

Oblivious to the political implications I went ahead with the job. But politicians have longer memories than their constituents. I had previously, on our closed-circuit video, made fun of the Minister for the Gaeltacht's poor command of the language of the Gaeltacht. There were now two political black marks against me.

Thus on the night of the Carraroe showing of the film the local Garda arrived at the door asking to see my licence to show films. No such licence existed. The only legislation the State had ever bothered to enact concerning film was the Dance Hall Act of 1935. Nobody could dance in our cinema because the seats were bolted to the floor. The Garda, a decent man named Rice, mentioned the suspicion that

I was raising funds for the IRA! I was summonsed to appear in court on the Dance Hall charge. It was a petty case of political harassment and the Garda was the messenger: don't mess with the Minister, the message said.

George Morrison of *Mise Éire* fame brought a sample of old flammable nitrate film as an exhibit in my defence. This was the dangerous stuff for which the British had legislated in 1904 and which had long fallen into disuse.

George intended to ignite an inch of it and detonate it in court as a smoke bomb – a game we had played as children. The demonstration would show the difference between it and the modern safety film which I handled.

Perhaps fortunately, George did not get the chance as the case was summarily dismissed with no blot on my escutcheon. Nevertheless some of the mud stuck and forever afterwards I was considered locally to be somehow not politically kosher.

Officially, I was bordering on the subversive. When some maverick IRA man named 'Mad Dog' McGlinchy was being sought high and low throughout Ireland there were only three houses searched in Conamara. One of them was mine. The Special Branch found and formally confiscated a child's popgun which did not work.

President Cearbhall Ó Dálaigh had a private peek at the film in the Project Theatre in Dublin and wrote a complimentary note to me. Film critic Ciaran Carty had kindly described it as 'the Irish film I for one have been waiting for.'

But the film was not really respectable until the Northern war was over. It has never been shown on RTÉ but TG4 is more daring and has shown it twice. When Channel 4 showed it they cut out the credits for Sinn Féin. Meantime Eamonn Smullen wanted to show the film in a Republican drinking club in Belfast and brought Joe Comerford and myself up there.

The film also seemed to confuse that audience. A lady turned to us and asked: 'What are yiz? Some kinda antellectuals?' While we were there the club was raided by the British Army who moved silently and grimly through the crowd. I found it strange that there was no heckling, not a voice raised in protest and deduced that, yes, there is something frightful happening in this part of Ireland. We were accommodated that night in the house of a man named Billy McMillen whom I gathered had been shot by the rival Provisional IRA. In Ireland the first thing on the agenda is the split.

I noticed a man in the tiny back yard of the house carrying a revolver, presumably to protect us. It felt as if we were in a film. We were escorted to the eight o'clock train the next morning by Smullen, the gentle man who had asked me to make the film.

At no stage did I feel in danger. I think I must sleepwalk through life, incapable of taking anything seriously, not even the darkness. All is at arm's length. It still surprises me that *Caoineadh Airt Uí Laoire* has become a kind of icon in the lexicon of Irish filmmaking. In recent years it was exhibited for a month in Trinity's Douglas Hyde Gallery. It was also featured in the Irish Museum of Modern Art as an example of the work of modern Irish artists.

A couple of years ago it was restored and Joe and I showed it in Derrynane, the Kerry home of Daniel O'Connell's family which features in the film. In the introduction I mentioned the film's small budget.

Poet Theo Dorgan was present and later in the pub said to me: 'I know where that £6,000 came from. I think I even know the post office from which it was stolen.' I still hope he was joking.

A Letter on the Irish Film Industry
(The Irish Press, 21 June 1975)

On 16 June 1975, John Boland in the Irish Press *reviewed the festival premiere of* Caoineadh Airt Uí Laoire *and said it 'had its moments but was spoiled by pretentiousness and self-indulgence. Not content with telling its story it had John Arden mouthing clichés and the performers being enthusiastically undisciplined. There were ideas here, but no-one seemed to know how to give them any coherence. Still, it was a brave first attempt.' Below is Bob's reply.*

I have read your Cork Film International Festival reporter's comments on the film *Caoineadh Airt Uí Laoire*.

I know his opinion was a sincere expression of bourgeois aestheticism, a condition I understand and sympathise with. I mean, that's the way we are all conditioned – by TV commercials, extended 'art' commercials, feature films which substitute a passing technical titillation for content.

But if he can take time off from his more suitable duties as an ordinary reporter and think about films seriously, perhaps he could read in full the comments of Louis Marcorelles, a member of the Cork features jury. I quote briefly:

> The movies we make shouldn't be a stale repetition of the output of Britain and America. Our movies should watch the people, listen to the people and feel their dreams. They should be a way of reflecting the country and interpreting it. A way of facing its problems. Cinema is not important if you want a peaceful life with no problems. Look what is happening in the top corner of your island.

Given a large budget and the duty to produce some pretty pictures to be subliminally associated with commercial enterprises such as Embassy cigarettes, BP oil, Shell, *The Liverpool Post* and Waterford Glass (all featured at Cork), it is easy to please the likes of your reporter. It certainly won't, as Marcorelles suggests, 'create an original national cinema which will be rooted in the people and enable them to discover their own national identity.'

The latter is very difficult, as so many Irish filmmakers have discovered. But as long as these same filmmakers are encouraged to escape into the bright prison of commercials by comments such as your reporter's, the illusion of an Irish National Cinema will remain precisely that.

To conclude, may I amusedly refer to one specific comment made by your reporter on *Caoineadh Airt Uí Laoire*. He mentioned John Arden 'mouthing clichés'. But this is precisely what the character played by Arden was supposed to do.

Is it possible that this part, that of an incompetent aesthete, English-speaking and representing a colonial culture was the only character with whom your reporter could identify, and was consequently insulted. In that case, again, he has my sympathy.

Bob Quinn
An Cheathrú Rua
Conamara

James McKenna and *Cloch*
(James McKenna – A Celebration, 2002)

The story of the making of the film Cloch, *published in a tribute to the sculptor James McKenna, edited by Desmond Egan and published by Goldsmith Press.*

In 1975 Cliodhna Cussen asked me to make a film about her group of stone carvers who were about to have a workshop in Kilkenny. I asked her to name one sculptor, through whose individual efforts I could personalise the work of the group. Without hesitation she named James McKenna. It was a good choice.

He was a dark, short and powerfully built man who stroked his chin whenever he answered my naive questions about his art. His accent was an odd mixture of down-to-earth Wicklow and polite

Dublin. His conversation was punctuated with nervous eruptions called laughter. This gave me an impression of tension, a controlled energy. It was fortunate that the McKenna personality had a physical and emotional outlet in his chosen craft. If he had not pitted this energy into cold stone I felt that otherwise the extremely gentle James might have physically assailed the planet itself. In a sense he did but he needed additional different outlets for this energy. He wrote poetry, composed the musical play *The Scatterin'* – whose first performance I had seen years before, and latterly he had decided to learn the piano. The epitome of the restless soul and a dream for a filmmaker.

I brought my camera to Kilkenny and observed a one-legged quarry man cutting and lifting James' chosen piece of limestone from the ground. In rain and sun, I saw the sculptor meticulously pencilling in the proportions of his proposed full-size figure and beginning to chip away. It reminded me of film editing where you imagine the final shape of the work and proceed to remove what is superfluous. James gave me the key to the process with a brief anecdote:

Every day a postman observed a sculptor working on a stone in a field. When the final figure was revealed, the postman asked the sculptor: 'How did you know she was in there?'

That was my first, last and completely adequate explanation for the strange process whereby human beings attempt the impossible: to breathe life into the inanimate. It is the nearest we get to behaving like gods and McKenna never ceased his defiant attempts to approach this divine state.

The roughed-out stone was finally wheeled on a handcart to the courtyard of Rothe House in the centre of Kilkenny City. Here James resumed his labours, this time in the convivial company of his peers, George and Justin Laffan, Noel Hoare, Bríd Ní Rinn, Cliodhna Cussen & Co. Gradually a female shape began to appear. James was very conscious of the grain in the stone, its pressure points, strengths and weaknesses. It was a revelation to me to realise that stone had characteristics similar to wood. He left what appeared to be long tresses at the back of the figure and was sensitive to suggestions that it gave the piece an Egyptian look. 'I don't know why people always say that,' he would complain. 'The "hair" is purely there for support.'

The week ended before he was finished the piece. I went home to Conamara and continued working on the film. Months later I asked Cliodhna Cussen where McKenna's piece was. 'He's still working on it,' she said. I shot a final sequence for the film in James' back garden in Chapelizod and gathered all the sculptors to discuss the work. The film was completed and its premiere was introduced by Cearbhall Ó Dálaigh in the Project Theatre in 1975. I moved on to my next job and didn't think of the piece until a year later when Cliodhna mentioned to me that it was still lying unsold in James' garden. Through viewing it constantly on my editing machine I realised I had fallen in love with the figure. I contacted James, asked how much he would sell it for, struck a price and paid him on the never-never over the next twelve months. We brought the piece home to Carraroe in a van, erected her in the garden, beside the road, and named her Limestone Biddy. For months our amusement was watching through the window as the passersby slowed down, stopped and gazed in wonder at this semi-naked woman. A couple of drunken brothers knocked her over one St Stephen's night and chipped her nose. I collected the minuscule bits from the weeds and still have them in an envelope, waiting for a stone plastic surgeon.

One day a young man stopped, looked and came in. 'That's very like sculptures in Limerick University,' he said. I felt it was a fine compliment to the sculptor. James had indeed prepared some massive pieces for that University (and was highly disappointed by the way the University had placed them). But the untutored eye of the student had recognised the unique style of James.

Twenty-five years later – and one house move which involved Limestone Biddy being transported ignominiously by a device for rescuing cows and cars from ditches – she still stands in my garden. I have photographed her, painted her (with James' approval), planted montbretia and other assorted flowers at her feet, used her as a landmark for visitors and generally felt proud to have the spirit of McKenna somehow represented here. James never saw the piece again. I hope that he realised one of his children had found a good home.

Notes on *Poitín*
(London Film Festival, 1978)

Poitín *received its British premiere at the 1978 London Film Festival where it was selected as an 'outstanding film of the year'. This is Bob's programme note for the screening.*

This is the first short feature film ever produced in the Irish language. Its entire cast and crew are Irish. It is based on a story by Colm Bairéad and directed by Bob Quinn, an independent Irish filmmaker. The film was made possible initially by Arts Council recognition in the form of the first ever film script award.

The story concerns an elderly poteen-maker in Conamara who employs two agents to sell his produce, a fiery and strictly illegal native brew. The police waylay the agents and impound a consignment of the drink. The agents break into the barracks and steal it back. (Details like this are based on fact). The agents sell the bottles at a fair and decide that their daring entitles them to keep the proceeds. They go on the spree and, having been refused more drink in a bar, decide to look for more poteen, this time for their own consumption. They rashly invade the cottage of the poteen-maker, terrorise his daughter and inevitably suffer the old man's vengeance.

The locations are quite authentic and the poteen-still which is featured in the film was actually in operation. The proprietor simply stepped aside for Cyril Cusack for a few minutes.

The director, Bob Quinn, who has lived in Conamara for the past seven years describes, the film simply as a belated attempt to counter the stage-Irishism of *The Quiet Man* which was made 25 years ago in the same area and seems to dominate people's idea of life there.

Cinegael, the name under which Bob Quinn makes films, has been located in Conamara for five years and has produced eight films. The best known of these, *Caoineadh Airt Uí Laoire*, is a drama/documentary which received critical acclaim at home and abroad, notably at Pesaro, Italy, a festival of progressive cinema. It is shown regularly in Ireland and the United States and provokes strong reactions, positive, negative and confused, wherever it is seen.

'Burn that film': Responses to the Television Premiere of *Poitín*
(RTÉ, 1979)

The text of a document provided by RTÉ to Bob that illustrates the public reaction to Poitín *when it premiered on RTÉ 1 on St Patrick's Day in 1979.*

From: Tony Lyons, Press & Information Executive
RE: *Poitín* – First Broadcast on RTÉ. Summary of telephone reaction received on Saturday March 17 1979 on RTÉ 1.

Poitín (12 calls)

Three callers complained they could not read the bottom line of the subtitles and asked for it to be altered.

Other comments were:
- 'Disgraceful and disgusting.'
- 'It's a national disgrace.'
- 'It's a direct insult. St Patrick was a decent man.'
- 'Disgraceful that visitors should see that film. No one should tolerate that.'
- 'You have no sense of decency. That film was not suitable for family viewing.'
- 'What part of Connemara was it filmed in?'
- 'Very unsuitable for transmission at such an early hour.'
- 'Burn that film and don't let it out of the country.'
- 'Great film, thanks for showing it.'

Part II

View from the Periphery
Ón Imeall Isteach

How to Make it in the Media
(Hot Press, 1985)

Recently I turned fifty and on reviewing the first quarter of my life decided that my attitude had been too negative, always bitching and bellyaching about the system and doing nothing to change it. Usually reliable sources confirmed this.

When I had the opportunity, when I was in a potentially powerful position as a TV producer, I simply walked away from my problem. My feeble excuse was that it is useless to attack from the inside; you can too easily be reminded that the system pays your salary. Much better to shout imprecations from outside the gates: people will think you are a noble fellow, you will get plenty of publicity, and that's good in show business. But this tawdry explication is no longer good enough for a man at an age when he should be seeking respectability. That is why today, for the first time in a quarter century of media practice, I will be positive and give solid advice on how to get into the media.

Of course, this advice will be limited in that most of my experience has been in the context of RTÉ. But insofar as all organisations run on the same principle – that of dynamic conservatism – and all broadcasting organisations engage in precisely the same nonsense, this is perhaps not as great a disadvantage as it might first appear. Therefore I proceed.

There's a lawyer of my acquaintance who became a judge in California. When asked how he achieved this dizzy height he told me the following: One day his secretary passed him a staff circular requesting that everybody keep more punctual hours. He threw it into a newspaper basket with the remark: 'I spent twenty years kissing the ass of the Governor of this State to become a judge, not an alarm clock.'

Therein lies the essence not only of how to get into the media, but how to get on in the media. A mean spirit might call it sycophancy. I call it becoming a social being and the way forward is simple: cultivate the media bosses. Find out where they drink, hang out there, hang around them, hang on their every word, hang in there and hang the consequences. Their growing familiarity will naturally breed their contempt, a critically important achievement because you are becoming the kind of personality they need around them, which is to say, Superiors need Inferiors. In this, as the more perceptive among you will note, the media are quite properly a reflection of the world at large. Just as, for instance, as Liam O'Leary has said, a politician is an arse on which a man has never sat, so also are the functionaries who block your way into the wonderful world of the media. There is, however, one significant difference. A politician has occasionally to humiliate himself by asking for your vote. The media boss never, ever, repeat never, has to do that. That leads to the Golden Rule: The correct and only attitude with which to approach a broadcasting executive is – prostrate.

Is that enough? It is not.

Let us work from the individual upwards. The first essential for the aspirant to the world of broadcasting is Good Taste. He or she demonstrates this by having been born the child of middle-class parents. It matters not what dastardliness you get up to after you are born, you have proved your Good Taste by the initial decision to be born in the correct circumstances. Even if you move from Dublin 4 to the Northside, even if you live in sin in an artisan's cottage in the inner city, even if your conversations are peppered with 'F—s', they can't take it away from you. You are the Right Stuff.

Now, in the bad old days about twenty years ago, before this self-evident truth emerged, the system was careless. It admitted many young people of doubtful origin who confused the selection process by displaying oodles of talent. They could sing, dance, read and play music, had worked on the stage, could actually read books, might even have written one or two, had been occupied as photographers, magicians, actors, even journalists, and took to broadcasting like ducks to water. Inevitably they proved quite unreliable and most ended rather badly in the backwaters of the service, or in middle management where they could least harm the corporate image, or worst of all, became freelancers, some even going to pagan England to become household names.

What changed this situation? What steps were taken to ensure reliability in the employees of the public broadcasting service?

The answer was staring personnel managers in the face: that unique invention called third-level education. As, by and large, only the genetically tasteful could afford such an expensive item it became a simple matter to make such a qualification a *sine qua non* for entry to the key broadcasting areas. Third-level education had already proved effective in taking passionate young people with ideas and imagination and turning them into grey, careful, career-conscious smoothies. Indeed I understand the universities themselves no longer maintain the pretence that their function is the pursuit of truth.

So, a third-level education ensures that you are properly defused, ready to enter the broadcasting brothel in the guise of a eunuch.

Is this an exclusive rule? It is not. Broadcasting organisations, being essentially PR-oriented, hire the occasional minority or Connemara man and point to him or her with pride, as evidence of non-discrimination. They sometimes even hire women.

Besides these two essential qualities – class and education – are there any other necessary criteria in the selection of programme personnel?

There are. Politics is also crucial. One could not seriously expect a Sinn Féin Councillor to be made Director-General of RTÉ. The screen image would not be right. Come to think of it, the screen image is non-existent. But I have personally no doubt whatsoever that if such a person dropped the awkward Sinn Féin prefix and adopted that of 'Worker' his case might be reconsidered. A political background, I assure you, is not necessarily a disadvantage, other things being equal. Presumably it would not be as easy for an ex-secretary of the Labour Party to jump straight into a plum job on television if a Coalition government was not in power!

Some unkind people use the word nepotism to describe the network of tribal and political relationships that can exist in such organisations. But would it not be ludicrous to expect the people who work there not to meet, fall in love and marry, whatever their sex? The problem only arises when they start to breed. When variations on the same surname appear, there is cause for concern. But then, in our society, doctors think their children should get preference in medical schools so the principle is probably reasonable in broadcasting too. The moral is, be realistic. If your local director-general or programme controller has an eligible son or daughter – seduce them.

Thus, at the individual level the world of broadcasting is at the young person's feet or, should one say, in your hands.

I will not dwell on self-improvement such as, in RTÉ, adopting a Northern accent or a west-Brit twang. But be prepared to change your accent at the next General Election.

So much for the individual. What about groups: struggling independents, video or film collectives? This is not quite so straightforward for the obvious reason that you are not just selling your bodies. With the help of God, you wish to sell your souls. Today these are not very marketable commodities. In broadcasting, souls are like aniseed balls – six a penny. But there is hope. Ironically, the more impoverished, young, striving and inexperienced you are, the more likely you are to be aided by the Organisation.

The reasons are: (a) You can be patronised; (b) Guilt: Their conscience is saved by giving you money and facilities; and (c) Safety: They reckon you are too young to be interested in politics. Even if you are, there is a safeguard: your programme on rubber bullets or strip searches or your thirteen-part series on the re-conquest of Ireland can be shelved on the grounds of lack of technical finesse. But do not despair: you have made your statement. It can be shown one day when standards have dropped. It's still a free country.

What about well-established and independent professionals? Certainly they have an advantage – as long as they avoid delicate areas like abortion, contraception, religion, nationalism, divorce, celibacy, The Language, politics, homosexuality, urban decay, the Christian Brothers, drugs, etcetera. Those subjects can only prudently be handled by organisation people, who understand all the nuances and can maintain balance. But there is a big world out there and other areas that are wide open. For instance, ecology, that is, nature studies – a deeply satisfying subject where there can be no embarrassing utterances by the participants. At a premium here are articulate seagulls.

Next there is the Art Film. This can be shown before midnight and will offend nobody: nice panning shots and equally nice Shaun Davey music with a good ladling of sensitive dissolves. This is 'A Good Thing' and the *Irish Times* will look fondly on your effort.

A much neglected area is the Artsy-Crafty programme which is particularly inoffensive. Feature oulwans and oulfellas who are total anachronisms talking about their totally anachronistic lifestyle, if possible, in rural areas. If they have a smattering of Irish so much the better. They will offend nobody and broadcasting executives can sleep easily in their offices.

If you feel, as a courageous and energetic filmmaker, that these areas are too limiting you are free to enter the field of Drama, particularly if you deal in pre-1950 settings and show the Irish as rural, gullible, shifty, tipsy, quaint, pious, predatory, sexually naive and either praying or slaying. If this is your forte there is plenty of scope and you are sure of half your budget from Channel 4 and a personal endorsement from Hugh Leonard.

In summary, the scenario is very optimistic. It is simply a matter of facing the reality of present-day broadcasting and bringing a fresh viewpoint to it. Anybody who cannot do this is a sorehead and probably hasn't any talent in the first place.

Remember, some are lucky enough to be born mediocre, some achieve mediocrity, but nobody has mediocrity thrust upon them. They must work at it.

In the final analysis there are only two certain ways to get into broadcasting: the first is to become a priest and give a *Thought for Today*; the other is to buy a good suit and join the meteorological service. *Next week: How to Break into Films.*

Sean-nós Singing and Conamara's Boats
(The Atlantean Irish, 2005)

In 1986, Bob published Atlantean: Ireland's North African and Maritime Heritage, *a book based on his* Atlantean *trilogy of films exploring connections between Ireland and North Africa. The series won a Jacob's Irish television award. An expanded and illustrated version of the book was published by the Lilliput Press as* The Atlantean Irish: Ireland's Oriental and Maritime Heritage *in 2005. Below is Chapter 2 in which he sets out his main thesis.*

On the periphery of Europe, midway up the west coast of Ireland, lies a region called Conamara. It occupies the area to the west of Galway City and forms the northern shore of Galway Bay. A much-visited part of a small island on the edge of Europe, it protects England and Wales from the full force of the Atlantic while at the same time deflecting the warm waters of the Gulf Stream northwards to Scotland. Conamara takes the brunt of the attack from the Atlantic. In the arc of its ever-changing skies the onset of whatever weather is in store for the two islands can be detected daily. In 1970 I exiled myself to this unpromising region and have made it my home ever since.

When visitors to Conamara extol the desolate beauty of mountain, bog and lonely lake, it is clear to me that they have not experienced the place at all. They have been shepherded by some tourist brochure northward through a countryside that looks well from a bus – particularly because there are no people to clutter the view. They have been consciously steered away from the coastal region, South Conamara, still the most densely populated region in rural Ireland although much less than its peak of 500 persons per square mile in 1841, before the Great Famine. North Conamara is more dramatically beautiful but relatively unpopulated; South Conamara is crowded and relatively untidy. In addition, the inhabitants speak Irish, show a disconcerting indifference to modern tourism, and sing songs that fall uneasily on Western ears.

South Conamara is about as far west as you can go in Europe. The people here are more familiar with Boston than Dublin. In the 1840s a local man is reputed to have packed his entire family into a small traditional sailing boat and, with a plentiful supply of salted pork, escaped from the Famine to North America – 4,800 kilometres away. The exploit was repeated by the intrepid Paddy Barry in a Galway Bay *húicéir* only a few years ago. These adventures serve to highlight the most significant yet most ignored aspect of Conamara and its people: their obsession with boats and the sea. They seem to be the only large and identifiable community in Ireland that realises we inhabit an island. For certain reasons, rooted in the colonial experience, the Irish of recent generations have all but ignored the sea. They even abandoned their small merchant fleet to creditors in distant ports some years ago. Consequently, most reporters on Conamara tend to overlook its predominantly maritime personality. In contrast to the rest of Ireland, where boating is essentially a suburban hobby, a rich man's sport or part of the neglected fishing industry, the average Conamara person has a feel for the sea. On every Sunday afternoon in summer, crowds still gather in the various bays and harbours to celebrate the survival of their own traditional craft: the *húicéir, gleoiteog, púcan* and *curach*.

On such festive occasions the sense of history is palpable, but sublimated to present enjoyment. The main attraction, apart from hotly contested rowing races in *curacha*, is the sailing competition. The most spectacular of these features the *húicéir* or *bád mór*, literally 'big boat'. It has a massive oak construction, a dramatic tumblehome or belly, dark heavy sails of canvas and can be up to fifteen metres in length. The sight of seven or eight of these boats scudding along in a brisk wind generates ripples of knowing comments among the onlookers ashore.

On the boats themselves the atmosphere is tense. Some skippers may have had their ships in dry dock for a few days in order to grease the hulls – I certainly witnessed one, the late Johnny Jimmy Mac Donncha, laboriously applying margarine for minimum water resistance to his *An Mhaighdean Mhara* (The Mermaid). His sons still proudly race the boat.

The races have been suspended in the past because of the dangerous rivalry and doubtful tactics occasionally employed. One outlawed technique was to send a sharp piece of flint whizzing across to rip into a rival's taut sail. This was considered fair when a rival had cut inside and 'stolen your wind'. It is part of the mythology that many years ago, when a crew member fell overboard and was clinging to a trailing rope, the skipper was so desperate to win the race that he cut through the lifeline, leaving the man to be picked up by the next boat, which the skipper knew was commanded by the unfortunate victim's cousin.

In these races the satisfaction lay not simply in taking part. Winning was everything and it was based on a sound economic tradition. These big boats were used for carrying turf from bog-rich Conamara to places that had none, the limestone islands of Aran as well as south Galway and Clare. Whichever boat first reached the small harbours made sure of the inside berth beside the quay wall. This made the unloading easier, saved hours of waiting and ensured the best price for the turf. The tradition of this trade is commemorated every August when a fleet of turf boats, with billowing brown, black and red sails, sets sail from a pier in Carraroe and races across Galway Bay to Kinvara, in County Clare.

It is hard to reconcile the massive beams and generous scale of the *húicéirí* with the intimate lifestyle and organic architecture that, up to recent years, the people themselves cultivated. It is as if all sense of grandeur was siphoned off from domestic life and channelled exclusively into these boats. Perhaps this was how the people showed their pride in themselves when in all other areas they were modest, even reticent. The small thatched cottages and tiny plots of land were undemonstrative. The fact that this lifestyle has been largely replaced by modern bungalows and cars, while economic dependence on the sea has diminished, underlines the interrelationship between these two aspects of Conamara life.

The presence and impact of the sea expresses itself first in the physical environment: a series of islands and peninsulas hewn out by the Atlantic, the topsoil stripped off by the gales that begin in September and sometimes do not ease until March. This indented coastline means that virtual neighbours, a half-mile apart, might have to travel thirty kilometres by road to visit each other. As against this, the presence of shops, post offices, pubs and travel agents on the remotest tips of these islands and peninsulas suggests that it was not always thus. The location of these services makes no economic sense until one stops looking through the windscreen of a car and realises that the logical connection between these places is the boat.

Within living memory practically all commuting and transporting was seaborne. Water was not a barrier but a lifeline. Even social life depended on the *curach*. On summer evenings young people would pile into these canvas boats, row to the next island or peninsula, dance all night and row home at dawn. There is sad evidence for this custom in the memory of occasional drownings; these were more likely if the indigenous brew – poitín – was indulged in. Even in the context of this illegal drink, and the efforts to suppress its manufacture, there is evidence of the native regard for boats. Poitín was – and still occasionally is – made on the islands and rocky shores of freshwater lakes. When the still is raided, the natural escape route is over water. The local forces of law and order would constantly bewail the fact that the powers that be would not supply them with a fast boat to engage in hot pursuit. Officialdom took a long time to realise that we are all surrounded by water and as a result captures were rare. The Conamara person's respect for boats has a practical as well as a sentimental basis.

This took on importance when I began to wonder about the strange music of the area: sean-nós singing. It is a pity the term is so imprecise; sean-nós simply means 'old style'. Nevertheless, the performers and their dedicated audiences know, with ferocious precision, what is meant by the term: an ascetic, unaccompanied form of solo singing that at its best has not succumbed to the emotional sogginess of pop music. It may not be too much to claim that whoever can be moved by the writing of Samuel Beckett has the capacity to enjoy sean-nós singing. In it, passion is pared away to reveal the extraordinary courage at the heart of the human being. Describing the most heart-rending events in song, an intelligent performer's face will betray not one wisp of emotion. This singing, at least in Conamara, defies comparison with the drawing-room tradition and its sentimental offspring. There are no dramatic high notes, no hushed tones, and no build-up to a pyrotechnical climax; instead the good singer will concentrate on minuscule decoration.

In this there is an analogy to be made with the art of manuscript illumination. At their best, singers like Darach Ó Catháin and Seán 'ac Dhonncha could sing with a subtlety compared to a page from the Book of Kells. Under a microscope some of the lines on those pages are miraculously fine. The art in them seems to be to conceal art; the satisfaction seems to be in the achievement rather than the acclaim. Similarly with the good sean-nós singer: in performance the singer seems to escape into total introspection, as if communing with him or herself rather than with the audience. In this way the audience is drawn into the singer's semi-trance. As if to make sure he does not forget their presence, and also to reassure him of their support, one of the audience will grasp his hand and move it rhythmically in a winding action.

Inevitably, this extraordinary art form is withering. Many of the songs relate to the sea, be they accounts of lovers lost or terrifying storms. As the maritime dependence of the people has lessened, so the musical form degenerates. This seems a more fundamental cause than that customarily offered: the decline in the use of spoken Irish. However, the singing is still the most popular event at the annual gathering of Irish speakers, the Oireachtas.

I encountered this music on the radio as a child in Dublin. It was quite alien to my urban ears, which were accustomed to Italian opera, the lighter classics and the pleasant treacle of Bing Crosby. Indeed, sean-nós singing was an occasional object of ridicule on stage and radio, being used as a symbol for an allegedly backward rural tradition that sophisticated urbanites should deride. In my father's house, sean-nós was switched off.

Twenty years later in Conamara I found it was the most popular form of musical expression. It was still difficult to enjoy. It defied all of the conditions I had been led to believe were essential to enjoy music: it did not easily lend itself to harmony; it had none of the simple rhythms of European classical form, nor the dance rhythms of folk music. Also, it seemed to go on and on, endlessly. No matter how musical a person was – and I prided myself on my musical ear – it was impossible to pick up the style quickly and perform even remotely well. Although Conamara people stated that it could be learned, they added that it could not be taught. In other words, one would have to apprentice oneself to a singer and simply listen for years before acquiring the words, melodies, or styles of ornamentation. Even then, much would depend on the performer's inventiveness, because no two singers embellish a song in the same way.

It became clear that this form of singing was an artistic response by a highly integrated community to a particular – and precarious – lifestyle in a long-settled environment. But this description does not match the conventional explanation of the origins of the people of Conamara. They are usually thought to be recent arrivals, descendants of the seventeenth-century victims of Oliver Cromwell and the famous dictum: 'To hell or to Connacht'. The explanation matches neither the Conamara sense of identity, the people's ancient singing style, nor their highly developed tradition of boat handling and design.

When I read descriptions of the place as 'lonely', 'remote', or 'out in the wilds', I looked out of my window and saw fifty houses across the lake. On Sundays I saw traffic jams outside the church. Social life was consistently more intense and gregarious than in the average city suburb. Whatever the depressing results of American sociologists' sallies into rural Ireland, their findings simply did not fit Conamara. Neither could those people who wrote the travel brochures about the place have spent much time here.

The social structure was so intimate, the channels of communication so efficient, that it was unwise to criticise persons behind their backs: your audience might very well be their cousins. The traditional naming system was biblical: surnames were shared by so many that it was wise to know, as well as the person's first name, those of his father and grandfather. This must have caused people in official agencies to tear their hair out; it was a sure way of confusing the computer. I found myself living in what felt like a slightly foreign country. Luckily, I had no private means and was forced to work with the people. This meant learning the language – quite different from the 'book Irish' I had been taught in school – and this helped when I began studying sean-nós singing.

On examination, the music did not at first appear to be simply a survivor of a long-forgotten European tradition. The late and highly respected composer, Seán Ó Riada, in the course of three radio lectures, contended that sean-nós was not European, nor could it be understood in that context; it was much closer to oriental forms. Irish art had never adopted the forms 'spawned', as he put it, by the Graeco-Roman renaissance. The best way to understand the music, he said, was 'to listen to it with a child's fresh mind'. In other words, dismiss all preconceptions. Failing that, he suggested, one might try to hear it in terms of Indian music.

Sure enough, there happen to be faint resonances in sean-nós that would remind one of Indian music. And, of course, this would fit with the conventional Indo-European explanation of the origins of the Irish. However, when pressed as to how such music could have arrived in Ireland, Ó Riada suggested it might have come through North Africa and Spain.

Ó Riada was a classically trained musician, had composed film scores, wrote some of the most important symphonic music in Ireland, formed a folk orchestra whose influence was seminal in the popularisation of traditional Irish music, and the famous Chieftains folk group owes its origin to his inspiration. Not only was Ó Riada also an admired jazz pianist, his sophisticated company was much sought after. His analysis of sean-nós should not be dismissed; his tragic death at the age of forty halted a fascinating line of enquiry.

Generally speaking, when Irish people listen to the music of the Middle East and North Africa they experience an odd, aural equivalent of déjà vu. Charles Acton, late music critic of the *Irish Times*, once wrote an extensive article on the subject:

> If one has listened for hours in the desert of an evening to Bedouin Arabs singing narrative epics with as many stanzas as any long *aisling* [Irish vision poem] and then returned to Ireland and heard a fine sean-nós singer using the same melismata and rhythm, one finds the resemblance between the two almost uncanny. So too, if one listens to *canto jondo* [of Spain]. (*The Irish Times*, 4 November 1976)

Mr Acton went on to say that he put this idea to Joan Rimmer, an ethnomusicologist of authority. Her crisp reply was: 'Well, of course.' He concluded: 'The connections between the Arab lands and southern Europe, Spain and Ireland are, apparently, commonplace to scholars of her eminence.'

The famed collector Alan Lomax shared this perspective:

[I] have long considered Ireland to be part of the Old Southern Mediterranean–Middle Eastern family of style that I call bardic – highly ornamented, free rhythmed, solo, or solo and string accompanied singing that support sophisticated and elaborate forms. (letter to the author, 23 September 1985)

One of the greatest exponents of sean-nós singing, the late Seosamh Ó hÉanaí, was described by the writer Máirtín Ó Cadhain as singing such songs

effortlessly, one after another, in a manner which strongly reminds one of Gitano singing in the caves of Granada. In fact his splendid figure and face is the southern Spanish type. There is a strong tradition that survivors of the Armada remained along the Conamara coast. (LP sleevenotes, *Seosamh Ó hÉanaí*, Gael Linn, 1969)

The Spanish connection made sense; Irishmen always looked to Catholic Spain as a possible saviour. Salamanca had educated thousands of Irish priests. Spanish Arch in Galway commemorates the busy trade between the two countries. Even the typical Conamara dance called 'the battering' is the nearest thing possible to Spanish flamenco. But contact with 'the Arab lands'? Such an outlandish suggestion had never been made in my presence. It was completely at variance with conventional history, which took all of the divergent characteristics of the Irish, both negative and positive, and dumped them into the romantic category: 'Celtic'. The suggestion that sean-nós had a respectably authenticated connection with the Arabs was startling. Not world-shaking, of course, as the music has a relatively small, loyal audience of aficionados and these are principally located within the Irish-speaking areas of Ireland.

An acquaintance of mine spent three years in University College Dublin acquiring a degree in music without once hearing sean-nós singing. Little attention is paid by musicians of the classical or even 'contemporary' school to this folk idiom, despite the fact that it is more subtle than a Scarlatti sonatina. I am aware of few serious Irish composers who have considered the form with insight; they include Frank Corcoran and Roger Doyle. Dr Seóirse Bodley has also perceptively written:

> The real oral tradition of sean-nós is often obscured for many listeners by several factors. There is often confusion in the public mind between: (a) the genuine sean-nós or oral tradition, and (b) songs that are sung in Irish but without the style and without the traditional ornaments or tone quality. This does not mean that one objects to the songs of the Irish Language Revival, but that a clear distinction must be made between them and sean-nós proper. (*Irish Folk Music Studies/ Éigse Cheol Tíre*, Vol. 1, 1972–73)

In the tightly-knitted garment of Irish 'Celtic' culture, there now appeared to me to be loose threads. If sean-nós was (a) not European, according to Ó Riada, (b) to be distinguished from the mainstream of 'Celtic' culture, and (c) was alien to the majority of Irish ears, then where on earth did it fit? I have spent many years tugging at these loose threads: the garment when unravelled is less a seamless jersey of pure 'Celtic' weave than a more interesting coat of many colours.

The first question to be asked was: how could there be any contact between two such apparently remote places – between Ireland and the Middle East, between two such different peoples – the Irish and the Arabs? They inhabited different continents, had profoundly different religious beliefs and, judged by the perilous barometer of ethnicity, looked different. Besides, one group lived in the sun, the other on a misty island 1,600 kilometres away.

Yet listening at night with more attention to those obscure radio stations that sometimes trespass on our wavelengths with strange music from North Africa, the possibility grew. For instance, the folk orchestra that Ó Riada developed so many years ago, consisting of fiddles, pipes, tin whistle, accordion and a quite primitive drum called the 'bodhrán', did not, in retrospect, seem quite so remote from the distant strains of North Africa. Indeed, when I visited Iran in 1968 I recall being struck by the similarity between their 'classical' music and the Ó Riada invention. At the time I attached little significance to it.

However, the goatskin drum or bodhrán, which Ó Riada rescued from obscurity in Kerry to become the basic rhythm section of most traditional Irish music groups, has its exact counterpoint in the *bendir*, the drum of Morocco. It was interesting that Ó Riada had, in creating a 'classical' folk music, unconsciously followed the example of the 'Persians'. Like them, he had respect for indigenous modes and techniques evolved over the centuries that only required the sophisticated humility of genius to recognise and adapt. Admittedly, Ó Riada introduced a baroque note by using the harpsichord, but he excused this as the nearest sound he could find to the early Irish harp.

A musicologist would get down to a detailed examination of the modes employed, the different scales, the instruments, and the chronology of these disparate manifestations of the same phenomenon. He or she would certainly soon realise the debt European music owes to Islamic culture: the violin's origin in the Middle East; the guitar's antecedent in the *ud* of North Africa; the influence of the Moors on the seminal troubadour repertoire of France; the possibility that Europe may have got its first idea for a definite pitch notation from Arabic scholars (in particular an Iraqi named Ziryab, who spent an influential period in Moorish Spain). There have been efforts to confine sean-nós to a respectable European context through comparison with Romanian and Hungarian musical idioms. Scholars who do this are invariably ignorant of the Islamic world, and of the impact the Turkish Ottoman culture has had on those areas.

However, these details are overshadowed by the practical objection of the distance between Ireland and North Africa, and the dangerous stretches of water between the two areas. Returning to Conamara, the objection does not seem insurmountable. Geographically, it is similar to the rest of the western seaboard of Europe: there is the same threatening Atlantic in common, the same cruelly indented coasts, the same peninsular layout. If the people of Conamara could develop an unparalleled tradition of seamanship to overcome the apparent social disadvantage of their physical environment, could the same principle not apply on a larger scale to the entire Atlantic coast of Europe? If Conamara regarded intervening stretches of water not as insurmountable barriers to social intercourse but the very common means of achieving this intercourse, could not the same principle apply on a larger scale? Just as the Irish-speaking minorities in Ireland constitute a cultural archipelago in a sea of English speakers (and are now united through the airwaves of Raidió na Gaeltachta), could not the 'isolated' regions of Atlantic Europe constitute a similar archipelago, writ large? This would then include the Welsh, Bretons, Cornish, even the Galicians, in a unity much more solid than that normally suggested for them. I hope it is not too soon in my argument to point out that Morocco is also one such part of the Atlantic areas.

To most Europeans – but particularly to most Irish people – the idea of significant contact by sea, in the presence of trains and cars and planes, is a little quaint, despite the fact that every single influence that reached Ireland in the past came by sea – as do ninety per cent of its imports and exports still. The Irish mind is so paralysed in matters maritime that the boats between Rosslare and Fishguard or Pembroke, between Dún Laoghaire and Holyhead, between Larne and Stranraer – that is to say the shortest possible sea passages between Ireland and Britain – are about as far as the imagination can stretch.

Only recently have the *nouveaux riche* of Ireland discovered how relatively simple it is to sail their cruisers to the sunny climes of Marbella and the south of Spain. But there have also emerged some true sailors. Paddy Barry honed his skills by sailing to Santander, until he finally made the big leap and sailed his *húicéir* to Boston and later to the Arctic Circle. In 1989 the Kerry-based Roger Foxall sailed the first Irish yacht into Leningrad since the Russian revolution. His return voyage lasted 111 days and took in thirteen countries. The pioneer of them all was Conor O'Brien, who in 1923–5 circumnavigated the world in the boat *Saoirse*.

To revive such daring was appropriate because, as sociologist Michael D. Higgins has pointed out: 'The migrant is the norm in coastal parishes. The deviant is the person who does not move.' Sociologist Kevin Whelan agrees: 'Looking at Cois Fharraige, for example, the variety of surnames indicates considerable mobility, especially from County Clare.' It is also borne out by finds on the remotest tip of the island of Leitir Mealláin in Conamara. Here the late Pádraig Mulkerns, an amateur archaeologist, found three groats from the reign of Henry VII (1490); coins identified as George II and George III; a Napoleon III piece; and many Victorian pennies, as well as a brass tap from a sixteenth-century wine butt.

Dr John de Courcy Ireland has laboured for years to restore to the Irish mind a consciousness of its sea-girt position. In a lecture in 1983 he passionately declared:

> *An té a bhíonn long aige, geibheann sé cóir uair éigin.* (He who has a boat eventually gets a breeze.) A proverbial statement like that does not emanate from a people that is a landlubberly people. Long before the Irish language, or a Celtic language of any description, came into this country of ours, we were a maritime people, and the blood that flows in every one of us here, every one of us in the country, is blood that came across the sea. I do not accept that because we have a reputation for holiness in this country, our ancestors were dropped from heaven. And you can go back to the very earliest moment in history and you find that the first people who came into our country came here by sea, and they laid the foundations of a maritime tradition that this country has, richer and older than almost any country in Europe.

At this point it would be helpful if the notion of Ireland as a remote and isolated place receded. Ideally, it might be replaced by the image of a traffic island or even a trading post, centre of a vast traffic in ships up and down the Atlantic coasts from the Baltic Sea to the Straits of Gibraltar. Such, up to recent times, was the position of Ireland and there are many testimonies to this fact. Instead of a nervous hedge-hopping to and fro between Britain and Ireland – spending the least possible time on the ocean waves – a picture emerges of the sea not as a barrier but as an essential part of the multifaceted culture of this island. It is appropriate that in Conamara, whence I derived this untypical perspective, there exists a more solid image of the idea.

The *púcan* has an unusual and distinctive sailing rig called the dipping lug, or lateen sail. This sailing rig revolutionised the art of sailing in the thirteenth century by making it possible to approach the wind from almost any direction. Hitherto the square sail had enforced long delays in port waiting for 'a fair wind', i.e. from astern. With the lateen a boat could be sailed almost directly into the wind and, by using the technique called tacking, could travel at the master's, rather than the wind's, convenience. Its incorporation by the Portuguese into their renowned *caravelle* design contributed greatly to that nation's pioneering exploration of the world.

Having sailed in a *púcan* all the way down the west coast of Ireland, I was familiar with this strange rig. But it came as a surprise to me to learn that it was an invention of the Arabs and was still in use in North Africa. From Egyptian travelogues one can see the equivalent of the *púcan* in the dhows and feluccas of the Nile. Even in Tunisia, fishermen still use it. At one stage the *púcan* was the most popular fishing boat in Galway. Apart from those in Conamara itself, a considerable fleet of such fishing boats worked out from the Claddagh, in Galway City. They were built, like the *húicéir* and *gleoiteog*, in skeletal/carvel style – that is to say, with butt-joined planks over a framework, as distinct from clinker design where the planks overlap. An expert on vernacular boat-building, Michael McCaughan, has detailed the stark contrast between the proliferation of the clinker design on the north and east coasts of Ireland and the skeletal/carvel design on the west (Conamara) and south coasts of Ireland, which, he suggests, may be far more ancient, perhaps going back to pre-Roman times.

I shall conclude with an observation made in 1984 by a maritime observer, Arthur Reynolds, about a fine maker of miniature traditional craft in Conamara, Pádraic Ó hEidhin:

When I called to his home I noticed that he also makes wooden fish traps for taking rockfish or ballan, popular with the Aran islanders and local people. Surely the use of traps for fin fish in Conamara must be unique in Ireland, *even though many Middle East and Far Eastern fishermen work with nothing else.* [my italics]

Waiting for Gaddafi
(Cassandra Voices, May 2019)

A chapter from Bob's memoir, later serialised in Cassandra Voices, *telling of an experience in Libya in 1988 with Colonel Gaddafi.*

I was pretty sure I was going to die, sooner rather than later, one midsummer's night in Libya's desert. It was 1988. A cousin of Colonel Gaddafi, a military man, was driving us to meet the Great Man himself. In the darkness, we had turned left off the tarmacadamed main road between Benghazi and Tripoli, and were bumping over scrub and dunes on an invisible track, when the realisation dawned on me.

The convivial chat amongst my companions – an Irishman, an Englishman and my Arab interpreter – dried up, and silence filled the jeep. Suddenly it was quite clear: we were being brought out here to be shot.

I knew the Englishman had lied about his public school background. Had Gaddafi found this out and deduced he was a spy for the Brits? This was around the period Libya was supplying arms to the IRA.

I was mixing in strange company, but my excuse was scholarship: my work on the Irish/North African connection had brought me to the regime's attention as a person sympathetic to Islam, and who might also be sympathetic to Libya and its leader.

My interpreter told me that twelve months previously he had turned down an offer to become Minister for Information: 'You don't say no to this man, but how could I work for the regime, having seen friends hung in the public square?'

He too had good reason to be nervous. He was the one who introduced me to the concept: 'Bone in my meal' – meaning there's a fly in the ointment or, life is great except for one tiny thing.

We two Irishmen could not think of any reason why they should try to get rid of us, except as awkward witnesses. On the other hand, maybe we had corrupted his aides by persuading them to smuggle our hard liquor into this strictly dry country. Worse, I had allowed one of them to polish off half my vodka (he explained that vodka didn't leave a smell on his breath). Were they suspicious because I wrote my daily notes in the Irish language, and their regular surveillance of my room frustratingly divulged nothing?

One morning, after crying off on an excursion, I answered a knock on the door to find three burly and embarrassed men. They carried one towel between them and pretended that was the purpose of their visit. They entered, installed the towel, and departed sheepishly.

Perhaps I had not shown sufficient enthusiasm in the discussions about writing the leader's biography. Yes, it's true. This was an exploratory visit. In preparation I had read most of the existing accounts of the man. The indigenous works were grossly sycophantic, the foreign ones mostly antagonistic, many written in British tabloid style.

Apart from a few objective demographic and economic descriptions of the country, I found only one account, *Qadhafi's Libya* by Jonathan Bearman, with a foreword by Claudia Wright, which struck me as fair-minded.

Perhaps I had insulted the Great Man at our first meeting when I spoke in Irish, leaving him and the interpreters upstaged until I translated my own words? I knew I was privileged. Five years earlier Kenneth Clarke, a Minister for Health representing the Thatcher Government, had hoped to meet Gaddafi but was fobbed off with functionaries. My guides said the access granted to me was unparalleled in their experience. But I already knew flattery as the *lingua franca* of North Africa.

There again, it might have been my direct question: 'How, sir, with the absolute power at your disposal, have you not become corrupt?' Could the interpreter have translated that as an accusation? No, not likely, because Gaddafi replied: 'But I do not have absolute power. The people have it.'

Hence the nervous silence as the jeep groaned and bucked all over the place. The military man seemed unsure of his path: he constantly peered around into the blackness, and occasionally up into the dark sky. I followed his glances into the dark and thought: 'Yes, this would be a handy spot to lose four bodies.' I had already seen the Kalashnikov resting handily on the floor beside him.

The driver suddenly jammed on the brakes. 'This is it,' I thought. But all he did was get on the radio, and apparently ask for directions.

We resumed our helter skelter ride, and an hour later saw lights across the scrub. A circle of car headlamps greeted us. Should we be relieved, or was this to be some kind of show trial and execution?

At the far side of the circle stood a figure straight out of Sigmund Romberg's 1926 Broadway musical *Desert Song*: a tall sheikh in flowing robes.

I have to confess that my first ever 'encounter' with North Africans was in a musical comedy in which I sang and acted in 1961, and in which I was described by the music critic of the *Irish Times*, the late Charles Acton, as 'the only unconvincing character on stage'; a comment which fortuitously saved me from making a greater fool of myself in the theatre for the rest of my life. This did not, of course, prevent me from exposing my inadequacies in other areas.

A quarter of a century later Acton penned an enthusiastic endorsement of my *Atlantean* speculations, saying he was entirely convinced of an Irish-Bedouin musical connection. We never met.

The real sheikh who now faced me was Gaddafi. I realised this was his answer to my question about avoidance of corruption: the implication was that he was at heart a Bedouin, a man of the desert. The utter cleanliness of the desert kept man pure.

He answered my first question – about Bedouin incorruptibility – by handing me a jackrabbit and a pigeon which, to judge by their warmth and the tiny pulse I could still feel in the rabbit, were only recently sacrificed. These gifts did not reassure me.

I thought I might as well get a photograph and sought his permission. He gestured to his Bedouin costume and half-grinned: 'If they see me dressed like this they will certainly say I am a terrorist.'

A rug was spread on which we sat, in front of a small fire. Our host lowered himself onto a stool, deftly slipped into place by an armed female bodyguard, one of his so-called 'revolutionary nuns'. He did not even glance behind him. 'Now that,' I thought, 'is the confidence of power.' She also draped a cloak around his shoulders and made sure we kept a respectful distance. Then, of all things, he poured us each a cup of tea.

In an effort to avoid staring, I ventured that in his youth in the desert he must have often drunk tea round a fire like this. 'No,' he said. 'We did not have the luxury of tea in those days.'

That put me in my privileged Western place. Conversation with this man had not been easy. Perhaps he just wanted to be stared at.

Then I had an inspiration: I remembered that the feast of Abraham's sacrifice of his son Isaac was imminent. It had seemed to me that Gaddafi's father was sparsely mentioned in accounts of his life – even though the father lived to the age of ninety-five – whereas the leader's mother was very prominent in despatches. 'Aha,' thought I, 'maybe there's something Oedipal in the background.'

'I wonder,' I said, 'about Abraham and Isaac and your relationship with your own father.'

'I share your wondering,' he said and refilled my cup.

No more questions for the moment, your honour.

The Englishman referred to an alleged whipping episode of Arab boys by the Brits in Egypt.

He asked whether this had fuelled the leader's anger.

'Not especially,' he replied, 'I saw all of humanity being whipped, I saw cruelty towards humanity everywhere.'

I realised this man should have been a film director. He did in fact finance the epic *Lion of the Desert*, at a time when oil revenue was unparalleled. His four months of army training in England were largely spent at Beaconsfield – now the location of the National Film School. The elaborate scenario he had set up for us was a masterpiece of wide-screen cinema. Only the dialogue needed a little polishing. We were flattered at the show put on for us but, needless to say, were, quite literally, a captive audience out there in the desert.

There was a certain amount of polite conversation which did not last long. My fellow Irishman made a reference to Samuel Beckett, quoting the phrase 'Imagination Dead Imagine', which resulted in blank looks all round. I'm still not quite sure what his point was.

I enquired, fairly disingenuously, whether Mr Gaddafi saw himself as a kind of philosopher king in the Socratic mould. I forget the answer, if he gave one at all. The conversation was desultory. What must he have thought of these idiot Irishmen who spoke of literature and philosophy as if they were keys to understanding life's great mysteries?

In a practical tone, Gaddafi referred to a letter he had written to Kurt Waldheim about Bobby Sands and the hunger strikers. I mentioned the book *Ten Men Dead* by David Beresford with an introduction by Peter Maas, and he asked me to send him a copy. I never did.

After perhaps a half-hour he stood up. The conversation petered out. Our minds, I suspect, were running on parallel tracks miles apart, and consequently doomed never to meet. He seemed to be satisfied he had made his general point: that the ascetic life of a desert Bedouin was the ideal on which to base one's life and society. Mind you, the fancy suit, possibly Armani, that peeped out from under his desert robes slightly undermined the homily.

A large dormobile drove up. The leader rose, shook hands, vanished into its interior and off it trundled into the blackness. Our guide explained that the leader suffered from some arthritic condition; hence the dormobile. I was assured that I would have at least sixteen – a figure plucked out of the air – meetings with the man, and that if the biography was successful I would be commissioned to make a film of his life with an unlimited budget. With these dreams of grandeur we were left to face the uncomfortable ride home across the scrubland. At least we were still alive.

It wasn't the end.

On the way back a couple of jackrabbits were trapped in the corridor of our headlights. Our driver stopped the jeep suddenly, grabbed his rifle and leaped from the vehicle. Laughing, he began blasting away at the terrified animals. It was as if he was relieving the tension of the past few hours. He missed. I got out to stretch my legs and he offered me the rifle. I declined, much to his surprise.

We slept uncertainly that night wondering what other scenarios Mr Gaddafi had in store for us.

Some months later in the Crane Bar in Galway I met five American students bound for London to catch a Pan Am flight back to New York, and their University in Syracuse. I admit this may be hindsight, but even in the presence of my lively two-year-old, they seemed unusually subdued for young people. I don't believe in premonitions. Maybe they were just worn out with travel.

A couple of days later I heard about the horror of the plane crash in Lockerbie, Scotland. The news bulletin said many of the passengers were students from Syracuse University in New York. When it emerged that a bomb was the cause, the finger was pointed at Libya.

I did not refer publicly to my encounters with Gaddafi until much later. I feared my musings might endanger the people who confided in me there – despite their urgings at the time to tell the world. I hope it is safe for them now if I mention in passing that one of them brought me to a beach in Cyrenaica and said: 'When you go home, tell the Americans that this is the easiest place to invade.' Not far away was a place called Tobruk, which even I had heard of.

Interesting things happen to me in North Africa.

How the West Was Won
(Film Base News, October 1988)

In the late 1980s and early 90s, Bob contributed a number of articles to Ireland's two film magazines, Film West *in Galway and* Film Base News *(later* Film Ireland*) in Dublin. The articles, including this one, illustrate the contemporary debates in the emerging Irish film industry.*

I recall an image of a man with a twisted body, the result of adopting a posture for thirty years to execute his particular job in a nineteenth-century factory. I saw it in a medical book. Filmmakers must likewise now twist their psyches to keep working. This could be a permanent condition. The technology of filmmaking is not neutral (*pace* Jack Dowling). It is not an innocent tool to be manipulated by superior people. Insofar as it is designed by certain minds it ruthlessly serves the functions defined by these minds. In what does this design consist? Modern feature filmmaking is not a pretty picture. It is a voracious technology comprising above all money, plus its own closed-circuit memory, tradition and culture as well as profit expectations and last of all cameras, microphones and talent. This very technology defines that any other definition of filmmaking is Mickey Mouse, art house, pretentiousness, self-indulgent and all the other protective slanders that a controlling technocracy uses. Think of Paddy jokes; the same principle applies.

Insofar as Irish filmmaking is in its Gadarene swine phase, i.e. accepting the definition of the controlling technocracy, it must be examined from that perspective. In keeping with all aspects of Western capitalism – as distinct from Marxist capitalism – film technocracy must expand its production and consumption simply to survive. This expanding universe has peculiar, not to say contradictory, features. While, say, Irish film technocrats believe they are expanding into the UK market, they are in fact imploding into themselves and becoming forlorn satellites serviced by alienated and homesick technicians. While the UK technocracy thinks it is expanding into the USA it is also becoming a satellite.

Around what sun do these moth-like satellites flicker? Why, around the glowing orb of private and international capital which not only bypasses the fictions called nations but mainly consists of a laundry service for mafioso, drug wholesalers and tax evaders – including our own.

Just as an imitation Marxist could write, hopefully, for Hollywood, so also can 'Irish' film accommodate itself to the above circumstance. It is an ideal scenario at least for those agents who used to be called running dogs (in China their function was licking babies' bums clean) but are now more kindly known as suitmen: people who have the jesuitical voices and brains to make deals – with anybody. (But is it really an achievement to get money from the UK or the Cayman Islands or elsewhere in order to make necrophiliac films, i.e. those that suck drama from the agony of the North in the name of 'understanding', films that essentially constitute acts of betrayal?)

In the end this 'accommodation' is futile for two reasons. Firstly, it means an Irish film every five centuries – or feels like that. Secondly, the basic schizophrenia of the action produces objects that must be swept off the screen. Schizophrenia? Yes. We live in a post-colonial, third-world country whose national aspirations were long ago hijacked à la

Frantz Fanon by its national bourgeoisie, resulting in a haemorrhaging of people exiting plus an unwinnable war against its own people. Yet film people pretend they are reasonable middle-class people – albeit with provincial origins – observing the peasants making a mess of things. They pretend that the psychological decimation of this island by its leaders, both political and intellectual, in conjunction with Maggie and NATO, is not the cause of our angst, but is something deeply personal like our Christian Brothers education or, agreeing with the *Daily Mail*, a fault in our genes. They join with our journalists in eating us alive.

Question: Why?

Answer: Because we can get real money to make nothing else.

Q: Real money?

A: Yes, money to make 35mm cinema features.

Q: Wait a moment. Surely there are other approaches, other scales of finance? What about 16mm?

A: Ah but. 16mm is only for TV. We are into the magic of cinema. Also it's the only way to be taken seriously.

Q: But don't you want the widest possible audience for your ideas? Doesn't that mean TV?

A: First, we're not really into ideas, more into the complete sensual experience that is a darkened cinema...

Q: Isn't that the height of self-indulgence?

A: Not really. TV is bland. Besides, it limits subject matter and approach more than cinema. Besides, there's Section 31.

Q: Do you mean that even if you could get money to make a non-revisionist cinema film Sheamus Smith or Ward Anderson would let the equivalent of Gerry Adams be heard in the cinemas?

A: I thought this was a serious conversation. Are you a Provo, or something?

Q: As a filmmaker, your options seem to be limited.

A: Not at all. I can go to film school in England, make a short about terrorism, get money from Palace or Channel 4 or somebody and get my name on a small feature about the inner city or small town drugs – plenty of scope for stunts – or dropouts with nostalgia for guns, or Irish yuppies in London, or whatever. Then I can get into commercials, hone my skills, prepare for the big one – have a script …

Q: Working title?

A: *How the West Became One*. You see, film is an international business, a universal language, cuts across cultural differences, drags us out of our provincial narrowness, as I was saying to Mickey O'Rourke!

Q: *Go raibh maith agat*?

To be facetious for a moment: what is recently clear in the truly desperate environment of filmmaking in this country is that success is now judged similarly to years ago when, as Donal McCann has said, we were thrilled if the snaps came out. The criterion of the success of an Irish film now is simply its appearance on the large screen.

Congratulations might be due on these grounds to the recent spate of Irish films – however compromised by their sources of funding, by the paralysing structures within which they were made – if they were not, without exception, triumphs of hustling and business acumen rather than of film itself.

Perhaps the moral is that it was ever, and ever will be, thus. The filmmaker makes a choice: to get his/her name in the trade papers or to make a decent film – on Super 8 if necessary.

MIPCOM in Cannes *or* What's a Nice Filmmaker Like You Doing in a Place Like This?
(Film West, Winter 1989)

The nearest thing to it I've seen is the 'souk' or marketplace in Tangier. Hundreds of stalls filled with gaudy geegaws, their owners blaring their virtues, in this case on TV screens. Imagine going to an Arabic market and trying to sell them something. That's what MIPCOM is like. If you're a salesman it's the place for you. If you're a filmmaker, stay away.

If one possesses a magnificent building on the seafront in Cannes whose principal industry is the famous film festival it is incumbent on you to fill it for the rest of the year. And that's what Reed Exhibition

Companies – the new owners of MIPCOM – do. They invite TV moguls, producers, cable and satellite companies, and broadcasters to come and – for a large fee – commune with each other. In September last they came, in their thousands. No small independent could afford to attend. So Euromedia provided an umbrella under which many independents could huddle, occasionally darting out to try and capture a buyer, persuade him/her to glance at their work, commit themselves to buy or at least look at a full programme back home. Miraculously, this occasionally happened.

The Irish independents had a further buffer against harsh reality in that Córas Tráchtála substantially contributed to their expenses. (But if you lost the magic badge that entitled you to pass the many bouncers, it cost you £70 to replace it.)

Being a coward I stayed away from all these thrusting personalities, left my producer to do all the dirty work and spent the time exploring Cannes. I saw *Batman* in French and visited the Isle of Lérins which libels itself by claiming that St Patrick stayed there before returning to Ireland. Still, the chanted Mass nearly made me revise my status as a lapsed atheist. I met a buyer from RTÉ, an old friend, on the Croisette and we had a great conversation about our hernias. Film was not mentioned. We are not vulgar people. I called to the church where Napoleon prayed for a comeback and heard a Breton choir singing out of tune, which restored my cynicism.

On Friday I attended the three hours of Peter Brook's latest epic called *The Mahabharata*. Every TV station in the cosmos, including RTÉ, was a backer. Amazing what a reputation will enable you to get away with.

In one of my occasional guilty forays back into the mêlée I heard a buyer from some American octopus express amazement that the American people were actually interested in some excerpts from Russian TV which her network had shown. I pointed out to her that her astonishment was a good reason for herself and all her out of touch fellow executives to resign their positions. She smiled. TV executives always smile – like tigers. I doubt if she'll buy my films.

Later I heard a colleague's voice raised at two other buyers and thanked the Lord I wasn't alone: in the wrong place at the wrong time.

Towards the end of the week panic was clearly visible in the eyes of some who took the whole thing seriously. All this time and money, for what?

Repeat: this is not a place for filmmakers. It's a place for salesmen and a lot of those I saw there, I wouldn't buy a used film from. But, believe me, that's what TV and film are all about – and why I've been trying to get out of it for years.

Television and Locality – Gaeltacht Community TV
(Celtic Film and Television Festival, 1990)

A piece from 1990 arguing the case for a television service for the Gaeltacht, published in the programme of the Celtic Film and Television Festival, which that year took place in the Donegal Gaeltacht of Gaoth Dobhair.

A Welsh television producer once told me that the reason they had S4C and that the Irish had not got its equivalent was that the Welsh were cuter. I doubted that. Why, if the Welsh were so cute, had they not achieved independence? Then I started thinking that the answer might lie in the question: It was precisely because of their close link with and cute manipulation of Westminster that the Welsh had achieved S4C.

Why has our proud autonomy of sixty years left the Irish language an orphan in the area of television? Clearly the first answer is that our political independence was illusory and the effort to pass a veneer of Gaelicism over this illusion showed and still shows the nature of the illusion.

The only people to understand this situation were and are the people of the Gaeltacht. They were at the coalface. They saw through the rhetoric. They saw where Irish got them: Scotland, Boston and London. In the sixties they fulminated, endeavoured to get through to well-meaning revivalists, limousine liberals and opportunist politicians. They were given Raidió na Gaeltachta to shut them up. It did.

However, in autumn 1987 a transient filmmaker and part-time electronic genius named Norbert Payne (son of a poet – wouldn't you know) built two transmitters in Conamara and put 'Teilifís na Gaeltachta' on the air for a weekend.

Why?

First, because he was waylaid in August '87 on a Galway street on a Sunday morning before the pubs opened and asked could he transmit a signal without wires and he said yes. Second because it was clear to everybody living in the Gaeltacht that the children there were learning Dallas-speak faster even than 'hopefully' or 'at this point in time' or 'no way' or 'make my day'. A schoolteacher in Conamara recorded the signature tunes of all TV programmes on RTÉ, played them to her primary school pupils and heard them identify all but those of the Irish-language programmes. As no household in the Gaeltacht normally has more than one TV set it meant that the parents were also ignoring Irish-language programmes.

Why?

For the same reason that Dublin audiences would switch off programmes if their sole *raison d'être* was that they were in English.

The Gaeltacht is not just some kind of well of linguistic spirituality to which one may refer when the weather is good. People actually live here when festival booze-ups are over. They make love here. They use caput Anglais, and the pill too. They are stratified in classes. They watch and listen to Gay Byrne! In other words they are as banjaxed as suburbians. What distinguishes them, however, is (1) their daily language (after Greek and Latin) is the oldest with a literature in Europe and it binds them into a community; and (2) the people of the Gaeltacht do not care a tinker's curse about this fact. They simply speak the language. Now as Dublin has its local TV service – well, from the Gaeltacht it looks like that – why hasn't the Gaeltacht?

Two Ministers of State in the present Irish Government were born and bred in the Gaeltacht (one, Máire Geoghegan-Quinn, has her bailiwick in Conamara, the other, Pat Gallagher, is local to this festival). One is definitely against Teilifís na Gaeltachta. The other is kicking for touch. (Guess which.) Fortunately the actual Minister for the Gaeltacht (Charles J. Haughey) has ever publicly declared in favour of a Gaeltacht TV service and earmarked half a million pounds towards it. Since then, silence.

Why?

Perhaps because Tallaght or Ballyfermot haven't a community TV service. Or Limerick. Or Cork, Galway, Lithuania, Estonia, Azerbaijan... Sorry, the last three have. And still they're not satisfied. That was a rhetorical question. All broadcasters know why there is no such thing as community TV. How could professional standards (and union rates) be maintained if every Ballyslapdashamuckery had its own TV station? The politicians have a more focused view. How could centralised control be maintained in such a situation? More importantly, how could Section 31 be maintained if every small community had its own TV station?

Broadcasting democracy is a dangerous concept.

At this festival in County Down some years ago, Seán Ó Mórdha of RTÉ was asked by Tommy Collins of Derry Film & Video why, if the broadcasters objected to the censorship of Section 31, didn't they defy it. Séan answered that if they did RTÉ would be closed down. Tommy asked would that be a bad thing. Séan asked for the next question. Thus the sub-plot is this: governments – all governments – dislike the public broadcasting ethos as solely represented in this country by RTÉ.

How to diminish its effect? Simple. Force RTÉ to transmit more Dublin programmes in Irish and pretend they are catering for the Gaeltacht. Gaeltacht people will certainly not watch such programmes, but statutory quotas will have been filled. They also will not have Teilifís na Gaeltachta. RTÉ will lose its majority English-speaking viewers to the Government's invention – TV3.

A political solution to a cultural problem.

The revisionism of Irish history in the last 20 years has clearly stated that we Irish are not capable of ruling ourselves, that we should never have left the British Empire; *Irish Times* – please note.

Acknowledging this, Meitheal Oibre Theilifís na Gaeltachta – the group that put the pilot Teilifís na Gaeltachta on air in 1987 and 1988

– is at present approaching the Prime Minister of Great Britain and Northern Ireland and requesting her to extend her Scottish largesse (£12 million for a Gaelic language TV) to Northern Ireland. Just as we do with the BBC we can pirate the Gaelic programmes from up there. The second tactic will be to organise a 'Lá Tostach' – a day of silence – when Gaeltacht people will prove their modernity by speaking any language but Irish. Will anybody in power notice, or care?

The third tactic will be to do a Gwynfor Evans and threaten a hunger strike to the death. Unfortunately, this is a riskier business ever since the fashion developed of letting such misguided people simply die.

But something must happen. And very soon. Otherwise the children of the Gaeltacht will continue replacing the language of their parents with the dialects of Bill Cosby and Kylie Minogue.

Miracles at Pesaro
(Film West, Summer 1990)

'We will pay for all your extras except telephone calls,' said the director of the 26th Pesaro Film Festival. Noting the disbelief in our eyes he said: 'Yes, even your drink.' Miracle number one.

Miracle number two is that the municipal authority of this small town on the Adriatic coast a hundred miles north-east of Rome paid for the entire ten-day event. Entry to the films was free, as were the headphones for simultaneous translation into French, Italian, English and Farsi. No charge either for the well-written brochures and booklets.

Miracle number three was a debate within the Irish delegation which started publicly at 10am on day seven, continuing informally until 5am the following morning, punctuated by lunch, dinner and a skinny dip in the Adriatic at 2.30am – and little other than surface wounds inflicted. Minor miracle was that the free drink had nothing to do with it. Kevin Rockett and I had to leave on day eight. For all we know the others, Paul Freaney, Alan Gilsenan, Richard and Anne

Kearney, Joe Comerford and Nicholas O'Neill, may still be yapping away in the perfumed nights of Pesaro.

The festival had three distinct sections: modern Irish and Iranian films plus British silent films. The last was the most interesting because we've seen our small output too often and because the Iranians seem to mainly make children's films. I normally avoid film festivals but went to Pesaro because it was the first to recognise *Caoineadh Airt Uí Laoire* fifteen years ago, so there must be more than starlets and sycophantic journalists involved. The instinct was right. These people take film seriously. There were excellent houses from 9pm until midnight. Questions were intelligent in the open forum, interviewers never mentioned budgets, concentrating instead on the art of film and the religious and political context in which they were made both in Ireland and Iran. They would, wouldn't they, I hear you say. But when comparable debate here is about the level of my left toe, it was refreshing.

For the Irish forum, several people noticed the line-up at the table: the journalist, the philosopher, the historian and the Arts Council officer taking centre stage; the three filmmakers hanging onto the ends of the table. It just happened like that. We know our place. We touched gloves by all standing and reciting Donnelly's Concise History of Ireland: Is it true, is it true? / And the tears fell on the letter in his hand. / Too true, too true. / More trouble in our native land! What was said was predictable. Kevin Rockett gave his usual calm historical analysis; Nicholas O'Neill spoke as a film reviewer, so I can't remember what he said; and Paul Freaney was also optimistic. Joe Comerford said Irish filmmakers had been marginalised out of existence in an arena of post-colonial revisionism. Alan Gilsenan said it wasn't that bad, and anyway the individual artist should be more concerned with imagination and passion than with politics. I said the artist by definition was a standing prick, i.e. had no conscience. Richard Kearney said Comerford and I were cynical and romantic (both at the same time) and gave long analyses of *Angel* and *Maeve*.

The real debate, as usual, came afterwards. It was agreed, surprisingly by all, that the Arts Council should give money only to 'lunatics' who hadn't a chance in hell with the suitmen. The role of the

Catholic Church was of course dissected. Conflicting aspects of this institution were defended surprisingly well by Dr Kearney and Paul Freaney. In another context Fr Des Wilson of Belfast was described as the greatest intellectual in Ireland. Vivienne Dick's status in America was reinforced by P. Adams Sitney, an American expert in underground cinema, who joined the group and reminded us how shabbily she had been treated by the late Irish Film Board. The highlight of it was at about midnight, when there was a passionate plea from one of the group for sex in Irish films. Asked why he didn't make such a film himself he proudly claimed to have made a Super-8 porn film years ago, in which one male gave another a blow job in a front garden in Sandymount.

And the question arose: how difficult is it for Irish people to say 'I love you'?

Listen, there's a real world out there, outside the pressure chamber of this small island, a place where Irish people actually talk freely, honestly and without malice. It's called Pesaro.

Once Upon a Script
(Film West, Winter 1991/92)

Bob's account of his experience with the European Script Fund scheme, part of the then EC's Media '95 programme.

It was called *Beautiful Isle of Somewhere* first of all, and then it was called *The Immigrant*, and now it's called *Celts*, which means at least it is still alive. I made my last film in 1975, and in 1976 another last film, another last film in 1977, another last film and so ever since then; every film I make is my last film.

I find film a very painful business; it depresses me, angers me and irritates me and it is too much like hard work. This is also intended to be my last film and I hope it is.

The outline is based on a true incident on an island in the west of Ireland where somebody at the end commits suicide. So in that form it was awarded a loan by the European Script Fund in 1989. Two and a half years ago, it was turned down for an Arts Council Film Script Award.

The producer (Christy King) I adopted, or who adopted me, was a friend of mine from way back and is a great hustler. The two of us over the last two years have been working in tandem, he being a person who can talk to suitmen, I being a person who can't talk to suitmen. He has done all the travelling and talking and I have sat at home writing and ringing. So, I just want to give you an idea of the number of contacts we made and the results of them.

In 1989, Jeremy Home of Channel 4 turned down the idea with the comment that the island featured in the script was not one he would like to visit – I don't blame him. Christy then approached Simon Relph of British Screen London. He was favourable towards the idea but he was reluctant to be the first investor. That's the most common theme of all – everybody is afraid to put their toe in the water first.

The script was then submitted to Bob Collins of RTÉ, who suggested passing it on to Richard Staniforth who was then Head of the Welsh Film Board. He was approached because I was prepared to shoot this film in a Welsh, Celtic and linguistic context. Staniforth lost the script or didn't get it, so we sent him another one and he turned that down. Since then, Staniforth has been reincarnated in 'Persona Films'. I also sent it off to Bill Bryden of BBC drama, who kept it for six months and then turned it down.

Throughout this period, I had been working on the script. At the start I loved the idea – it was a grand melancholic, depressive idea with a suicide at the end, which thrilled me. However, over the last couple of years I have changed, the world has changed, and I have been tinkering at it, working at it.

Coming in contact with the Script Fund was one of the most helpful things that happened. I got a report from them which encouraged me to become more positive about my idea. This was an organic process, in that the more I became depressed with the problems of making the film, the more optimistic I became about the theme itself and decided, 'Why give up? Why commit suicide?', and so I developed it into something more optimistic. I have to confess that it was also in part a response to the attitude of people who have money and who are involved in film funding. They are, I think, more inclined to be interested in Walt Disney than in angst.

The revised script was sent to the new head of British Screen, Simon Perry, last September. A response is still awaited from him. I also got another report from the Script Fund, which was even more helpful, so I sat down and wrote the script again and indeed it is just on the presses at the moment. The brand new, ultimate – no, penultimate – script is called *The Celts* and has a great ending. You will stand up and cheer at the ending now.

Before this last draft, Mark Shebas in Channel 4 turned the script down again. Christy met a man called Pat Ferns of Primedia in Canada, who had worked with RTÉ on *Dick Francis*, but he said the budget was too small for him to be interested. This year it was re-submitted to Bob Collins of RTÉ, who still has no money for non-recent ex-staff independent projects. The Arts Council also recently turned down the reconstructed and rewritten version for a script award. They also retained £10,000 of the available award money, so I wonder, were they trying to tell me something?

By now the script resembles the original concept and it also has the new title *Celts*. An agent in London told Christy that it might make a 'Celtic *Cinema Paradiso*' and I am still trying to work that out. There is a friend of mine who has some deal with a crowd called WMG Telefilm Essen and suggested sending it to their office in Munich to a man called Hans Brockmann; I wrote, I sent faxes, and I got no reply whatsoever.

Another crowd called Druid Films in New York expressed themselves very happy with the idea and said that if we got an international star and told them how many millions we wanted to make out of the project, that they could work with us. I left that to Christy to work out.

I met Dieter Kosslick in July and he said that when I had a budget, to send it to him and he would help. Two alternative budgets were provided for him in Cork recently; one was £600,000 for a 16mm film and £1m for a 35mm film. This is all tremendously new to me because it is against my religion to spend more than £100,000 on the business of film.

I have a friend in distribution in Los Angeles, T.C. Rice, who has become the father confessor to many Irish independents. He has read the script, made some suggestions, and asked for a final copy of it to shop it around in LA. I am getting involved in a huge world here that I never had anything to do with before and I am not in the least depressed by this whole bad history.

After two and a half years, with a producer handling the film, it still has not been made. I now have to rethink my priorities and get back to my original role as a one-man band; producer, director, writer, editor, and the whole catastrophe that may happen. On the other hand, my producer is committed to putting £50,000 into this film upfront, which is very generous.

One last thing, to prove that I am not too pessimistic, I have decided not to bring back the original suicide in the first script, and I will play the part myself.

Smokey Hollow
(1991)

The first two chapters of Smokey Hollow, *Bob's fictionalised memoir of his childhood in Orwell Gardens, Dublin, published by the O'Brien Press. The name 'Toner', the surname of the family in the story, is the maiden name of Bob's mother Annie. Annie's father was Robert Toner, after whom Bob and two of his sons are named.*

I

The only thing you can do with bogeymen is pull the covers over your head and wish the night will hurry up so that the daylight can banish them.

You know their shadows are still up there on the ceiling and on the wall. They're peering down, but maybe they won't come near if you hold your breath and don't move, pretend you're already dead, fill your head with things like: Janey Mack me shirt is black, what'll I do for Sunday, go to bed and cover me head, and not get up till Monday.

Listen. Not a move. Now I lay me down to sleep I pray the Lord my soul to keep and if I die before I wake I pray the Lord my soul to take. Anything to stop thinking of them. But it's no use; when you've used up all your poems and prayers they're still up there and you're clutching the covers waiting for them to pounce.

Even with his eyes squeezed shut Dominic could always see them plainly. Now one of the shadows was big and black like the huntsman with the hatchet that creeps up on Snow White in the forest because the ugly oul' bitch of a queen has ordered him to kill the girl so that liar of a mirror will be fooled and tell her she's still the fairest of them all. The big dark shadow looms over Snow White and she cringes back. Oh feck, he should have closed his eyes for that bit. He knew it would give him nightmares but he couldn't take his eyes off the screen.

In this nightmare the victim was Bern, his big brother, and the huntsman shadow was his father. Snow White was tied to one of the brass knobs of the bedstead, wriggling like a fish while the huntsman unbuckled his belt. It didn't matter that in the pictures the huntsman was really soft-hearted and let Snow White off with a warning. He got into terrible trouble with the queen that time. He wasn't going to let the next kid off so easy. Dominic huddled deeper into the blankets, examining his conscience, desperately identifying his own sins, wondering which of them would justify him being the next for the hatchet. He heard their mother coming up the stairs at a run. Relief. She'd chase the bogeymen away.

– James, don't. He's learned his lesson.

– I'll learn him more.

The belt thwacked sickeningly against the door jamb as the huntsman practised his swing.

She would be standing at the narrow turn of the stairs, looking through the bannisters. Her eyes would be tired, her face slightly drawn. In her wedding photo in the glass case in the sittingroom she was darkhaired and pretty, but bearing and rearing five children, sewing all their clothes, darning all their socks, keeping the house clean to the exacting standards of her tradition had taken their toll. Dominic would not in the future ever be able to conjure up the sound of her famous silvery laugh because he heard it so rarely. He was more accustomed to sighs or doleful tones as she led the family rosary, the only supplicant to kneel upright.

– He won't do it again, sure you won't, son?

– I'll make damn sure he doesn't.

The belt slapped against the door again. The victim wriggled furiously.

– All I ask is a bit of peace when I get home. All I get is squabbling kids. I'll put an end to it once and for all.

– He's sorry, aren't you, son?

– Yes I am, I am.

He still had not been hit. Abject grovelling was the key to salvation. The anger went from the huntsman shape. The victim went limp.

– I'm warning you, me bucko. Next time you won't have your mother to save you. I'll take your solemn life, I swear.

Bern escaped into bed. Snow White was saved. The huntsman was only pretending, had a heart after all. Dominic raised his head from the covers and peered around the room. The shadows were gone. He heard the parents going downstairs, the third step from the end squeaking as usual, blunting the seriousness of the procession. Before the sittingroom door slammed, Mr Toner called out a final warning.

– Not another sound from any of you.

They waited ten seconds of murmuring from the room below to make sure he wasn't listening at the foot of the stairs to catch them out. Then they relaxed. The reprieved criminal, Bern, made a deprecating sound. His bedmate, Joe, began the whispered interrogation while the youngest listened.

– Did he get you?

– Not at all.

– Go on. He nearly killed you.

– Missed me every time. Couldn't get a decent swipe. He only hit the door. He always does that. He's an oul' softy.

– Didn't sound like it.

– Sure he's only trying to frighten us. Anyway, how would you know? It was me he was aiming at.

One of the girls came on tiptoe from the boxroom.

– Are you all right?

– No thanks to you.

– I only asked, snotty.

– None of your business, anyway. You told him I peed on the cabbages.

– I did not. Mammy saw you herself.

– Only after you told her, you little bitch.

– I'm telling what you called me, you brat.

– Go away, wet your knickers.

– I'm telling on you.

They froze as a door opened and the voice bellowed.

– Go asleep this minute or I'll come up those stairs three at a time. I'll mark you all and that's your last warning.

The sister fled back to her room. There was silence. Since Mr Toner had bored a hole in the ceiling of the room below – to let some of the warm air penetrate upstairs – they had no privacy. It was a well-meant attempt at primitive central heating but it made no difference to the temperature.

Normally he would come up to tuck them in and make the sign of the cross on their foreheads. He would straighten their knees, tell them to sleep on their sides, their arms pillowing their heads in a salute. That's the way soldiers sleep, he'd say. You'll never have backache that way. It was also a check that they weren't fiddling with themselves. You were never too young for sins of the flesh. There were other checks too. They learned to recite a prayer in the morning:

Angel of God, my guardian dear,
To whom God's love commits me here,
Ever this day be at my side,
To light, to guard, to rule and guide.

When they realised that this angel could also snoop on their most private conversations and actions they ceased to invoke him. Nobody likes squealers.

Immediately he left they would pull up their knees, replace their hands between their thighs to warm them and resume the armchair position which allowed heat to be shared.

When Mr Toner went downstairs the master storyteller, Bern, would resume. He had the advantage of seeing more films; the obligatory retelling of these, much embellished, formed the substance of his tales. *Reap the Wild Wind* was a favourite, especially the part where the octopus grabs the diver in the sunken treasure ship, breaks his air line, strangles him, then drags him struggling down to his dark lair. Dominic would cover his ears for that part even when Bern said the diver was the bad guy and he had it coming to him. The chap always got the girl, except in *Geronimo* and *Custer's Last Stand*. When the younger ones eventually saw the films for themselves they were not nearly as entertaining.

The boys' room had two beds, a double for Bern and Joe, a single for Dominic, the youngest. Their two sisters slept in the small front room and the parents occupied the room in between. It would be years before they would dare trespass on that sacred territory with its black wooden bedside locker which contained only a pile of silvery badges in the image of doves, representing the Holy Ghost. Mr Toner was a member of some confraternity run by his priest cousin. He never got around to distributing the badges.

On winter mornings it was lovely to be wakened by the sound of the radio and know you didn't have to get up yet. Mr Toner was often due at work in the brewery at six o'clock, especially approaching Christmas. And little thanks I get for it, he used say. Nowadays they wouldn't recognise work if it jumped up and bit them.

Mr Toner made the porridge the previous night and had only to heat it up for his breakfast. While he shaved, the radio murmured the morning litany that would constitute part of the memory of most children living in the British Isles in that period: Lundy, Sole, Fastnet, Shannon, Malin, Iceland, Faroes, Dogger which Dominic thought was the Dodder, the river that flowed at the back of their garden. The names were indelibly imprinted on their memories and so was 'Lilliburlero', the tune that announced the news and which their father said the English had stolen from them.

The ritual never varied, six days a week, summer and winter. They waited for the radio to be switched off, the voice calling softly up the stairs, 'I'm off, Mam.' Then they heard the back door opening.

There would be a pause while he collected his bike from the shed, then the creak of the side gate, the clatter of the front gate and they could go back to sleep until it was time for Mrs Toner to heat up the porridge for them. When he was first married their father owned an old Harley-Davidson motorcycle and a sidecar which he built himself and into which the first babies were crammed. They saw the photo of the machine in the glass case and hoped he would get another, but he never did.

The Toners lived in a cul-de-sac of about eighty houses built in Council style by some socially aware town planner in the thirties. He located the scheme in the middle of one of the poshest suburbs in Dublin. Whether the intention was to improve the manners of its working-class inhabitants or to apply a little Bolshevik jab to the local bourgeoisie it would be difficult to say. But lest there be squeals of protest – or possibly as a result of protests from the respectable residents – a facade of ten or eleven more opulent houses was erected at the entrance to the ghetto. These effectively camouflaged the swarming little development. Delicate sensibilities, not to mention property values, were therefore protected. It suited the residents of the cul-de-sac too because they prided themselves on being house owners, not Council tenants. These were utility houses, built by a private developer and purchased on long-term mortgages.

The Toner family arrived in their grandfather's pony and cart in the year the Second World War started. They had escaped from the less desirable area of Drimnagh whose address automatically branded them as Council or Corporation dwellers. In those straitened days degrees of poverty were perceived more sharply than distinctions between rich and poor. Nothing changes.

Dominic was barely old enough to remember the excitement of the journey on a moonlit night, the cart crammed with children and the smaller household goods, their mother holding on to them for dear life while Granda Hope urged on their very own snow white steed with flowing mane called Kit, after Kit Carson of course, who in daylight was an undersized, overburdened, dirty-grey animal with sores on its knees. It had a long tail that whipped at their faces while their Granda cursed it, 'Will you hup outa that, you lazy streepeach.'

On the short, steep hill down to the cul-de-sac, which would later be perfect for toboggans, they felt terror, sure that the pony would slip and they would go tumbling over its back. No such thing happened and they were greeted by Mr Toner and the older children who had earlier that day cycled across the south city suburbs of Harold's Cross and Rathgar to meet the furniture van. Dominic, already half asleep, went out like a light.

II

The new home was paradise, halfway between city and country. There were plenty of other kids and friendly neighbours. The river lined it on one side, squeezing the rows of terraced houses like toothpaste against the mini-escarpment of the Churchtown hill. Although this gave it a tucked-in character which Drimnagh could never have, it also made it the most unsalubrious location for miles around: a damp, low-lying area which caused the river to flood the houses down at the end every few winters. The nice people living in the surrounding areas nicknamed it Smokey Hollow because on summer mornings the settlement was shrouded in mist and in winter the smoke from coal fires gave the same effect. Fog always remained thickest over the Hollow. To the children, this gave it a magical dimension.

It also gave them the opportunity to get their own back on cranky neighbours. They would tie a long piece of thread to a door knocker, feed it out as delicately as a fuse, then, retreating towards the safety zone, tug sharply, hear the knocker rattling as the thread broke, destroying the evidence. It was thrilling simply to stand still and know they were invisible, to hear the screeched imprecations of the householder as he or she peered uselessly into the grey blanket.

The children familiarised themselves with the neighbours by means of a simple game played every night after lights out:

– Who lives in number sixty-one?
– The O'Briens.
– Wrong.
– The Murtaghs.
– Wrong.

– Give up.

– The Woodisons.

– What! They do not. They live in number sixty-three. I was there only yesterday.

– You're wrong.

– Wanna bet?

And so on until they fell asleep.

The first row the Toner kids had with their new neighbours was about who was going to play the devil in the play in Lynch's shed. It was really Joe's row but they were all dragged in because the previous night they had been regaled by Bern's version of *The Three Musketeers* in the Classic cinema.

– So, said Joe to Bern when the row broke out. One for all and all for one, right?

– Oh all right, said Bern grudgingly. There was no backing out even if Bern hadn't the faintest interest in play-acting and particularly in stupid plays about ghosts and devils.

Every play in Lynch's shed featured a ghost or a devil. It was the best thing about the plays. In fact it was the only substantial thing that happened. All plots were improvised and whether they were about nagging wives and drunkard husbands, policemen and robbers, mad professors who had sold their souls to the devil and were going to blow up the world – no matter, all led up to the point where the kid lucky enough to get the part draped himself in a sheet and leaped out from the wings bellowing at everybody that he was the devil or the ghost, whichever suited the narrative. This was the cue as well as the excuse for everybody to start shouting and roaring.

The key to the role was the sheet. Whoever could provide the costume automatically got the part. Mothers refused point-blank to lend such expensive items. They always got dirty and invariably got torn. If the sheets were newish it was out of the question. If they were old and patched the neighbours would know whose it was. So it had to be taken without permission and returned with nobody the wiser. Whoever had the nerve to do this deserved the part of the ghost/devil.

Joe, waiting in the wings as it were, was perceptive enough to see this as a shortcut to acceptance in the gang and airily declared it'd be no bother to get one. He was duly promised the part. But when the day of the performance came he turned up and glumly reported failure. The mothers' grapevine had heard about the play so the linen cupboards and hot presses were policed too tightly.

There was only one solution and Davy Lynch knew it. It was his shed and he was overall impresario, playwright and chief actor. With a black look at Joe he slinged up his garden path. They saw him disappear into the kitchen and waited despondently for the indignant sounds of refusal from Mrs Lynch.

When Davy appeared with the sheet in his hands everyone was very impressed. The day, and the play, were saved. That's when the row started.

– Good man yourself, said Joe. Let's see how it fits.

– Of course it fits, said Davy, draping it over his own head.

Joe took a deep breath.

– No messing now. You said I could be the devil.

Davy lifted the sheet to reveal his incredulous expression.

– Are you codding! I got the sheet. I'm the devil.

He dropped the sheet over his face again and uttered an experimental growl.

– Don't annoy me, said Joe patiently.

– And you don't annoy me, said the devil.

– I'm warning you, said Joe.

The devil waved his arms derisively and turned his back on Joe. What was a frustrated actor to do?

– You're only a little shit, Davy Lynch, muttered Joe and directed a kick at the devil's backside.

The devil yelped, turned and kicked back wildly. He caught Joe in the goolies. Joe yelled in pain, crumpled briefly, then straightened up and lashed out with his fist at the part of the sheet where Davy's nose should be, and was. It was a direct hit, evidenced by a red stain seeping through the sheet. The devil had a bloody nose. Joe ran for his life.

That wasn't the end of it. His fellow actors pushed Davy's head back, placed a bit of tin at the back of his neck and eventually stopped the nosebleed. Then they discussed what to do. The sheet's condition could be blamed on Joe Toner and compensation could be worked out between mothers. Joe would certainly get a hiding. In the meantime … the red stain on the sheet was fascinating. It would be a shame to waste it.

They decided the show must go on. But as the devil was sort of like Dracula and didn't have any blood in his veins – or so the Slag Kelly said – the sheet would be used to represent the ghost of a murdered man. The temptation of a real blood-stained sheet was irresistible.

Back in the safety of his own garden, five houses away, Joe brooded. He would never be let in, even to watch the show. But he knew that security at the shed always became lax once the play started. That's when he demanded Bern's cooperation and together they concocted a plan of revenge.

The local children crowded into the shed for the performance. They were a noisy, jostling, catcalling lot. Even babies were there, bawling before the thing started, before the ghost even came out to frighten them. They sat on planks placed on wooden boxes. Those in the front row passed the time by ducking their heads through the sacks which served as curtains and bobbing quickly back to avoid the vicious kicks from the cast within.

The play started. It was a complex plot which neither the audience nor the cast could understand because no lines were audible. But Davy, playing one of his many roles, swaggered convincingly across the ten feet of stage dragging at a stolen cigarette and it was clear he was the detective brought in by the worried-looking woman, Maisie McGee, in a superlative performance marred only by the calls to show them her knickers. Various characters made entrances and exits, looking here and there for stolen jewels and bumping repeatedly and violently into each other, because that got the laughs.

There were numerous fights and one stabbing when Davy had to stagger interminably all over the place, dying for a long time. Then there was an interval where Ginty Scully tried to sing 'The Moon Behind the Hill' and was booed off the stage.

A rumour started among the audience that there was no ghost at all, otherwise why would they bore people with Ginty Scully who hadn't a note in his head. They began to stamp their feet.

– Give us our money back, they chanted, which was unjust because very few of them had paid the entrance fee – a jamjar on which Davy hoped to collect the penny refund.

So the climax had to be advanced a little in the play. It was Davy's big moment to don the sheet. On the corrugated roof of the shed, Bern and Joe crouched. They could follow the action easily by listening to the din and peering through the holes left by long-rusted nails. At the precisely correct moment, as Davy was about to make his big entrance, they lit twisted bits of newspaper and pushed them through a gap in two layers of the corrugated iron, directly over the stage area.

These missiles contained pieces of nitrate film, obtained from Mr Toner's workshop. They were the most effective stinkbombs of all, as was instantly recognised by the experts in the audience below. Not only did the bombs stink foully, they produced a satisfying volume of smoke.

No previous ghost ever produced such pandemonium. Both the stage and the seating were wrecked – rather, reverted to their normal status of planks and barrels – in the ensuing mêlée. Babies even stopped crying and gazed in wonder at the entertainment. Miraculously nobody got more than normal abrasions and the only real casualty was Mrs Lynch's sheet which was trampled in the rush. It was later agreed that it was the best play ever, and everybody congratulated Joe and Bern on their daring.

They even congratulated Davy on his inspired stage direction and he had to pretend that it was all arranged, but privately he told Joe it would be over his dead body if Joe ever appeared on stage again.

– It's only for sissies anyway, muttered Joe, smug that he didn't have the job of bringing home a bloody as well as torn and dirty sheet.

It was a kind of initiation rite for Bern and Joe as well as their siblings. It showed that you didn't mess around with the Toners, and on that level they fitted with ease into the community.

Across the stepping stones at the back of Toners' was a field with a long avenue of young pine trees clearly designed for hide-and-seek. On hot summer nights it was used also by courting couples, mainly army privates from Portobello Barracks who brought their mots on the tram from Rathmines to Dartry and persuaded them to walk in the field. But this was Hollow territory. People intruded at their own risk, and were fair game for the older children who could evade or ignore the evening chorus of parents calling that it was time to go to bed. Hollow children knew every bush, every tree in the field, could slip like wraiths through the twilight, cupping their mouths to say 'woooo, wooo' or whistle in brilliant imitation of the Indians they saw in the Classic, all to terrify the mots and drive them closer into the embrace of the soldiers who, in all equity, should have paid them and, in a sense, did.

Because after the evening's sport of pestering the recumbent and oddly moving shapes – Donal Barry, whose family came originally from the country, so he should know, said the mots were milking the soldiers, whatever that meant – the children would return in the morning to find the occasional coin. They sometimes also found a kind of balloon which wouldn't blow up and which was greeted with horror by their mothers: 'Throw that dirty thing in the fire. I hope you didn't put it in your mouth.'

They shared the river with fishermen, courting couples and the occasional dead dog that floated down from Rathfarnham. It was superb for swimming. There was a bridge from which they could dive and a waterfall under whose sheet of falling light they could sidle and imagine themselves as Tarzan. Its banks provided shelter for bands of Robin Hoods, Jesse Jameses and Apaches who used the long stalks of wild rhubarb to repel townie gangs.

A mile away, Pogue's Valley was overflowing with blackberries, an asset to the permanently hungry kids. It was also on the route home from Saturday afternoon matinees in the Classic in Terenure. Then it became Death Valley to accommodate all the miniature cowboys and Indians who galloped through it, slapping their own backsides like the cowboys did when they were chasing stagecoaches or getting away from the posse.

There were convenient orchards for 'boxing the fox', places to keep out of sight when mitching from school and a sewage pipe which could be thrillingly penetrated in summer with the light from stolen boxes of matches. There was a row of six trees opposite their back window, one of which, as their father pointed out, contained a gorilla in its branches, who stayed motionless and menacing from a distance but always vanished when they climbed the tree!

To traverse this row of trees without touching ground was the initiation rite into the various gangs. If girls wanted to join they had to prove they'd done the task by leaving a miraculous medal on the top of the ultimate and most difficult tree. Mrs Toner got fed up supplying them with the medals. She also got fed up with the girls asking her to make shorts for them – not slacks which were considered 'fast' – so that they could climb the trees without those brats of boys looking up at their knickers. Few girls ever fulfilled all the conditions, which was just as well because their presence inhibited the boys when they wanted to recite the latest ditty:

There was an old lady, God bless her,
Who threw her leg over the dresser.
The dresser was sticky,
And stuck to her mickey,
And no one could dress her, the messer.

Once a foolish visitor from the country, a cousin of the Houghtons, attempted it and fell fifteen feet. He was lucky the barbed wire below broke his fall. He bounced safely, screeched that he had been pushed by the next initiate but couldn't prove it and was judged to be not the right material for the gang – a crybaby as well as a culchie. The child brought an interesting scar home to Clare.

Halfway down the cul-de-sac itself there was the Circle, a roundabout which was a kind of village green without grass. It was perfect for rounders, and cricket played with a hurley stick. Once the Council tried to sabotage these games by planting a shrub in the centre. It survived one unhappy season. The circumference of the Circle was the race track. One wonderful August during the war a man from Belfast brought his two children to visit their cousins in number forty-five. He was very rich and organised races with cash prizes of pennies and tuppences. There were also many consolation prizes of a farthing, the coin with the kingfisher which was pretty but could buy only two aniseed sweets, better known as Nancyballs.

The children felt sorry for the visitors not winning any of the races but, after all, the strangers had full-time access to a rich father, whom they addressed musically as 'Dohray', presumably Belfastese for Daddy. One of the children tried this name out on Mr Toner, in the hope that it might loosen his purse strings too, but all he got was a quare look, a ruffle of the newspaper and a shake of the head that said: Blessed God, am I rearing imbeciles as well!

Teilifís 1994 – Moltaí le cur os comhair an Choiste Bunaithe Teilifíse
(Film West, 1994)

Following the pirate television broadcast in Ros Muc in 1987, an extended political campaign took place regarding the setting up of an Irish-language television station. The following article contains Bob's suggestions for the new channel, directed towards the committee that was appointed to oversee the establishment of the station.

Teilifís Pobail – seirbhís áitiúil don Ghaeltacht an bhunaidhm a bhí ag an togra seo i dtús ama. Ní hin a bheas anois ann. Tá an bhunaidhm méadaithe (sáraithe?) ag an Aire i dtreo is go mbeidh seirbhís teilifíse ar fáil i nGaeilge don phobal i gcoitinne, seirbhís náisiúnta.

Níl an 'pobal i gcoitinne', is é sin an pobal náisiúnta, ag iarraidh seirbhís teilifíse i nGaeilge ach tá seans maith ann go bhfuil siad ag iarraidh seirbhís ar a mbeadh corrchlár taitneamhach as Gaeilge. Is rud eile é sin. Ach iad siúd, an mionlach, a bhfuil tuiscint acu ar an scéal; iad siúd atá ag obair ag an *gcoalface* agus a fheiceann an chaoi a bhfuil rudaí, tuigeann siad sin gurb é an riachtanas is práinní ó thaobh slánú na Gaeilge de, go gcuirfí seirbhís teilifíse rialta ar fáil do ghasúir.

Ní fhéadfadh an tseirbhís a d'fhógair an tAire, bíodh sí olc nó maith, a bheith ina macasamhail de Raidió na Gaeltachta. Ceaptar go minic gurb é Sianel Pedwar Cymru (S4C) an eiseamláir is feiliúnaí dúinne, sé sin raon iomlán cláracha i nGaeilge measctha le cláracha i mBéarla (nó i *Sanscrit* le fotheidil). Ach tá an t-uafás airgid ag S4C agus ní fhéadfaí an sampla uilig a leanacht. Caithfear díriú ar na riachtanais is práinní. Mura mbeidh an bhéim ar ghasúir ag an tseirbhís, ar ghasúir na Gaeltachta go speisialta, ní dhéanfaidh an tseirbhís teilifíse nua leas ar bith.

Tá chuile dhuine ar aon intinn faoi rud amháin: mura bhfuil na gasúir sa nGaeltacht ag labhairt a dteanga féin, níl ach an bás i ndán don Ghaeilge mar theanga bheo pobail. Is géarchéim náisiúnta í seo a gcaithfear aghaidh a thabhairt air, sula mbeidh sé ródheireanach.

Sa gcás seo níor chóir mórán airde a thabhairt ar bhaill an NUJ, a bheas ag iarraidh a gcaighdeán maireachtála a choinneáil leis an tseirbhís nua agus níor chóir aird a thabhairt ach oiread orthu siúd a bhfuil sean-nósanna dolúbtha costasacha na teilifíse acu. Ba chóir cuimhneamh chomh maith, nach le freastal ar na comhlachtaí nua neamhspleácha teilifíse, atá ag faire ar chuid den 'aicsean' ar mhaithe leo féin, atá an tseirbhís nua teilifíse dá bunú. Is cuma faoi thuairimí na '*professionals*' le Gaeilge líofa, nach mbeidh ag iarraidh drannadh le cláracha do ghasúir, mar nach bhfeilfeadh sé dá ngairmeacha pearsanta féin.

Ní le brabach a dhéanamh ná le fostaíocht a chruthú ná le margadh a shásamh atá an tseirbhís nua teilifíse dá bunú. Seirbhís Phoiblí atá i gceist agus is iad gasúir na tíre an pobal is tábhachtaí, ar chóir don tseirbhís freastal orthu. Chuige sin, b'fhéidir gur chóir *Teilifís na nÓg* a thabhairt mar theideal ar an tseirbhís nua!

Molaim mar sin:

1. Nach mbeadh ar an tseirbhís nua ach cláracha do pháistí. Tá buntáistí faoi leith ag baint leis an gcoincheap 'páistiúil' seo. Bheadh daoine fásta ar bheagán Gaeilge in ann breathnú ar na cláracha seo le feabhas a chur ar a gcuid Gaeilge. Bheadh ar RTÉ a dhualgais don 'phobal Gaeilge líofa' a chomhlíonadh i gcónaí agus cláracha ar nós *Cúrsaí* a fhágáil ar Network 2. Tá scata beag Gaeilgeoirí ann a bheadh ag iarraidh íomha shofaisticiúil a léiriú ach iad siúd a bhfuil gasúir acu, ba chóir go dtuigfidís an cás.

2. Ná bactar le seirbhís nuachta 'náisiúnta' ná 'idirnáisiúnta', ar an gcainéal nua seo. Ní hamháin nach bhfuil spéis ar bith ag gasúir óga i bpleidhcíocht na bpolaiteoirí, i GATT ná i Greencore, ach tá muid uilig bodhraithe ag éisteacht le *'bulletins'* chuile leathuair ó thrí sheirbhís raidió agus dhá sheirbhís teilifíse cheana féin. Is iad na hiriseoirí an dream is mó a bheadh ag iarraidh seirbhís nuachta ach ná cuirtear san áireamh iad sin, mar ar is mhaithe leo féin atá siad, cosúil le dream proifisiúnta ar bith.

Le hoideachasóirí a shásamh, d'fhéadfaí clár gearr mínitheach faoi chúrsaí an domhain; trualliú timpeallachta, gorta san Afraic, srl. a chur ar fáil do na gasúir.

Chun aird tuismitheoirí a tharraingt ar an tseirbhís, ní mba dhochar roinnt bheag 'nuacht áitiúil' a chraoladh – d'fhéadfaí a chinntiú go mbeadh *camcorder* Hi-8 i ngach baile fearainn sa nGaeltacht, ag bailiú ábhair. Tá chuile fhormáid teilifíse inchraolta.

Níos tábhachtaí ná sin tá clár a mhíneodh na meáin chumarsáide do ghasúir ag teastáil. Is scannal é an easpa oideachais sna scoileanna faoi láthair agus an t-aineolas faoi na meán cumarsáide atá i measc daoine óga.

D'fheadfaí trealamh simplí a thabhairt ar iasacht do dhéagóirí agus saoirse a thabhairt dóibh a rogha clár a dhéanamh. Arís, tá chuile fhormáid teilifíse inchraolta. Ná bac leis na '*professionals*' sa gcás seo. Tá deis ann in 1994, seirbhís nua-aoiseach a bhunú nach mbeadh ina macasamhail de nó cosúil le chuile sheirbhís thuirsiúil teilifíse atá ar fáil sa 'chéad domhan'. Tá an córas teicniúil athraithe as cuimse, ó tháinig RTÉ ar an saol 30 bliain ó shin. Ach faraor níor tháinig aon athrú ar chor ar bith ar bhundearcadh na seirbhíse sin. Cuir daoine óga i gceannas na seirbhíse nua agus cuir muinín iontu agus ná bac leis na seanfhondúirí agus ár gcuid 'freagrachtaí' leadránacha.

What Happened to the Bishop?
(Film Ireland, February/March 1994)

In 1987, Bob produced a silent film titled Budawanny *about an island priest's housekeeper becoming pregnant and the subsequent fallout. The film was eventually developed into* The Bishop's Story *in 1994. In this essay, he tells the full story of the two films.*

For the first time in my life I am nervous about writing exactly what I think, feel and remember. The timidity in the heart of me, long camouflaged by an abrasive shell, is emerging like an attic picture; the 23 years of wearing a protective Conamara cloak of resilience is peeling away and leaving me exposed to myself and inevitably to others. Intimations of mortality are making me question the energy that drove me headlong into *Sit Down and Be Counted*, *Caoineadh Airt Uí Laoire*, *Poitín*, *Atlantean* and all those other vain acts of defiance. They changed nothing. The ancient women are still gathering fuel in vacant lots.

In 1980 Pádraig Standún, a priest with a vow of celibacy, sent me a manuscript entitled *The New Generation* and said I could have the film rights for a penny: 'after all, I want to be able to tell my grandchildren that I once actually sold film rights.' When in 1983 he rewrote and published the novel in Irish as *Súil le Breith* it had become a lean and best-selling story of doomed love between a priest and his housekeeper. The wonder of it was his unpatronising treatment of real (as distinct from *Quiet Man*) peasant/fisher life. His use of dialogue in Conamara Irish made 'quaintness' impossible and his unfashionable respect and love for secondary characters in a rural setting was refreshing.

Because I was in the middle of my *Atlantean* odyssey it was a year before I sat down and filleted it for the exact bones of the story. What emerged was almost melodramatic: a fragile relationship set against the iron tradition of institutionalised religion. It appealed to me because it revealed the unique tolerance towards sexual peccadilloes that I had long discovered existed in Conamara and which survived in no other community in this theocratic State. There were few grey areas.

The story was black and white, freshness versus tradition, innocence versus the monolith. There were no anti-heroes, no ambiguous sex, no vicarious violence, no Northern backdrop. It appealed to my desire for clarity. It was also incident-packed, a godsend to the relatively superficial medium of film. I imagined a Hollywood version and immediately ran in the opposite direction; copy everything American except its films.

I decided to approach the novel as a sculptor would a piece of stone; itself a wonderful object but amenable to transformation. The process is to slowly chip away whatever is not essential to the chosen new form or whatever cannot be accommodated by this form, i.e. film.

I reduced the idea to simple pictures, tried to do without sound (my real love), and dialogue; snip, snip went my nose (and no loss either); I am spite-d, spite-d, complained my face (good riddance). I was going back in time, reducing the story to the original elements of cinema. There would be no crashing zooms, tracking shots or fast focussing, no overwhelming score, no shouting or shoulder-shrugs from the repertoire of American brat-acting. But it was impossible to avoid some sort of dialogue. The narrative wasn't so simplistic as to allow the characters to be utterly dumb. They had to speak. But without sound, how? Solution: dialogue captions. A silent movie! I had reinvented the wheel.

And all because Joe McMahon of Galway had months previously brought me to a season of black-and-white silent classics. I noted that these films had no trouble moving an audience without spoken dialogue.

The film would be an exercise in spartan values, a minimalist film on a minimal budget. I would use all locals with (like *Poitín*) perhaps a sinewy backbone of pros. I would do the job on Clare Island, an old refuge of mine. Its distance from the fleshpots would keep the crew, if not moral, at least far from the flaccid precedents of Dublin – that Taiwan of international features where, as Roger Doyle said to me, they don't make films, only career moves. The project would be as pared down, lean and clean as the story and the form I had chosen. It would be a doddle, to be shot in twelve days. Oh, all the plans we dress our dreams in!

Years afterwards on a bridge over the Corrib, Lelia Doolan asked me could I ever produce anything straight. No, I answered sadly. I can't even lie straight.

What perversity is it that poses as so-called originality? A low threshold of boredom, a desire not to do the same thing twice, not to repeat, not to imitate. Heaney says: Keep at a tangent. I once saw an autistic child masturbating and its minder told me to ignore this 'attention-catching device'. In the film and television sewer down which are flushed billions of audio-visual objects, you are forced to swim against the stream or your work will end up a comfortable, anonymous and rapidly disintegrating turd in Dublin Bay. Thus, with this possible self-deception that one is defending the vulnerable and attacking the unassailable you continue to try to do something that a chimp has not done before, or, given a modern editing suite, could not do now. Of course you run the risk of being dismissed as just trying to be different. If the cap fits …

The working title became *End as a Gander* because a man in a pub told me the phrase 'choking the gander' is a euphemism for sexual intercourse; '*la petite mort*' and all that. The enamoured priest would be the gander.

In 1984 I told Michael Algar, chief executive of the old Film Board, what I intended. To my surprise he did not cough discreetly and say he would get back to me next century. He was my first encouragement for this exercise in cinematic regression. I was incited enough to apply for a development loan of £10,000. Meanwhile I shoved the scenario into the Arts Council competition and they liked it too – £15,000 worth.

The only person who didn't fully approve was me. The story was classic, would make people laugh and cry, but was, in the form to which I had reduced it, too straightforward to me and, believe it or not, too enjoyable! A puritan by upbringing, I decided that if the audience was going to enjoy itself then it must pay for it. They must learn something, too. Entertain in order to educate. Educate that you may be free. Not complete arrogance, by the way; just a hangover from my public broadcasting days and the ethos of responsibility I had learned there (this old-fashioned idea has long since been mangled to death in RTÉ). I was a bit stumped as to how I might restore some of the novel's serious intent and change the course of Irish religiosity.

Then Deus, in the form of Pádraig Standún, did an ex machina trick and sent me the manuscript of his next novel, *2016 AD*.

I loved it, thought it was Beckett in Irish and almost preferred it to *Súil le Breith*. Best of all, and the solution to my puritanical conundrum, was that Tom Connors, the brave and sincere priest in *Súil le Breith* had grown in this novel into a cynical and faithless bishop. The end of his love affair thirty years before, too much sacrifice, not to mention putting on the wisdom of a higher ecclesiastic, had made a stone of his heart. I thought: Standún is a genius. The story was already a sugar. I now had the pill.

I wrote a prologue in which the bishop intones a monologue revealing his pragmatic, hypocritical attitude to religion. When Pádraig read it he said: 'I couldn't have put it better myself.' Then he mused and added: 'You're getting a bargain, you know; two novels for the price of one and that itself only a penny.'

Who would play the priest? I imagined a silent movie wouldn't really need professional actors, just intelligent, personable ciphers whom I would move like pawns through the simple story. Like ninety per cent of modern films but without the personality cult.

In steps Donal McCann. Into my house that is, stepped a man who is nobody's pawn. We drank and chatted about old times, *Poitín* et al. McCann asked about what I was up to. I told him, asked would he be interested. 'Sairtinly,' he said.

We have never discussed this but I believe that there was a good reason for Donal's ready acceptance: the silent movie. He thought it would be less demanding than the usual film. At least he wouldn't have to learn lines and therefore wouldn't be distracted from studying his part in the now-famous *Juno and the Paycock* which was scheduled to happen immediately after the shoot. It would be a good warm up for such a demanding stage role. Trouble is, no film is either simple or undemanding.

I asked Brendan Neilan of RTÉ for the name of a handsome female cipher who could look anything from 23 to 30. I found Maggie Fegan acting in St Francis Xavier Hall in Dublin and mad keen to appear with McCann. From my occasional Conamara repertory company I got Tom Sailí Ó Flaithearta and Johnny Chóil Mhaidhc plus my neighbours, 76-year-old Freda Gillen and 16-year-old Susan Flaherty. I looked for a smallish dog but settled for our own rough collie, Laddie.

It was against my principles – and my pocket – ever to spend more than £100,000 on any film. The nearest I'd got to it before was *Atlantean*, which was actually a trilogy of films. But all I was sure of early in 1986 was £15,000 from the Arts Council, a strong possibility of £15,000 from Channel 4 and a vague possibility of £15,000 from RTÉ. These figures are, I realise, a nonsense to driving filmmakers nowadays. So it goes. Dramatically, Michael Algar rang me up and asked how soon could I go if the Film Board put up £50,000. Pause for a moment.

Now, I said.

My assumption was that the Film Board had suddenly realised that no films were in production for 1986 and a silent movie was better than no film at all. I went to the ITGWU to pre-empt irritation and told them the budget. Pat Keenan said: 'Sure that's not a film at all.'

We were off. The budget was £80,000. I began to round up the usual suspects for crew. My old comrade Seamus Deasy was game. He reminded me that in May 1986 it would be exactly 20 years since we shot our first film together – on Clare Island. Shane O'Neill, sick of the big budget and concomitant egos of foreign features, jumped at the chance of doing something small and at home 'for whatever you can afford and for nothing if necessary.' Martin Duffy, film editor, had just gone freelance from RTÉ and was all set to establish himself in Dublin but sacrificed it to spend two months editing in the 'wilds' of Conamara – he had never been west of Leixlip before – as long as his young son could join them. These people reinforced what I had long known: Irish film artists get their greatest satisfaction from working on Irish films. If there is any continuity in the trade they will work for modest fees and quite regularly give their services for nothing – as I later found out.

On 23 May 1986 the core cast with all the crew and equipment embarked on Chris O'Grady's boat at Roonagh Quay and vomited its way across the three-mile channel, Freda praying, Tiernan MacBride – ancient mariner that he is – reassuring everybody, Miriam Allen wondering how much it would cost, Martin O'Malley hanging on to his motor bike, Tom Conroy clutching the paraphernalia of his one-man design and props department, Laddie barking at the seagulls.

Donal was waiting on the island pier.

'C'mere,' he said, without preamble. 'D'you know that scene with the kids. Remember how I used to amuse your kids? Here's what I thought of doing….'

He proceeded to describe exactly the gags I too had remembered. That happened constantly. We seemed to be running on tram lines, in telepathic harness. Maybe we share a similar desperation. That's why I credit him as Consultant Director. More actors should demand this credit. Once when Maggie forgot my stricture that there was to be no 'acting' in this minimalist film, I turned angrily on Donal and accused him of the sin. As prearranged between us he stormed off the cottage set. I followed him and we giggled outside. Maggie was perfect after that. Indeed Peter Brook himself was wowed by her performance. She has a French quality, he said. Of course, McCann got the best actor award…

The twelve days went beautifully. The sun shone when we wanted it, the rain came on cue, even a fog descended on precisely the right day. The small crew was made for adaptability. I drew the storyboard every night.

There were minor irritations. When the wind tripped a switch on the cliffs the island generator would stop and a very fit Robert Quinn (Connacht schoolboy half-mile champion and himself conceived on this same island 16 years before) had to regularly tear across the island to get Michael Bob to start her up again. When the pre-booked Whit weekend visitors turfed us out of the hotel everybody slummed it in two small cottages. A mainland priest resisted MacBride's persuasions to lend us his alb for a film of 'that book', as he called it. A more broadminded one in Lecanvey came to the rescue. Donal wore Pádraig Standún's spare suit. He also had to make do with patent leather shoes on which he slipped frequently in the mountain search scene. Johnny Chóil Mhaidhc reassured him: 'Sure didn't Jesus fall three times!' McCann's reply was unpriestly.

One of our extras broke his ankle. Another was carted off with appendicitis. One of the key islanders (who besides acting powerfully was our sole means of transport) threatened to withdraw because he thought we were making a pornographic movie which would offend his parents. A desperate phone call to Standún brought him sailing across to make reassuring noises. Old friend I might be but only the priest could be believed.

Wise Freda asked me who she was supposed to be. I said Mother Church and she chuckled and said you're an awful man. Then the islanders beat the crew in a game of soccer.

Soon the disasters concomitant with every film began. This was the first film I had ever insured against mishap. It was on the Film Board's insistence. I now believe insuring ensures disaster.

Tiny flashes on the rush prints which we were assured by the laboratory were innocuous were finally established by Martin Duffy in Carraroe to be irreparably on the negative. Probably fifty per cent of the film was affected. An assessor flew from London, agreed to a minimum £23,000 worth of damage. Secretly I was not displeased. It meant we could return to the island and re-do a number of scenes, repeat a couple of unsatisfactory shots, pick up a number of cutaways, and relax. Martin Duffy's ingenuity could cut around a lot of the flashes. However, Donal couldn't come because of *Juno* so one long scene (the cottage night vigil) had to be 'rewritten' and shot without him.

Worse was to come. The bishop's monologue was to be done in Dublin. Donal was under severe pressure with *Juno*. McCann is demonically single-minded about his job. 'All I can remember ever wanting to do is act,' he told me. Every performance must be perfect. But this time he was exhausted, had had a harrowing three days.

We were so transfixed by his performance, by the fact of his acting at all in the circumstances, that nobody, not even the make-up girl, noticed that under the lights his perspiration was washing away the carefully applied powder and paint. At the end of the day

Deasy pointed out that instead of aging, the bishop seemed to have become younger. Dismayed, we watched the rushes that week and realised it wouldn't work. And because of Donal's stage commitments – a long run of *Juno* – it was too late to re-do it. In an effort to salvage something I asked Peadar Lamb to do the part.

Peadar heroically stepped into the breach and produced one of his finest performances on film. But the entire irony of the film – the sincere young priest turning into a bitter and cynical bishop – which would have carried my otherwise turgid words, was lost.

Meanwhile our dog Laddie was killed outside the house. Donal and I were nearly goners when the roof of my local pub caved in beside us. We called it 'The Curse of *Budawanny*'. More seriously, a van containing all of our costumes and stock for the re-shoot, a couple of cameras and a consignment of tiles for Ciara Cullen on Clare Island, was stolen in Dublin. There was no insurance for that.

There were good things. Martin found an unlikely cutaway with which he made sense of a particular scene. My youngest, Marcus, was conceived during the shoot which proves it wasn't all work on the island. Then my battered four-plate Steenbeck, on which Martin ground his teeth every day, gave up the ghost and editing shifted expensively to Dublin.

But losing Donal as the bishop was the main disaster. I think that was the point at which I lost interest in the film. It was not what I intended, was irretrievable. My 'catastrophes *ansicht*' meant that hereafter I was just going through the motions, finishing the job from habit. Martin Duffy kept it, and me, going. Roger Doyle produced a marvellous score, 70 minutes of music all based on two stuck-together notes on my ancient harmonium. Tony McHugh did a lovely mix.

I had retrieved the negative from the first laboratory and given it to Filmatic who produced a fine print. An unanticipated problem was that to get a no-join optical print incorporating the bishop's colour sequences would mean sacrificing Deasy's lovely black & white photography. There was really no choice. I doomed myself to forever showing the film on a cumbersome double-headed projector.

To revive my flagging interest for the premiere in the Royal Hospital, Kilmainham, I decided to make the film a vehicle for an attack on the grossness of commercial cinema, the helplessness of critics and the general bastardisation of this medium, the art of the twentieth century. I invited only art critics.

You can imagine how the film reviewers felt; my onslaught was described as an attention-catching device.

Ho Hum.

The film, which was really a work in progress called *Budawanny*, got a best actor award in Portugal, was rejected by the Celtic Film Festival and was the success of the Cork Film Festival; it represented European cinema on a tour of America and was generally well received. Tom Hayes said it was 'wickedly clever', Louis Marcus and Paul Durcan praised it generously. I showed it for a week to great audiences in the Academy in Dublin and for two months in the Taibhdhearc in Galway. But each time I projected it I said 'damn', 'blast', 'if only', and much, much stronger language.

Then I tried to forget it …

On 19 May 1992 Seamus Deasy rang me and said; 'Isn't it incredible. Truth is stranger than fiction. You'll have to do the job as you wrote it.'

He was referring to the undignified departure of Eamonn Casey from his bishopric in Galway, an event strangely rehearsed by the original idea of the film (and that's where any similarity ends).

'I know,' said I. 'I've been wanting to do it for six years. What about money?'

'We'll work for nothing,' he said.

And so eventually he did. As did his brother Brendan and his son, Shane, as well as Shane O'Neill and Robert and Martin and Tom and as many of the original crew as were free. I rang McCann to see would he do it.

'Sairtinly!', he said.

Begging letters raised €9,000; a bank mortgage on my house raised €10,000. The bishop scenes were rewritten to make my words less indigestible; they were turned into a two-hander between Ray

McBride and Donal. On the first day Ray arrived with an abscess-swollen jaw which he endured for a day and then was admitted to hospital. A week later we tried again.

I put the characters into a drying-out house for tired clerics and shot for the first time on 35mm; in black and white because I didn't want to have the same double-headed problem. I was too clever. When after many tribulations to do with re-photographing some of the old 16mm material (during which the borrowed £9,000 went down the Swanee) I discovered the best bet was to print it in sepia on colour stock. I could have shot the new material in colour after all!

The low threshold of boredom raised its head again. It wouldn't allow me simply to repeat the old silent movie format. I also wanted to introduce a dimension of the language in which Pádraig Standún wrote his novel and whose omission I had long felt guilty about. It's not often you get a second chance. What about producing the First Bilingual Silent Movie in history? Making the dumb speak? Or as McCann put it, change Cinegael to 'Ciúinigael' and make a film for Gaeldumb. And that's what happened.

Why do people inflict such punishment on themselves?

The crazy decision meant months of tedious work in Telegael and Screen Scene, getting local actors to reinvent (in Irish!) the lines that the silent actors mouthed eight years ago (some of the lines were unrepeatable anyway). It meant creating an entirely new soundtrack, adapting Roger Doyle's music to the new concept, getting Máirtín O'Connor to exactly reproduce on his *bosca* an intricate melody and rhythm invented by Roger for the Fairlight synthesiser. It meant post-synching every line of Donal and Ray on that extraordinary thing called an audiofile, manned by a patient young man named Enda Boner who earned a new credit, Sound Design.

Making the film on 35mm for cinema was just as significant a decision. Long ago when I was interested in these things I advocated that if ten Irish films, shot on 16mm and relatively small budgets, were made annually at least one of them might merit the 35mm treatment.

Modest as ever, I decided that *The Bishop's Story* was the one. If *Budawanny* was the Old Testament, *The Bishop's Story* would be the

New, the fulfillment of the old. Is that blasphemy? (Hey, it's a good publicity line; look at Rushdie. This is the kind of thinking 35mm induces).

Seriously, in 1986 I still believed drama on television was the best way of getting ideas across to the widest range of people. Now I have resigned myself to the fact that that medium has become – apart from a good way to see old films – a showreel for safe personalities and an endless chat and quiz show which asks no serious questions of itself. It is for being on, not for watching and it is run by suitmen and, increasingly, suitwomen. The cinema might be escapism but at least its primary purpose is not yet to sell cornflakes. In 1969 I was angry about TV and the abuse of potentially the greatest educational force in history; now with the medium at an unwatchable nadir I am merely sad. So when Deasy suggested we shoot on 35mm and aim at theatrical viewing I jumped at the chance.

35mm costs at least two and a half times as much as 16mm in every department – which includes expectations. All film eats money; 35mm gorges itself on it. Help came from a lot of quarters like Údarás na Gaeltachta, Gael Media and, again, the Arts Council and my bank.

But what made the remake of the film ultimately possible was a man from Derry named Tommy Collins who produced *Dragon's Teeth*, *Hush-a-Bye Baby* et al. When I had spent six months raising money and losing what I did raise on abortive tests by incompetent labs and optical houses he had a look at the script and material and said: I'd like to have a bash at it. I think it would be worth it.

We need these Northerners.

He plunged into the dense thickets of European media bureaucracy and after eight months swam his way successfully to agreements with EURIMAGES and EFDO. There was at least as much creativity, tenacity and downright pigheadedness needed for his role as there was for my eight years of actually making this object called *The Bishop's Story*.

And that, as *beagnach fíor* as I can make it, is the history of one film. It's probably a function of age but I don't believe anymore that film is worth such time, energy or capital, financial and emotional. Do you? You are young.

Perhaps I am at the stage when, as I can roughly gauge the amount of these valuable commodities left to me, I do not intend to squander them anymore on film. Of course I am aware that one must be doing something, that making and watching films keeps a lot of part-time psychopaths off the streets. But as television, my first teacher, is no longer available to the likes of me I'll stick to making single-frame films and, of course, writing valedictories – timid and not-so-timid.

Fourteen years after Pádraig Standún sent me his manuscript the film is finished. I watch it now dispassionately. I know it is precisely what I intended but I have no idea if it works. I can't actually see the film any more. There are cataracts in my mind's eye. I can hear the film alright and just worry if this or that touch is too subtle in an already avowedly minimalist piece of work. I care and also don't care. It's like watching one of my children grow up and become distant from me. I can't afford to care too much or there will occur meltdown in this core of blancmange.

Film Art: A Credo
(Film Ireland, 1996)

An article published ahead of a conference titled Art and Cinema that took place at the Irish Museum of Modern Art in November 1996.

It bores me to repeat what I've been saying for twenty years. We tired Westerners can distinguish between forms of writing, can see the difference between toilet graffiti, poems and novels; can even identify sub-categories. Alright, with increasing difficulty.

But so brutalised is our cinematic taste that a fillum is a fillum is a fillum whether it's by Alanna O'Kelly or Stephen Spiegel. They're all fillums and we bring the same childish expectations of fairytale escapism to them.

But all fillums aren't art. Like Edna O'Brien said, many 'novels' are just knitting. And most fillums are a waste of petrol.

So, define a fillum as a work of art.

It is a finely made challenger of assumptions, an invitation to see differently. But.

Insofar as ninety-nine per cent of filmic objects made in our American-colonised world are: (a) propaganda for 007-type notions of freedom and democracy; (b) persuasive arguments for individualism, hedonism, and various other -isms that are presently popular and profitable and above all P.C.; (c) celebrations of violence; and (d) made by the haves as distinct from the have-nots; is it even worth considering fillum as an art form?

Yes. Why?

Because more than ever film needs an injection of non-pragmatic vision. And artists who happen to have chosen film as their medium deserve to be identified and encouraged, at least in the short period before they take the Hollywood shilling. Otherwise, as present trends indicate, we will make imitation films (both cinema and TV) which will be no good here or over there.

Also otherwise: those few film artists who haven't yet become geriatrics like me, or brilliant humorists like Damien O'Donnell, will become an irritation – a kind of Gallanstown or Summerhill – to the precarious consensus of Irish distributors, exhibitors, journalists, national broadcasters, Film Boards, Arts Councils, Trade Unions, all those who while fighting noble rearguard actions against Murdoch-type monsters, and their apparatchiks, may trample personal vision into the mud of the battlefield.

No matter how difficult, it is time to start making delicate, painful and essential distinctions between commercialism and film. No matter how many suitmen and women say film is a business as well as an art form – and approach it exclusively as a business – baggage must be jettisoned. Baggage like production companies, PLCs, 'windows' in our schedules, faxes, carphones, mobile phones, creative accountancy, production portfolios, deals, options, properties – all the bric-a-brac that enables clerks call themselves filmmakers and makes film artists curl up and die.

Imagining Conamara
(*Arguing at the Crossroads, 1997*)

An essay from Arguing at the Crossroads – Essays on a Changing
Ireland, *edited by Paul Brennan and Catherine de Saint Phalle
and published by New Island Books. The book was produced to mark
L'Imaginaire Irlandaise, a celebration of Irish culture in France in 1996
organised by Doireann Ní Bhriain.*

I was driving from Galway to Foxford, Co. Mayo, two years ago with
my neighbour, poet and playwright Johnny Chóil Mhaidhc and as
is my custom in Mayo I got lost. After many side roads, turns and
returns to the pilgrimage town of Knock which has some kind of
magnetic attraction for lost souls we finally got back on the right road.
Johnny turned to me and said, '*Má's oileán beag fhéin í Éireann, is tír
an-mhór í.*' For a small island, Ireland is a very big country.

Unless you are a journalist or tourist, i.e. trading in clichés, it
is sensible to accept and celebrate the extraordinary detail of this
country. Every generalisation about the place can be simultaneously
true and false.

Yes, we have great hatred, little room; but being human are
capable of much charity.

Yes, we are xenophobic, but strangers usually experience a warm
welcome.

Yes, we are at base illiterate peasants, but we have produced one of
the great literatures in Europe and, after Latin and Greek, the oldest.
And that's apart from writers in the English language!

Yes, we were (may still be) a broken people but we were the first
to achieve independence from Empire.

Yes, we are anti-intellectual but we are presently the most generous
country in the world towards individual artists.

How can the observer resolve these contradictions?

One approach might be to try to imaginatively reconstruct the
humanity of one's own village, street or apartment block and from that
microcosm deduce the nature of the larger world. The extraordinary
variety of opinions and personalities that can live within affective

distance of each other is always a salutary sample of the variety of the world. One should, and usually does, base one's *weltanschauung* on the local. You are as likely to be an inch as a mile from an accurate universal perception – but you will certainly be closer than those villains who categorise us all as A, B, or C for advertising purposes.

Thus I choose to imagine Ireland as it is and as it might be through the prism of a part of it in which I have lived for the past twenty-five years – a period which, happily for the purposes of these words, roughly coincides with one of the greatest periods of social change that has ever hit this small island.

Where I live was a century ago a place of thatched cottages, donkey transport, subsistence living and poverty. Electricity preceded me to this village by only ten years. The area is called Conamara. It is described as a Gaeltacht or Irish-speaking community and it is located in the West of Ireland.

However, the donkey is now obsolete.

Conamara is now, for good or ill, alive with pubs, discos, Walkmen, microwaves, TVs, National Lottery mania, traffic jams every day in summer, after Mass every Sunday and at three o'clock every weekday when parents pick up their children from school.

About thirty miles away is the county town called Galway which is officially a city and reputed to be the Athens of Ireland but I can't vouch for it, being only an occasional visitor there. Galway City has not sufficient symphony orchestras, art galleries, schools of music, museums, corps de ballet or opera companies to attract me regularly.

Come to think of it, it does not possess even one of these amenities. Instead it has recently had an explosion of hotels and apartment blocks. And tourists.

The place in which I live is utterly rural and not sufficiently pacified to attract package tours.

Twenty-five years ago I decided to leave Ireland. I'd had enough. I wanted to emigrate again, take the *bád bán* finally, get away from the claustrophobic religiosity and worse, the Anglo-American serfdom of my birthplace, my culture, my country. I thought of New York, San Francisco, Nova Scotia, Montreal, Munich, Tehran, Paris, Moscow, London, Leeds and all of the places I had known in my itinerant life.

None of them looked vaguely like an improvement on Ireland, bad as it was, so I decided to emigrate inland.

An interior émigré?

Sort of. I became an immigrant in my own country, to this place, Conamara. At least here the Irish language, Gaelic, was everyday speech and might constitute, I hoped, a linguistic bulwark against the worst excesses of Coca-Cola speak or even the pretentious London and New York-aping nonsense that passed as respectable social and literary criticism in this country (it still does).

That was 1970.

A quarter of a century later I am still here in Conamara, which is due to a peculiar combination of the force of inertia and the fact that I still can't think of a better place to live.

In my first few years here I became increasingly irritated by the image the outside world had of the place: painters and tourists had described it as a wilderness of lakes and bogs and mountains and big mountainy men and little fresh faced colleens and Paul Henry landscapes and poitín makers and dole men.

It was a patently false image.

But it was analogous to the expectations that the French and Germans and Americans had of the larger island, Ireland itself. This was good for tourism but was more a product of the adman's necrophiliac imagination, the tourist's memories and the Dubliner's weekend fantasies than anything approaching reality.

I found South Conamara to be full of people who didn't read the *Irish Times* but knew Boston and London intimately, who weren't obsessed with 'the media', had no interest in the gossip from Dublin 4 but knew their local politicians' every move as intimately as they knew every rock and field around them, the forty ways to cut turf, the lines of a boat, their neighbours' business, the weather in the sky. They also knew how to work the system.

They were and are the largest bilingual community on the island; they were as much at home on the sea as on the land and their popular music was a weird unaccompanied singing which bore more resemblance to a mullah's call to prayer than to the Beatles. They knew nothing of European classical music. Initially I thought they had no sense of rhythm; they found it hard to carry a 3/4 beat when they occasionally strayed into country and western. On the other hand, I found the internal rhythms and nuances of their own singing utterly alien to my Chopin/Bach/Debussy background.

They were as different from the denizens of Dublin as Orangemen are. But the Pale would never and probably never will acknowledge this. Conamara people are as alien and as alienated from pan-Celticism as the abandoned working class suburbs of Dublin.

Overcoming my own urban cultural egocentricity took a long time.

You recall the early imaginings of a child?

It thinks it can't possibly have sprung from those awful people, its parents. It must have been born of kind, generous, non-authoritarian Princes.

Well, I began to project such imaginings onto Conamara and its people. They couldn't possibly fit into the narrow, puritanical, timid, suburban island of the Ireland I knew. A parish priest I met confided in me that his parishioners weren't like 'us'; they were more like pagans, he said. This cheered me up greatly. The late Patrick Lindsay said he had retired to Conamara because there was a touch of savagery there which he found amenable. He came from Belmullet, Co. Mayo.

I once said to a friend in Conamara that she wasn't civilised. She was highly insulted until I explained that I meant she was not city-reared and therefore hadn't a strait-jacketed mind like me. It was my kind of compliment but I doubt if she has yet forgiven me.

What is the point?

Freedom, that's what. However much these people might be constrained by living in small, almost tribal circumstances, their behaviour displayed a freedom of action and independence of mind, not to mention an initiative, that I was not accustomed to. For a start, they were more widely travelled than any comparable group on this island. As a community they knew Boston, Chicago, London and Huddersfield more intimately than Dublin – possibly even than Galway. They didn't emigrate. They simply went to their extended family: uncles, aunts, older brothers and sisters, grannies and grandads who had carved out a space for them amidst alien corn.

They constituted a sharply etched diaspora within the larger diaspora of general Irish emigration.

They had, and still have, that most rare commodity – a sense of who they were. Good, bad or indifferent, it might be based on intermarriage, on hundreds of uncles and aunts and brothers and sisters and cousins scattered from Carna to Camden town; it might smack of tribalism, but it undoubtedly had and still has a sense of community.

This tribalism or sense of family is a bit like presently unfashionable nationalism. You dismiss its reality and power at your peril and as ineffectually as if you outlawed sin.

This sense of community did not mean that Conamara people didn't squabble. I have seen men trying to tear the heads off each other one night; next day I have observed the combatants chatting amiably at a bar counter. I have heard of a man returning to a pub thirteen years after he was bounced out of it, to seek redress. There might be inter-familial tensions, based on wrongs of a hundred years ago; there might be the occasional eruption when drink was taken, but they still lived close to each other, still walked the same roads, went to the same funerals and weddings and sailed in the same races.

Why?

Because they knew that, whatever the slings and arrows from outside, however the politicians and development authorities might want to organise their lives, no matter how much money the EU might pour in, when the billion was eventually squandered, whenever the last cobweb factory closed they were still stuck on the same patch, were still going to have to rely on one another. *Ar scáth a chéile a mhaireann na daoine*. People live in each other's shadows.

If I was giving a sermon I would say there was a moral there somewhere for the rest of the tribes on this island.

However, I want to talk about the Royal House into which I imagined my neighbours all those years ago. It was wilful, I know. I wanted to distance them from what I perceived as the awfulness of Ireland. Just as the celtophiles in the nineteenth century imagined the general population of the island to be descendants of so-called Celts, to distinguish them from mother England, I looked for clues, things that distinguished Conamara people from their imposed post-Famine romantic image, and at the same time linked them with other places and people.

If you look hard enough you'll find evidence for any hypothesis.

I found plenty of evidence: sean-nós singing, styles of boat building, linguistic affinities, local customs, maritime traditions, related stories.

The result was three films and a book called *Atlantean: Ireland's North African and Maritime Heritage.*

These suggested that we owed as much to the various Mediterranean cultures, be they Coptic or Islamic or Berber, as we did to our cold northern neighbours, including the Vikings. My findings were treated with silence by academics, with contempt by some traditionalists and with delight by intellectual anarchists.

The most positive reaction was from a brave historian in UCG who said to me it was the single most important intellectual event in twenty years in this country. On the other hand a famous female Irish-language poetess described it as a compendium of nonsense.

But the real reward was more interesting. You know the story of Jacob's folly? The one about the lazy farmer who won't lift a finger and just dreams of winning the lottery? In a dream one night an angel tells him there is treasure buried under one of his apple trees. He has 200 trees. So he begins to dig around the roots of the trees and after much toil and sweat finds – nothing. Disgusted, the farmer retreats to his bed. But the following autumn he has the best crop of apples in the region and makes a fortune selling them.

The treasure I found from my apple trees was a personal perception of Ireland which makes it to me the most interesting place on earth.

Firstly, it is an island with a deeply indented coastline. This makes it a paradise not just for drug smugglers. Historically, an endless insular coastline means it has been open to every influence under the sun, be it Gallic tribes, Barbary pirates, Vikings, Normans, Tudors, Arab whalers, Huguenots, Palatines, Italian postmen, Welsh mercenaries, Scottish Gallowglasses, megalithic argonauts, seeds from the Caribbean, American PhDs and multi-nationals, German fence-erectors, Coptic monks, Quaker do-gooders, Roman missionaries,

Spanish Armadas and Russian trawlers. The island is like a circle, a defined enclosure with an infinity of external contacts.

As John de Courcy Ireland put it:

An té a mbíonn long aige, geibheann sé cóir. He who has a boat will get a breeze. A proverbial statement like that does not emanate from a landlubberly people. Long before the Irish language, or a Celtic language of any description came into this country of ours, we were a maritime people, and the blood that flows in every one of us here, every one of us in the country, is blood that came across the sea.

Probably an unfortunate modern analogy would be Sky TV. You can't stop it. It becomes, for good or ill – usually for ill – part of what we are. So every visitor – invader if you like – has contributed to the make up of this island population. It is not a melting pot, though. Only huge empires can aspire to such an anti-human homogeneity. We are a compendium of tribes.

I first got that perception in Conamara and I found it very liberating. It lifted a veil from this island, made it seem less narrow or cut-off, more varied and interesting. It meant that we were not some tiny, homogenous bunch of Celtic Catholic Gaeilgeoirs bravely and irrelevantly surviving on the periphery of Godless Western Europe. This was how customarily we presented ourselves officially to ourselves.

But neither were we a nation of poets, saints and scholars, irritable Joyceans, urbane Wildeans, mad Beckettians or hairy Yeatsians in every street and pub. We were neither Celtic aristocrats nor secondhand Britons. We were, in fact, a healthy mongrel race. Now, if it's a choice between mongrel and thoroughbred, well, give me the mongrel every time. They are not robber barons and they don't interbreed to the point of insanity.

So I have imagined, like Yeats' Fisherman, a construct of Ireland that enables me to continue living here, a place of infinite variety of temperature and temperament. When one expression of our beliefs temporarily depresses me (such as our adoption of the 'free market' mentality) I lean on another equally temporary but presently attractive trait (our belief that we are undergoing an artistic renaissance).

Thus my affection for this island and its people exactly counterpoints our weather. Very changeable. Its personality is amenable to a million constructions. That makes life interesting.

Now here's the bad news.

We're losing our infinite variety, the endless array of personality and idiosyncrasy that has made this island interesting to not just me. Like the Catholic Church we are losing our mystery.

Listen to children in any village in Ireland and you will notice a peculiar thing: they are losing their regional accents. This is more noticeable of course with middle-class children. That has always been their parents' ambition. But it is now happening to children from less prosperous strata. Their voices and accents are converging in a kind of TV cartoonspeak. This is a good thing, you might say; it breaks down regional barriers, minimises their perception of others as strange and threatening, gives all children a common language.

The trouble is, the dialect is imposed. It is a kind of *vox Americana*, and it is the linguistic environment which, thanks to television and the cinema, most Irish people now inhabit.

Having English as the majority language accelerates the process in Ireland. The potential for this was a trickle thirty years ago when 'Irish' television first hit this island. Now it has become a torrent.

Among teenagers and yuppies one of its variants has been clearly identified as the DART accent – referring to the prosperous South Dublin area served by the commuter rail system. Some call it the Fürstenberg accent, referring to an upmarket beer whose appalling taste was overcome by an expensive advertising campaign.

Is an accent shift so important?

I think so. It indicates a move away from something, a move towards something else. It is away from the indigenous; towards the cosmopolitan. Away from the rooted; towards the transient. Away from the local; towards the distant green hills. Away from self-confidence; towards a sense of shame.

It is a rejection of the dreary familiar. In this sense it is Joycean. In this sense teenagers are Joycean, even though they know nothing of him. As Joyce (like the early Abbey Theatre) could not have indulged his hedonism without the patronage of romantic maiden ladies, neither can our teenagers indulge their rejection without the romanticism of Brussels which pays their education fees or the utopianism of television soap operas which provide them with new self-images, new dialects.

Adults are undergoing the same transformation.

Their rejection expresses itself in this accent shift. Is this so significant? I believe so.

I imagine it to be analogous to the unprecedented language shift that happened in this island after the Great Famine. The shift from Irish to English. That shift was based on more than words, words, words. It betokened a final collapse of faith in the physical land and the culture that had nurtured the people for millennia. Mass hunger and death will encourage people to examine their basic premises. The land was basic and was found wanting. The Irish language was rooted in it. It had to be jettisoned too. Into the cultural vacuum poured organised religion, a continental Jansenism purporting to be Catholicism. (Now that Catholicism is also being jettisoned here, what will pour into that vacuum?)

Is this a fair comparison? Too dramatic? Juxtaposing a fairly superficial shift in the way a language is spoken with the wholesale abandonment of a language itself? All we can do is try to grasp straws in the wind, to find out what is happening to us, what is bewildering us, why we are frightened.

Because we are frightened.

Frightened of what?

Of drugs, rave parties, joyriding, muggings, housebreaking, rapes, child abuse, consumerism, unemployment, high-level corruption, tabloid journalism, all of the ills we see on television which signal our emergence as a modern Western state, a member of the rich man's club.

All of these ills are making us cower behind locked doors and BMWs, smoke alarms, community alert schemes and calls for more law and order. Fortress Ireland is emerging. We are suffering from the Westerner's disease of information obesity: we know instantly and intimately what's wrong, can describe it in detail but like the eunuchs in Don Juan's Hell, are increasingly rendered incapable of action by the rain of facts that deepen the drought of the will.

One of the great ironies of Ireland today is the number of well-heeled foreigners who are buying property (and passports) here on the assumption that this is a simple, Catholic, unspoiled, slightly backward country in which they and their children will be safe from the social excesses contingent on their own triumphant capitalism. Little do they know that they are inadvertently helping to transform their chosen haven into just another dangerous part of the world.

This amuses me. Perversely it reminds me of the behaviour of some Conamara people when they enter powerful enclaves. In 1987 I made a series of films on my émigré neighbours' existence in London. I found many chameleons who had adapted to their new circumstances, had adopted English accents, condemned IRA outrages in tabloid-speak, became invisible to the watchdogs of the Prevention of Terrorism Act. By contrast, and much more attractive, were a group called the flytippers among whom were some of my neighbours' children. These young people lived in the cracks, the interstices, the gaps in respectable society.

They were people who had assessed the situation in London as precisely as Indian immigrants to Mexico City, the ones who knew within weeks precisely how much public officials need to be bribed to achieve anything.

My ex-neighbours saw instantly that Mrs Thatcher's building programme in inner London required a more efficient building rubble disposal system than the London public authority was capable of providing. They moved into the breach.

Dumping sites were inadequate. They were also thirty miles from central London. The flytippers immediately grasped the solution. They hired lorries, collected the rubble from Mrs Thatcher's Tory friends' development sites and promptly dumped it, more efficiently in gardens, on quiet streets, in basements, outside Wormwood Scrubbs prison, all under the eyes of respectable, law-abiding citizens in central London. They were enacting the logic of capitalism: you can do anything as long as you are not caught.

They were mini-multi-nationals. Some were caught. They laughed at the fines. The rewards enabled them to do so.

A few were caught and did time. They became cleverer. So it goes.

I am torn between condemning their lack of a sense of 'civics' and admiration for their daring. On balance I think positively of them: they were faced with a hostile culture, the adoptive culture of their own rulers; they were following in the footsteps of their navvying parents who had come to London without any English and suffered ignominy as a result; the flytippers were wary of social entrapment.

All of these stray thoughts are stimulated by Conamara.

Lest I be accused of romanticising this place and its people I should say that I am writing this in the grim afterbirth of Christmas, on a cold and wet January night. There is a gale battering the house. The nearest cinema is thirty miles away. My newly planted trees are leafless, defenceless. The phone is kaput. Soon the electricity will go. I could venture a mile to the pub where I will find only a handful of men brooding into their pints. Every winter it is the same. I confess that every winter for the past twenty years I have sworn that I will leave in March. But something stops me.

For instance, recently there was an '*airneán*' – a song and story session – in the pub: my own son was among the musicians, and I am still warmed by the occasion. There is some kind of unwritten law in the best of these sessions – at least in this area – that causes people to behave, to become sensitive to unspoken rules of attention, respect, sensibility. It might have been something as simple as the absence of amplification – no large black and threatening loudspeakers which make small talk impossible, force normally quiet people to shout. Here the musicians – Johnny Connolly leading three melodeons, two flutes, a fiddle and the respectful bodhrán – had only their subtlety to capture attention in a crowded hostelry. And they did. Even the inevitable bodhrán – which is usually recommended to be played with a penknife – was kept muffled by its owner so that it would not dominate. Middle-aged people, unable to resist the complex rhythms, broke into little self-conscious dances; grown men held hands and sang long songs. An 86-year-old began to formally recite a story which went on for half-an-hour. It was from the 2000-year-old Fianna epic.

He was given the compliment of total silence. A stray, out-of-season German said she had never experienced anything like it.

As usual, in the middle of it, I realised that such occasions were the reason I have endured here so long.

I store up these to leaven the occasional bleakness such as tonight and to think how such events may, for all I know, be repeated all over this island – although I doubt it.

I am reminded of the Swedish attitude to America: 'To hell with the United States, I want to go back to Minnesota'. In the same spirit, you can keep the concept 'Ireland'. I prefer the concept 'Conamara'. And I hope every man and woman from the Shankill Road to Andersonstown, from Killarney to Dublin 4, from Bagenalstown to Buncrana and every other locality in this island which has pride in itself thinks the same.

It is the only answer to the *vox Americana* – or the *vox Bruxelliana* for that matter.

Part III

Maverick
In Aghaidh an Easa

Maverick
(2001)

In 1995, Bob was appointed by Michael D. Higgins to the RTÉ Authority, the board that governs the national broadcaster. He resigned without serving the full term and, in 2001, published the book Maverick: A Dissident View of Broadcasting Today *about his experiences. Below are the first three chapters.*

I

The Lone Ranger

Ke-mo sabe?

At 10am on the last Friday of June 1995, the nine members of the new RTÉ Authority, accompanied by their officers and servants, assembled round a polished oval table in the boardroom on the third floor of the administration block in Donnybrook, Dublin 4.

That morning marked the 541st meeting of the RTÉ Authority.

The new chairman sat with his back to the window, the director-general and the assistant director-general on his right. The director of corporate affairs and the recording secretary covered his left flank. Behind the five of them, through the plate-glass windows, full-grown sycamores and chestnuts luxuriated in their summer dresses. We eight ordinary members sitting opposite that window had the best view. Studying the movement of those trees, their seasonal greening, browning and shedding, would while away many a moment of ennui for me over the next four years. Peering over our own shoulders were portraits of past chairmen and directors general of RTÉ: Eamonn Andrews, Ed Roth, Kevin McCourt, Tom Hardiman, Todd Andrews, Dónall Ó Móráin, Sheila Conroy, P.J. Moriarty and company.

I felt as out of place as the Lone Ranger. Even as I had approached the building, when I saw a besuited figure waving at me, I thought I was going to be told to leave the environs, that it had all been a mistake. In the sixties, some programme-makers called this building the Reichstag. Its symmetrical driveways were somehow reminiscent of a Nuremberg rally. The building then housed all those not at the coalface of programme-making. It still does. It is now known as the Montrose Hilton.

It was actually Tom Quinn, the director of corporate affairs himself, who was welcoming me and directing me towards a reserved parking space. I exchanged greetings and carefully backed my trusty banger in, wishing I had brought Tonto with me from the Wild West. My old compadre and his Indian friends were way out beyond the walls of Montrose, mercurial in their loyalties, malleable with liquor and trinkets, more or less pacified but still vaguely threatening. I was on my own now, pardner.

Once a month I would push through the same swing doors, take the same lift for a three-hour session of windmill-fighting followed by a sumptuous lunch. It should have been a five-year term. To avoid suspense you should know that after four years I decided that even one more year as a marginalised bit of a rubber stamp was too much and I resigned. The reason I endured it for so long was old-fashioned stubbornness; for historical reasons, many thought I would not last more than six months. The Lone Ranger was not known for lingering, even for the sake of his cherished cause of public broadcasting.

Broadcasting in Ireland has traditionally had a public service ethos. 2RN was founded in 1926 as a branch of the Department of Posts and Telegraphs. It begot Radio Éireann, which begot Radio Teilifís Éireann, a semi-state statutory body which was launched on New Year's Eve 1961 in the Gresham Hotel in Dublin. I was there, seconded with my fellows from the RTÉ sound department to help with seating in the Gresham for all the great and good of Irish society.

Outside in O'Connell Street, it snowed while tenor Patrick O'Hagan tried to entertain the great unwashed. Inside, the Gresham was luxury itself. Although I was not among those entitled to eat upstairs, I stole a menu to see what I was missing: Dublin Bay Prawn Cocktail, Filet of Sole Nantua with Vin Tourat, Supreme of Chicken Gourmet with Beaujolais, Petit Fours and Liqueur or coffee. (I still have the menu, which shows what an inveterate hoarder I am.)

In the Gresham that night the honoured guests – including, I believe, the young King Hussein of Jordan – resembled famine victims. We youngsters were astonished at the resulting chaos, at the undignified scrambling for seats, at the gluttonous and free scoffing and drinking by the cream of Irish society. We soon abandoned the distasteful scene, retreated to the basement of the hotel where there was free food and drink for us, too, possibly to reward us for our discrimination.

At midnight Charlie Roberts, the inimitable floor manager, clutching his headphones and clipboard and trailing a cable, dashed on stage and bellowed, 'Cue 1962.'

Teilifís Éireann was on the air, having been blessed on screen by President Éamon de Valera and the Primate of All Ireland, Cardinal D'Alton. Dev said the following:

> Never before was there in the hands of men an instrument so powerful to influence the thoughts and actions of the multitude ... On the other hand, it can lead through demoralisation to decadence and disillusion. Sometimes one hears, when one urges higher standards in information and recreation services, that one must give the people what they want. And the competition unfortunately is in the wrong direction, so standards become lower and lower.

His words may have been prescient, but that was only Dev talking in the twilight of his career. We were young and optimistic. I had returned from a job teaching Berlitz English in Germany and was delighted to work in such an ambience of youth, energy and creativity.

Montrose, the new studio building designed by Michael Scott, was not yet ready, so we had beavered away for the previous six months stockpiling programmes in a warehouse in the centre of Dublin. A couple of streets away in Henry Street, the Senior Service (as Brendan Cauldwell named Radio Éireann), if a little apprehensive about all these new developments, continued on its solid reliable way in the GPO. The Tower Bar in Henry Street and Madigan's pub in Moore Street were still the most attractive aspects of work for some of those talented radio people.

But the atmosphere in television was youthful and ebullient. That phase actually lasted a number of years until the rot set in, and in 1969 I left the place. Shortly before I returned to join the RTÉ Authority, an old hand in the organisation said to me, 'Bob, you thought it was bad when you left. That was paradise compared to now.'

Contrary to the contemporary belief that RTÉ in the sixties was run by perverts and deviants – which earned the place the name 'Fairyhouse' – we were actually, or at least relatively, innocent. The most daring breakthrough for many of us was an all-night drinking party on Good Friday, a day when all the pubs traditionally closed. I retain a copy of a page from an early *RTÉ Guide* because it lists my one and only play for radio, *The Image*, which starred a woman, Celia Salkeld, in the role of God. Overleaf there are more important details: the TV programmes on RTÉ's single channel. They begin at 5.30pm and end at 11.30pm.

It starts with *Fadó Fadó* for children, has *Gaelic Report* at 7, *The Treaty Debates* at 8, *Féach* at 9.50, and ends with *Outlook* presented by Fr Leon Ó Mórcháin. There were only fourteen minutes of cartoons, some of which, as I remember well, were incomprehensibly brilliant works from Czechoslovakia. Ah, the innocence and unchallenged Irishness of those days. Little vestige of it remains on television, but some gems like the *Thomas Davis Lectures* and *Sunday Miscellany* incredibly survive on radio, alongside the gentle dinosaur which is Ciarán Mac Mathúna's *Mo Cheol Thú*. I can't imagine why, if our past is officially now a different country, we hang on for dear life to such relics of 'aul' dacency'.

My first job in television occasionally placed me in the small Studio Three where I would roll the prerecorded Angelus tape, followed immediately by the signature tune for the news – a version of 'Baa, Baa, Black Sheep' by Dohnanyi. I would then feed in sound effects from the BBC library to accompany the (mute) film reports. I still remember the catalogue number of the most useful record: No. 3/6. It consisted of murmuring voices in an echoing room. From what one could decipher, they were all saying 'rhubarb, rhubarb'. The sound fitted most news reports perfectly.

In the two years I spent at this undemanding job, which also involved swinging a boom microphone on dramas and general cable-bashing, I would use up superfluous energy by writing short stories for the *Evening Press* and features for the radio service. In 1964 I was offered two jobs by RTÉ. One was as programme assistant for sponsored programmes in radio; the other was as producer/director in television. How different life would have been if I had chosen the first. But I spent several fulfilling years producing studio programmes and film documentaries, some of which were good enough to represent RTÉ at international festivals. By 1968 I had reached the conclusion, rightly or wrongly, that my work was only serving to ratify the commercial abuse of public broadcasting.

I formally resigned from my staff job in RTÉ in October 1968, bought an old car and drove to Tehran and back. Poverty then forced me to become a contract producer for RTÉ. That was a mistake. The following May, 1969, I did the unpardonable. I hijacked a crew, brought them across country to Clare Island and promptly sent them home with a short note denouncing all of RTÉ's commercial and organisational works and pomps. It prompted an upheaval in RTÉ which resulted in the resignations of Jack Dowling, producer, and Lelia Doolan, head of Light Entertainment, as well as a book entitled *Sit Down and Be Counted*. In his introduction to this 'cultural evolution of a television station', Raymond Williams wrote:

> … consider also the contemporary events in Paris, where in the attempted renewal of the society, by students and workers, the well-trained radio and television service suddenly found its full voice and began speaking as it needed to speak and not as in expediency it had found convenient and manageable. With the failure of the general renewal, a serious revenge was taken on the professionals involved. Many of them were dismissed, and, as in the case of Prague, too few of their colleagues elsewhere showed the necessary solidarity and support.

Then I became a dishwasher in London. Dowling, Doolan and myself briefly returned to RTÉ for an infamous appearance on *The*

Late Late Show in November 1969. Afterwards I was singled out (by an anonymous caller) as 'a rudderless intellectual drop-out who can't see the wood for the trees'. This judgement may still be true. When Gay Byrne demanded, on air, to know why I had bothered to appear so broodingly on his show, I responded that he had offered me £25 and an air ticket from London; and that these were my only reasons. It was a great many years before I was invited back on the show.

However, if a character reference were needed for the three people who left RTÉ in that eventful May of 1969, one could do no better than quote the flattering memoir of the then chairman, Todd Andrews: 'Sad to say, those who left the service were highly intelligent people, well informed and animated by the best of sociological and national convictions.' Despite the headaches the event caused RTÉ, it did not prevent the station from involving itself in co-productions with me over the following thirty years.

I believe my unlikely appointment to the RTÉ Authority in 1995 was a product of the sense of humour of the minister responsible for broadcasting, Michael D. Higgins. On 31 May the minister's adviser – Colm Ó Briain – had rung me at home to sound me out. In the light of my erratic thirty-four-year relationship with the national broadcaster, it was an astonishing invitation.

I thought for a moment and said yes. When the minister rang to confirm his decision, I told him it might be a mischievous appointment and warned that I might not express my opinions on such an Authority in as graceful a manner as he.

'That also has its value,' the minister said.

When Louis Marcus, an ancient workhorse of a filmmaker like myself, heard of the appointment, he sent me a postcard saying: 'Congratulations. The lunatics have taken over the asylum.'

On that lovely June morning, before we entered the inner sanctum of the boardroom, I met old acquaintances: Joe Barry, the director-general, had been the affable outside broadcast engineer when I produced *School Around the Corner* in the sixties. An outgoing Authority member, Gay Byrne, shook my hand and wished me all the best. I had been the youngest ever producer of his *Late Late*; indeed, the show first topped the audience ratings during my brief reign. I met

Carmel O'Reilly, secretary to the secretariat and once a neighbour of mine in Terenure, Dublin, and Daphne O'Donnell, secretary to the Authority secretary and wife of a technical genius named Kevin, now a lecturer, with whom I cable-bashed in the sound department in the early days. In a sense we were all old friends, although we had not met for aeons. It was like coming home. Joe Mulholland, still head of news, when told that it had been nearly thirty years since I dramatically walked out of my job in RTÉ, said in his phlegmatic Donegal burr, 'You never really left us.' I realised I was seen as a kind of poltergeist returned to bump into furniture in the daylight.

Dr Garret FitzGerald flatteringly greeted me by my first name. The ex-Taoiseach was described in the staff newsletter as having an interest in theology. It became clear that there was no better man to count the number of angels one could fit on the head of a pin. Des Geraghty was also there. He had once worked on studio cameras, and we had not met in all the years since Des played the tin whistle at a drunken barbecue in Dollymount. He was now, I gathered, a bigshot in SIPTU and president-designate of that organisation.

Bob Collins, the assistant to the director-general, whom I had met in the context of television for the Gaeltacht, answered succinctly when asked, in Irish, how he was getting on: '*Ag cosaint an rud do-cosanta,*' he replied. This could be translated either as 'protecting what is hard to protect' or 'defending the indefensible'. I opted for the latter interpretation. Within eighteen months Collins would succeed Joe Barry as director-general.

The other members of the cast were unknown to me: Bill Attley, soccer enthusiast and soon-to-retire general secretary of SIPTU; Anne Haslam, tax consultant from County Offaly and one-time Fine Gael election candidate, who would continually worry about my nicotine intake; Anne Tannahill, who, as befitted a canny Belfast publisher, rarely commented but made copious notes (when she resigned from the Authority in 1998, she was replaced by Pat Hume, a former teacher from Derry). There was a handsome woman, Maureen Rennicks, manufacturer of road signs in Mulhuddart, whom I can recall opening her mouth but once in my presence. She lasted six months, to be replaced by Patricia Redlich, an agony aunt from a

Sunday newspaper. At her first meeting, she spoke on 'creativity' to the assembled RTÉ Authority.

At least, I told myself, there is Betty Purcell, the staff representative. I knew her only by reputation. She had, with Seosamh Ó Cuaig of Raidió na Gaeltachta, taken an NUJ case against the disastrous Section 31 censorship to the Human Rights Court in Strasbourg. They lost, of course. As the only person besides myself with direct experience of programme-making, she would prove to be my sole ally on the Authority. This is not to say that Purcell did not have her own very distinct agenda. She had been elected by the staff on the promise of keeping them informed of the Authority's deliberations by means of a regular newsletter. One of the first things the new Authority did was to take this promise in its jaws, worry at it for a moment, then emasculate it. Result – no newsletter would be issued without official vetting.

The new chairman, Farrel Corcoran, professor of communications in Dublin City University, had invited me to meet him over a pint in Temple Bar a few weeks before. The professor seemed a nice man, and we had, not one, but two pints, after which I expressed the blunt opinion that RTÉ was out of control. The professor said he found the prospect of his new appointment intimidating, an attitude which, to my mind, he had difficulty shaking off. In the philosophic desert that was and is RTÉ, the professor's chairmanship has been described by a close observer as 'an academic too late'.

In this uncertain atmosphere began a period when I observed RTÉ trying to protect the elusive concept of public broadcasting from the attempts of certain politicians and huge financial interests to destroy it. In the process I also noted RTÉ's self-destructive contribution. It was a good microcosm of the parallel dissolution of that once-sovereign but increasingly confused entity known as the Republic of Ireland.

I admit to a moment of panic at that first meeting. I realised that I was in the company of people who measured their and others' every word; my natural mode of impatient rhetoric would have to be greatly tempered. I never achieved this ambition. It also briefly occurred to me that we, the RTÉ Authority, in this centralised state of broadcasting, might be considered to be the Politburo. It was a vainglorious idea. I soon found out that the real masters were the permanent officers of the Executive. I tried to imagine the jaundiced feelings of these veteran administrators as they viewed the motley collection of broadcasting amateurs and part-timers who had been foisted on them as 'the Authority'. There had been the tradition of overlapping Authority membership, to preserve some continuity of policy. But in 1995, the clean sweep of outgoing members meant that now there was an entirely fresh class of greenhorns to be slowly and painfully educated into the realities of modern broadcasting.

As I studied the faces around the table, an image of the pecking order came to my mind: a daily procession round the seven hectares of bog which constitute my garden in Conamara. I, the chairman, am conducting the regular inspection of tiny trees planted the previous winter. I am followed by Ceefor the cat, who is tracked by Beefer the bantam cock who fancies her; followed by Blackie the tom-cat who is inscrutable, followed by a black puppy, Óiche, who is largely ignored by the others. One or other of my various children might also trail along, reluctantly. As in this boardroom their acceptance of leadership is based less on respect than on self-preservation. Though fate has imposed on them a shared and quite transient territorial imperative, each is preoccupied with its own deeply personal constituencies.

A late vocation to ecology had induced me to plant trees, to counter in a minuscule way the depredations of the increasing number of internal combustion engines on this planet. One must start somewhere, however small. As well as cleaning the air, my trees would in coming years also serve to clear my brain from the toxic residues left by meetings of the RTÉ Authority.

On this midsummer morning in 1995, not long after the deliberations of the Authority began, I asked to be supplied with a copy of the daily television log. This is a meticulous computerised record of everything transmitted, from presentation announcements to programmes to commercials. It gives the precise second at which everything begins and everything ends. It reveals exactly what constitutes the quantity of output from RTÉ television; the quality is obviously another matter. But to study exactly what we broadcast every day seemed a reasonable request from a member of the group that was statutorily responsible for every belch of such a formidable output.

The affable atmosphere on the other side of the boardroom table immediately froze. Director-General Joe Barry knew exactly where I was heading: that it was not the programmes I wanted to study – I knew enough about them – but the commercial messages in between. He knew that, even after thirty years, my preoccupation with this aspect of broadcasting was unaltered and that my attention had increasingly become focused on the commercial exploitation of children. He decided to cut me off at the pass.

'No, we couldn't possibly let you have the daily logs.'

'Why not?'

'They are for internal consumption only.'

'But I'm a member of the Authority responsible for this organisation. Am I not now vaguely internal?'

'We're in a very competitive business. Suppose our competitors got their hands on it? We couldn't have such delicate information floating around outside.'

I ignored the implication that I might dash off to the nearest TV magnate and show him proof that RTÉ actually 'broadcasts'.

'The delicate information contained in the minutes and agendas, the bumf that pours out of this place – is that not floated through the post to me?'

'I'm afraid I couldn't approve of this. But we might arrange for you to study the logs in here.' He looked inquiringly at Tom Quinn, the Authority secretary and director of corporate affairs. Tom nodded agreeably.

I pointed out to the chairman that if I had the patience to sit for hours in front of my television set at home, I could tediously record this precise information myself – and was already doing so; that by its very nature it was already available to the public, quite apart from the 'competition', if they were interested enough. And the prospect of spending days in RTÉ studying logs under supervision was not one that appealed to me. I would feel like the journalist in *Citizen Kane*, reading archives under a gimlet eye in a bank vault. I asked the chairman if the nine assembled persons did not statutorily constitute the entity known as RTÉ? I had checked this out. Were we not, in fact, the RTÉ Authority, charged with hiring and firing officers and servants such as the director-general and his staff, and therefore entitled to instruct them to do our bidding?

Sharp intakes of breath. It may have been the first and last time that the formal relationship between Authority and its officers was ever spelled out in this room. The chairman instantly deciphered the message. I got the logs. The interchange was recorded in the minutes thus:

> There was also the question of access of information from RTÉ to Authority members [implying that 'RTÉ' existed autonomously from its Authority] and the need to strike a reasonable balance between members having access to information to facilitate policy-making and the possibility of *maverick* requests for various information [my italics].

I had already been earmarked as a maverick. But it was round one to me, and it taught me the first lesson: RTÉ is an organisation in the hands of a few dedicated semi-public servants who will fight tooth and nail to protect it from real or imagined attack from outside or inside. This means that even that body of temporary political appointees – the Authority that governs it – is a prime suspect. Todd Andrews, chairman in 1969, wrote: 'Clearly it was not within the competence of a disparate group of individuals such as constituted the Authority ... to produce a serviceable broadcasting policy.'

I recently checked my impression with John Carroll, ex-secretary of the then ITGWU, who had served fifteen years on the RTÉ Authority. He did not find my analysis of our insignificance at all fanciful, agreeing that three hours a month is inadequate to make informed decisions about such an organisation. I hope we were not quite as useless as the committee defined in the *New York Times* as 'a group of the unwilling, picked from the unfit, to do the unnecessary'. But we were not far off.

It is the nature of all organisations, public and private, to give information to the boards of directors exclusively on a need-to-know basis. I am sure that civil servants have the same attitude to those temporary occupiers of panelled offices of state: the ministers of government.

The loyalty to the organisation is admirable, but the siege mentality is worrying. This first round suggested to me that it was not considered good form to subject to close scrutiny the actual output for which we were responsible; alternately, that such output would not stand up to close scrutiny. Interesting times lay ahead. It helped greatly that I had studied the scripts of *Yes, Minister*, the BBC series about an analogous situation.

In retrospect, I must have been regarded with a certain suspicion. I was independent, had never been a member of a political party – although my class origin dictated that I should always vote Labour, for good and often for ill. I had no threatening personal ambitions, lived on an artist's stipend, had no need to touch the forelock or ingratiate myself with anybody, had been known to attack RTÉ publicly and trenchantly, often without premeditation. Worse, I was the only one on the new Authority who had ever directed a television programme or film (*pace* Betty Purcell who was hands-on editor of *Questions and Answers* and *Divided World* and whose efforts to become a producer/ director had been regularly stonewalled), and I had practised this trade for over thirty years. Worst of all, as detailed above, I had been one of the original thirty trainees enlisted to put Irish television on the air in December 1961. I went way back. Neutralising such advantages in this arena was the fact that I am a fulminator rather than a debater; my thought processes operate in so jagged and short-circuited a way that, having assumed that once is enough to express my point, I forget that people are only half-listening most of the time, being preoccupied with what they themselves are going to say next. I share this fault. But I also initially had the naivety to believe that if the truth of a situation is outlined and the remedy is obvious, something will be done. Ancient though I am, I have retained the idealism of a young politician who enters the system assuming that action will immediately follow a clear enunciation of the problem. This, as Sir Humphrey might say to Minister Hacker, is to assume that organisations or political systems behave in a logical way. Such an expectation is entirely optimistic and disproved by experience. As Garret FitzGerald once said in a pre-election situation, 'If people evaluate our programme, in logic they will come to us – if there is any logic in politics, which I doubt.'

After that first meeting, I bumped into one of RTÉ's finest Current Affairs producers, then strangely transferred to directing a soap opera. 'What is to be done about the mess?' I asked him.

'It's too late, Bob,' he replied mournfully. 'Joshua has blown his horn and the walls have tumbled down.'

My wilful interpretation of this was to decide that the walls of public broadcasting had been breached by the barbarians and that they were now inside, in control. I bore this analysis constantly in mind.

It was my first experience of moving in the so-called corridors of power, and my naivety was exceeded only by my desire to learn how things worked. Over four years I gathered a smattering of an idea of this convoluted process. Certainly I learned that knowing how to put a film or television programme together was of absolutely no value. A background of horse trading or, better still, poker would have been invaluable. Since I have no skill in either of these vocations, I sought advice.

There is an old warrior of my acquaintance named Hugh Duffy, now-retired chief executive of the Irish Music Rights Organisation. Duffy is a solid, phlegmatic pipe-smoker whose qualities of thoroughness, patience and attention to detail are exactly the opposite of mine. This may be why he has been a successful businessman all his life and also why we have remained good friends since childhood: there was never competition between us. He also once worked for RTÉ. When I asked his advice as to what to do in the new position, he said the following: 'Concentrate on changing one single thing at a time. If we all did this, we could change the world.'

Thus it was that the first simple thesis I experimentally nailed on the door of the RTÉ cathedral was this: TO TARGET YOUNG CHILDREN AS CONSUMERS IS CHILD ABUSE.

The lunch that followed that first meeting, by the way, was superb. The manageress who supervised it was soon to leave RTÉ and start a restaurant in a Conamara village near me. She would not be alone. Some other RTÉ people were just buying or building weekend cottages in the area and pushing up the price of sites so high that locals could not afford to live there.

II

The First Language

Mo chlann féin a dhíol a máthair.
Pádraig Mac Piarais, 'Mise Éire'

When Gay Byrne was safely off the previous Authority, he said in an interview: 'Teilifís na Gaeilge! Sweet Jesus, did we talk about Teilifís na Gaeilge.'

The new Authority continued the tradition. There was hardly a meeting over the next four years that the subject was not plonked in front of us. I have counted forty mentions in the minutes. I had to be restrained in my comments, having been a prime mover in the illegal origins of the project. All of the RTÉ Executive must have known of my original criminal involvement.

When Charles J. Haughey, then Taoiseach, was emerging from the RTÉ studios in the late eighties after a not-too-friendly interview, he turned to his companions and said, 'Never mind. We'll soon have our own fucking station.' One of his ex-ministers reported that remark to three of us in Conamara in 1988 when we were still agitating for a community TV service in the Gaeltacht.

When Haughey made the remark, Bob Collins was RTÉ director of television programmes and held the opposite view to us. In 1987, at a language conference in Dublin, he said he was opposed to the establishment of a TV channel devoted to Irish-language broadcasting. It was a good idea in theory, he said, but to talk about it in present circumstances was '*craiceálte*', meaning crazy. An Irish-language service would have to continue to be provided instead within the existing RTÉ framework.

That same autumn, oblivious to both RTÉ's position and the anti-RTÉ activities of Haughey's henchman Ray Burke, the people of Conamara were laboriously putting up a small and illegal TV transmitter.

It was erected during a windy and wet October night on the bleak slopes of Cnoc Mordáin near Cill Chiaráin. The transmitter had been built from scratch in my small back room by an electronic genius named Norbert Payne, son of the poet Basil Payne. He was assisted by Josie Mac Donncha, a local student of electronics.

Seventeen years previously the Conamara Gaeltacht civil righters had shamed the powers that be into setting up a community radio service, Raidió na Gaeltachta, by use of the same tactic. They called their achievement Saor-Raidió Chonamara. We called ours Teilifís na Gaeltachta and hoped to have the same impact.

For one weekend everybody converged on the community hall in Ros Muc to celebrate this signal occasion. Mary Bergin came to play her tin whistle. Cór Chúil Aodha travelled from Cork to perform. Gearóid Ó Tuathaigh, an eminent professor from UCG and later chairman of Údarás na Gaeltachta, could be seen dancing on screen. A local garda hung around the door of the hall, but did not interfere. My partner Miriam rang excitedly from home, fifteen miles away: 'We can see a picture,' she screamed. 'And there's sound, too!' We hardly believed it. It was as if we had invented television all over again – with two and a half cameras: one borrowed by Billy Keady, one brought on the bus from Derry by Tommy Collins, and the other an antique resuscitated by Norbert Payne. Christo Mhico's pub in Turloughbeg was jammed with happy punters seeing a live broadcast from a few hundred yards away. It was like the first moon landing. The transmitter lasted for just three days. In an effort to avoid interfering with RTÉ's signal, Norbert had incorporated a large number of transposers. They overloaded the apparatus, and on Sunday afternoon it emitted smoke and expired. That was the rather undignified end of that transmission. But the apparatus was briefly resuscitated, and in the next six months there were two more transmissions, from Carraroe and from Clare.

The operation was seen by RTÉ as an 'unfriendly act'. We were treated as pirates, even pariahs, or at least seen as giving comfort to the real commercial pirates, not the least of whom was Ray Burke. Much hair was torn out in Donnybrook. I understand that Bob Collins, in his then role as programme controller, let it be known that none of the ringleaders was to be interviewed on RTÉ. And we were not. There even seemed to be a reluctance in the RTÉ newsroom to report that the event had actually happened. As an independent contributor to RTÉ's schedules, I received a warning to distance myself from the operation. A senior executive bluntly told me that if I did not abandon what was seen as a pirate operation, it might influence their commissioning decisions in the future.

It did not mean, however, that a couple of Raidió na Gaeltachta colleagues did not continue informally helping us – which RTÉ must have guessed but could do nothing about. Naturally, there were some members of the NUJ who were vehemently opposed to our shoestring proposals for a community TV service.

This story is full of ironies – not least of which was the RTÉ *Cúrsaí* programme begging the Conamara pirates for a tape of their exclusive last interview with the suddenly deceased Dónall Mac Amhlaigh, author of *Dialann Deoraí*, who had spent much of his working life as a labourer in Northampton.

The first positive result was that Charlie Haughey approved of our initiative and earmarked half a million pounds for a future Gaeltacht TV service. It was Lottery money; apparently Haughey never paid for anything himself. At a formal dinner in the Royal Hospital, Kilmainham, celebrating the tenth anniversary of the founding of Aosdána, I wore a T-shirt with 'Teilifís na Gaeltachta' emblazoned on the chest. He pointed to it and said, '*Beidh sé ann*' (it will be there). Little did we know that we were pawns in the bigger war against RTÉ. Our field of struggle was local and linguistic; RTÉ's was national and economic; Haughey's was bigger than both.

This was part of the baggage which I brought to the RTÉ Authority. I was frequently reminded of these heady events in the boardroom. Discussions on the then proposed Teilifís na Gaeilge, now TG4, were rarely off the agenda. Although a wholly owned subsidiary of RTÉ – admittedly imposed on it by Minister Michael D. Higgins – TG4 has constantly been felt by RTÉ to be a thorn in its flesh, especially in the matter of the latter's obligation to provide an hour's programming every day. It was over inevitable squeals of pain that Michael D. Higgins in 1995 urged RTÉ to hasten the establishment of the station (in his first meeting with the new Authority), and a wonderful technical job RTÉ did in double-quick time! The snag was expenditure. Having had the residue of the £10 million CAP money which RTÉ had carefully squirreled away (the bulk was appropriated by the Department of Finance), earmarked by the minister as capital to build the station, RTÉ was now ordered to supply 365 hours programming to the station per year! The cost to the beleaguered national broadcaster would be at least £5 million per annum.

The odium towards this venture displayed by many people was not dissipated by the RTÉ Authority of which I was a member. In press statements and annual reports, it consistently associated, almost in a cause and effect relationship, the burden of TnaG with its own straitened circumstances. It is still doing so. The best-selling magazine in Ireland, the *RTÉ Guide*, buried the TnaG schedules in obscure corners of its pages. I protested regularly about these matters. The only injustice eventually remedied was that in the *RTÉ Guide*.

Not all Conamara people were happy either. The reaction of one Fianna Fáil man was gleefully noted down for me by a Raidió na Gaeltachta broadcaster: '*Foc é Michael D... Ní dhearna sé foc-all don taobh seo anyways... EVER... Céard a rinne sé, an foc-dog bradach? Alright... thóg sé foc-in monstrosity sa ngarraí sin thiar... do shower cuntannaí... nach bhfuil béarla ná Gaeilge acub.*'

Because minors may be reading this, I would rather not translate it. One does not have to be a sycophant to note the daring of Michael D. Higgins acting in the darkness of such a climate.

Nevertheless, most of us trooped over to Baile na hAbhann in January 1996 to witness the minister turning the first sod on the new station. He explained his personal sense of urgency in getting the station going: 'This decision had to be taken now or a crucial moment affecting citizenship, the Irish language and democracy would be lost for ever. The debate about Teilifís na Gaeilge is about national self-respect.' On the RTÉ Authority in the main there was a politically correct attitude to these efforts towards saving the first national language – as long as the Authority did not have to foot the bill! The government alone should do it. This meant foot-dragging by RTÉ until the financial i's and t's were respectively dotted and crossed, which made it impossible for TnaG to plan its programme schedules. Just four days after the sod-turning, there was a controlled explosion of anger in Donnybrook when the TnaG advisory committee (represented by Brian Mac Aonghusa and Cathal Goan) first met the RTÉ chairman and the chief executive. Recriminations were tossed back and forth. In the end both sides, because essentially they were in bed together, agreed that any blame for the contretemps could be laid at the minister's feet, and they ended up friends.

When I realised the sorry impasse into which our original idealistic effort had been led, I said to the RTÉ Authority that I almost regretted our piratical actions. The only one who nodded assent was Bob Collins. We had come to the same conclusion – for patently different reasons. On Halloween 1996, the occasion of TnaG's first transmission, we held our monthly Authority meeting in Conamara. I imagine that if TnaG had been established in the grounds of Montrose, there would not have been half the objections.

There was other opposition; it was not just political opportunists or even so-called 'west Brits' who were against an Irish-language community TV service. As I suggested at the time of our piratical activities, in an article in the *Irish Times*, the real enemies of the project were the Dublin Gaelic revivalists, who seemed to me to be saying, 'Why should we have pictures of Conamara people gathering seaweed imposed on us sophisticated Dublin people?' It seemed not to occur to these critics that Conamara people for thirty years had had images, equally irrelevant to their lives, imposed on them. The revivalist mindset never lost sight of the goal of imposing a veneer of halting Irish on the entire nation. In seventy years of such a state-backed aspiration, they had utterly failed. The real losers were the Gaeltacht communities who actually spoke exquisite and fluent Irish. As Senator Joe O'Toole has recently said, 'Isn't it daft to think that we have spent eighty years trying to get people to speak the language in the Galltacht while virtually ignoring the very people who speak and live the language daily in the Gaeltacht?'

The object of those who set up Saor-Raidió Chonamara and Teilifís na Gaeltachta was to try to salvage something from the ruins of the national revival policy. Joe Steve Ó Neachtain, a popular Conamara poet, playwright and actor, sanely observed: 'Let us not impose ourselves and our language on English speakers. Let us run a Gaeltacht TV service, and those interested can eavesdrop on us.'

As the first person to subtitle an Irish film in English (in 1977), I was pleased with Joe Steve's sane observation. The richness of Gaeltacht life should be made available to, not imposed upon, the culturally impoverished monoglot people of the Galltacht.

In 1987 a local community television service for the Gaeltacht was our modest ambition. It was eventually distorted into a grandiose plan to have a national and linguistically based service. The latter would initially ignore or gloss over the geographical reality of the Gaeltacht. The result – nine years later in 1996 – was a compromise: the TV station would be physically located in Baile na hAbhann in the Conamara Gaeltacht, but its philosophy, outlook and physical transmission would be 'national'. Like many compromises in Ireland, it fell between several stools and satisfied few. It would be called Teilifís na Gaeilge (not 'Gaeltachta'), thus emphasising its location in the ephemera of linguistics rather than in the flesh and blood of small Irish-speaking communities. Later it was rebranded as 'TG4' to pragmatically enhance its position on urban cable TV as a mainstream rather than a community broadcaster.

Compromise spawned paradox. When the new TV station was being reluctantly planned by RTÉ, the decision was taken that it would broadcast on UHF transmitters. Now, the only sizeable communities in this island who speak Irish as a first language, those people in the Gaeltacht areas of Kerry, Galway and Donegal, had only a VHF reception capability. Obviously this meant they could not receive a UHF signal unless they put up new aerials. Images of red-shawled '*mamós*' and becapped pensioners climbing up roofs all over Conamara occurred to us.

The rationalisations for this odd decision were explained to me many times on the Authority by engineers, senior executives et al. Even Joe Barry, an engineer by training, told me that the future would be on

UHF, that VHF would be televisually obsolete, that everybody would have to change eventually on to UHF. The hope was that thousands of households would dash out and buy new aerials, then clamber on to their roofs and install them to get a couple of programmes in 'book Irish'. There was a further Alice in Wonderland touch expressed at an Authority meeting: it was hoped that the advent of RTÉ's new competitor, the commercial station TV3 – also scheduled to broadcast on UHF – would be an incentive for Gaeltacht people to take the soup and buy a UHF aerial. I still have no TV3 reception, for which relief I believe I am to be envied – TV3 has not bothered to extend its signal so far west. In desperation the Executive proposed that there might even be some small subsidy offered to Gaeltacht viewers to buy aerials and join this global village, this brave new world of UHF. Nothing came of that.

A government-appointed technical subcommittee had been set up to examine the situation. Michael Grant was the chairman. The committee got the impression that a VHF service for the Gaeltacht was impossible. But it was learned that an RTÉ internal report had shown that this was not quite accurate: it might be inconvenient but it certainly was not impossible. Bobby Gahan of RTÉ claimed that the report was confidential, but when it was pointed out by Michael Grant that all of the committee's dealings were confidential (until this moment), the report surfaced – thanks to Bob Collins' sensible intervention. It made no difference. The engineers' minds were clear: provision of a VHF facility for the Gaeltacht would disrupt their plan – as well as their plans for VHF-carried digital radio. It was intended that the whole TV network would be UHF based. This systematic engineering perspective has dominated RTÉ for forty years, rather like Egyptian priests whose technical knowledge of the Nile's fluctuation enabled them to dominate millions of peasants. As Charles Curran of the BBC long ago pointed out, the BBC regional services are 'the result of engineering requirements and not of the people of those regions'.

Even though technology is never neutral, the engineers must not entirely be blamed. It was clear from the start that the priority audience was the cabled urban audience in the advertisers' prime category who might or might not have a smattering of what is laughingly called the first national language of the state. The viewers in the Gaeltacht were a poor last in this race. Eighteen months after the station's launch, only fifty per cent of Munster viewers had access to its programming.

One of the ironies of this decision was that with the advent of digital broadcasting – which will make community access broadcasting a serious possibility – it transpires that the VHF vehicle, whose obsolescence had been confidently predicted by the powers that be, would not be useless. When I asked Joe Barry from whence the original decision had emanated, I was told 'the department'. But an outside engineer then suggested to me that no engineers other than RTÉ engineers would have advised the department. This in turn suggested to me that a pragmatic decision had been taken by engineers, which suited the linguistic politics of urban Gaeilgeoirí, whose prime, if futile, ambition has always been to turn Dubliners into Gaeilgeoirí. Even if this meant that the baby – a community TV service for the Gaeltachtaí – was thrown out with the bathwater of VHF.

Our little adventure ultimately led to the establishment of Teilifís na Gaeilge (later rebranded as TG4). But it was defined as a national service with little technological and not much other social relevance to the community from whose womb it was untimely torn. Ironically, thanks to the careful steering of its baby steps by Cathal Goan, and recently by Pól Ó Gallchóir, TG4 has now emerged as the only Irish TV channel which, in my opinion, can unambiguously claim to represent the interests and tastes, as well as the intelligent idiosyncrasies, of the Irish people.

TG4 has survived everything and provides a crucial alternative to RTÉ – as well as being a useful stalking horse for the mother house in Donnybrook. It has been used as a laboratory to experiment with more efficient news-gathering practices, lack of familiarity with which in the first six months caused a series of appalling blunders and damaged the early reputation of the baby TV service. The station is also used – as independent programme-makers have found to their cost – as a means of RTÉ cherry-picking the TG4-commissioned programmes for next to nothing. Internal logic admits that RTÉ is entitled to such a concession: it makes its own superb archive freely available to TG4. That is little consolation to independent programme-makers who provide practically all TG4's non-news output from which RTÉ can pick the choicest morsels.

I hope I may be pardoned for devoting so much attention to these matters. My view from the Gaeltacht periphery of this island informed much of my perspective on the RTÉ Authority. In the ecology of Irish broadcasting, Raidió na Gaeltachta and TG4 may be considered to be the only species that are unique to Ireland, and like any rare species whose cultural hinterland is ever diminishing, they are hanging on by their fingertips. In the ecosystem of sounds, images and ideas which broadcasting should be, there is presently a monocultural preponderance of weeds, choking all educative possibilities, asphyxiating our cultural life and slowly toxifying our imaginations. Raidió na Gaeltachta and TG4 are essential detoxifiers.

On a personal note: these past thirty years in the Conamara Gaeltacht have been the informative and educational part of my life. They have given me an insight into the political and social contradictions of Irish life which I would never have acquired in the protected environment of middle-class Dublin and RTÉ. It has also been the richest cultural experience I have encountered – and I have lived and travelled from Iran to Germany, from Canada to North Africa.

Best of all, the fresh air has kept me, a decadent drinker and smoker, relatively healthy. When I was a harassed RTÉ staff producer in the sixties, my life expectancy was actuarially assessed at forty-five years, which gloomy prognostication I have defied for over twenty years. If Montrose gave me heartburn, Conamara saved my life.

III

The Age of Effluence

Shit happens.

Because I live in a rural area, my home is serviced by a septic tank. This fixture was originally badly constructed, developed severe transmission faults, and I never seemed to have the wherewithal to fix or replace it. Owing to faulty plumbing, its malodorous contents could occasionally back up into the bath. To protect my children from cholera or the black plague, I was obliged twice a year to open the access points and clear the sewage pipe that led to the tank. The task demanded a gas mask – alternatively, a windy day – and thirty feet of chimney-sweeping apparatus. This is a good exercise in humility, a pungent reminder of one of the fundamentals of human existence: at bottom, we are all equal. The job is analogous to that of certain monastic orders, each of whose members dig a little of their grave every day.

The lavatory on the third floor of the RTÉ administration building is also a great equaliser, a place where it is difficult for Authority members to maintain any natural or acquired pomposity. Real encounters take place here, and within this sacred portal one of my new colleagues, Bill Attley, told me a good story.

On a large building site in Donegal, the workers were all making solid money but found it hard to shed old habits like collecting unemployment assistance. The names under which they were employed on the building site were perforce all bogus, and this was a source of frustration to the local 'gaugers', the agents of the social welfare system. However, the latter showed commendable and, according to Bill, unusual initiative when they hit on a bright idea to circumvent this fraud. They dressed one of their younger and prettier female employees in a tight miniskirt and sweater and sent her pedalling her endless legs out to the site on a bicycle. Armed only with a book of raffle tickets as bogus as the workers' assumed names, she charmed the birds off their scaffolding. Every single man Jack of them bought a ticket from the beauty and carefully wrote his real name and address on the stub. These stubs were carefully and pleasurably perused by the local office of the Department of Social Welfare. It was the end of that scam – and of the workers' dole.

Attley, a committed trade unionist and then secretary of SIPTU, was illustrating to me the fact that even he was not blind to the vagaries of human nature and did not believe that all workers were saints, particularly rural workers who were not unionised. However, when it came to union members in safe public employment, the ones who mainly paid his and Des Geraghty's salaries, he was utterly fearless in their defence.

This became clear when I initially put forward my objections to child-targeted commercials.

With the help of the daily TV log, I made a detailed study of their frequency. At our second meeting, in late July, under the umbrella of a discussion on the Green Paper on Broadcasting, I insisted that the Authority have piped through to them in the boardroom one of the commercial breaks at that moment being transmitted by our own Network 2. They were thus forced to watch the endless procession of seductive messages directed at their children and grandchildren. I doubt if they had ever paid attention to them before; adults do not bother to watch children's TV. Perhaps a domestic event the previous week had added an edge to my assault: Miriam had presented me with yet another bouncing baby boy – her second, my fourth – whom we named Dominic, after the Order of Preachers. Together with the two girls, I had altogether produced six young targets for commercial consumption.

Fuelled by this thought, I energetically pointed out to my colleagues the symmetry between the Third World exploitation of children as sweatshop labour and that of our own children being brainwashed to buy the toy products of the same sweatshops from Hawaii to China. Two years previously, the Kader toy sweatshop in Bangkok went on fire. Because its young workers were locked in, 148 of them were burned to death and 469 more were injured. Among the charred remains were scattered hundreds of soot-stained Bugs Bunnies, Bart Simpsons, the Muppets and Big Bird from *Sesame Street*. Claiming that

RTÉ through its child-targeted advertising practices was encouraging this business, I formally proposed the following motion: 'That we, the RTÉ Authority, cease treating children as targetable consumers, i.e. as a market, and forthwith remove commercial messages from the context of children's programming.'

It was a crude tactic: to highlight the defencelessness of children, to make some kind of analogy between child abuse (which was all the rage in the Irish media at the time) and child-targeted commercials. Children are the soft underbelly. If I could achieve a questioning of the ethics of contemptuously treating them as consumers, perhaps adults might wake up and say, 'Hey, I'm an advertising puppet, too!' The battlefield of child-targeted commercials was the front I had tactically – but with a certain amount of passion – chosen on which to combat the excesses of global consumerism and its pernicious influence on good broadcasting.

But initially, what was Joe Barry's reaction to the viewing of the commercial break? He sat back smiling and said, 'I didn't think business was so good.'

However, Joe did not get the job of director-general for being a softie. One of the menacing phrases he used to me at the time in relation to this whole system of commercials was, 'You poke at this at your peril.'

Further, when he adroitly mentioned that the loss of revenue on curbing our child-targeted commercials could cost fifty jobs – which was an exaggeration – both trade unionists on the Authority were adamantly against such a step. Any reform, no matter how well-intentioned, that constituted a threat to jobs in RTÉ was absolutely out. Bill Attley was a man I would love to have had in my corner. Des Geraghty, too. But even the influence of these two powerful and articulate men was limited in RTÉ. Despite their suggestion that, proportionate to the attention given to agriculture on RTÉ, there might also be a programme devoted to normal trade union activities, no such step was ever taken. Gearóid Ó Tuathaigh of UCG had pointed out the same lack in RTÉ programming as long ago as 1984.

Following my line in practical terms, Betty Purcell proposed a moratorium on at least the Christmas toy advertisements which would lose the station not more than one per cent of its income. But the powerful worker voices on the Authority said we must first establish how the loss would be covered. This touch-kicking became a recurrent tactic when anything difficult was proposed.

The result of this first skirmish was that the director-general promised a full examination of the problem and a detailed proposal within two months. My motion would also be discussed then. After these exertions, I retreated to the lavatory for a smoke.

Perhaps it was my familiarity with septic tanks, perhaps a throwback to schooldays, but as the months rolled by the lavatory would become my refuge. When Patricia Redlich was in full spate, droning on about the recalcitrance of RTÉ staff and boring at least me to tears with 'nanny states' and 'hush puppies' and a litany of Thatcherisms, I would rise and head for this retreat.

The *Phoenix* magazine had an interesting item on her at the time of her appointment in March 1996. Being *Phoenix*, it may have been speculative. It said that she had been appointed to RTÉ directly by Taoiseach John Bruton, and she was reported as being close to Eoghan Harris, who had been an advisor to Bruton. This version, whether true or not, was never challenged. Realistically, Minister Michael D. Higgins would hardly have approved the appointment of a woman who shortly before had said in the *Sunday Independent* that the minister would not be unhappy if Saddam Hussein acquired a nuclear device! The *Sunday Independent* was forced to apologise.

Redlich brought to three the quota of Bruton appointees on the Authority, joining Anne Haslam and Garret FitzGerald, the first ex-Taoiseach to be so appointed. When in power he had strongly advocated the depoliticising of such appointments (and did so as recently as September 2000 in his *Irish Times* column). However, in 1995 times must have been hard, particularly after his recent flirtation with GPA, AIB and the whole damn catastrophe in which he speculated and lost hundreds of thousands of pounds, as well as his home.

The lavatory was also the place where I found my secret weapon. There were at least three occasions when certain members of the Authority were outraged by my actions and demanded my resignation. To staunch my wounds, all I had to do was recall some early words of the chairman to me as we stood shoulder to shoulder in the urinal: 'You know, of course, that it would take a vote of both houses of the Oireachtas to get rid of you.'

I had not previously known that. Since then I have wondered if the chairman ever regretted giving me that invincible shield of burning brass. It had been forged by Conor Cruise O'Brien in an amendment to the Broadcasting Act in 1976: the solo power of a minister to sack either an individual member or the Authority as a whole was rescinded.

The subsequent frictions on this Authority, with which I admit having not a little to do, reflected the tensions within the organisation. A survey of staff attitudes two years previously – after a bitter strike of programme people about cutbacks in camera crews – revealed that 64 per cent of the staff thought management passed the buck, 59 per cent thought they were indecisive, 56 per cent said they were bureaucratic and 58 per cent said they were inconsistent. Sixty-four per cent thought RTÉ was clique-ridden, 69 per cent thought it secretive, 62 per cent said morale was low, and 75 per cent thought there was a chasm between management and the actual programme-making operation. Thirty-five per cent of the staff thought that RTÉ fulfilled its public service obligations 'not at all'.

One RTÉ producer sorrowfully expressed the situation to me: 'RTÉ is like a dysfunctional family with alcoholic parents. The children run around lost and wild, not knowing where they are.'

Since that survey was conducted within a year of the devastating 1992 strike of programme staff, and on the assumption that things must have improved, I suggested to the Executive that the survey might valuably be updated. A question I would have included was this: which TV channel do you most watch? I would have laid bets that the majority of RTÉ staff concentrated their viewing on cross-channel and satellite services – from which they could derive useful programme ideas – rather than their own home-produced stuff. That was left for us deprived people in three-channel land.

Incidentally, the only group in this survey which seemed to be happy was management, 78 per cent of whom thought RTÉ was a good place in which to work. To paraphrase Mandy Rice-Davies, 'They would say that, wouldn't they?'

This was the atmosphere into which the new Authority was launched. It was a perilous stage for an ingénue such as me. As in domestic circumstances, there is always something of a love-hate quality in such relationships. Never interfere in a husband-wife row. I knew that I had to tread carefully.

I sought further advice.

Ben Barenholtz is an independent New York producer who has survived in the jungle of film and theatre for many years. He has produced for, among others, the Coen brothers, so he is no slouch. *Barton Fink* and *Miller's Crossing* are on his CV. On his annual visit to the Galway Film Fleadh in July, I took the opportunity to explain my position and ask for tactical advice on how to get a director-general to see things my way. Over our customary breaking of brown bread – washed down with a bottle of vodka – Ben said:

> Remember that a big shot has a job to keep, that he has an ego, that he has had to do awful things. Remember particularly that if he had any integrity he wouldn't be in that job in the first place. The tactic is to persuade the guy that his job will not be jeopardised by your proposal. Reassure him that he is great. Reassure him that everybody has to do awful things, that he shouldn't feel guilty. Certainly don't you make him feel any more guilty. Tell him what he wants to hear. Then tell him new ways of not losing money.

This was sound advice which was effectively transmuted by me into the following: tell the chief executive that his job is not the most important thing in the world and that I couldn't care less anyway; try to undermine his ego; make him feel as guilty as hell for the awful things he is doing. Finally, tell him he must lose money.

In defence I submit that as a member of Aosdána, the Irish parliament of artists, to which I was the first filmmaker elected, I was entitled to use artistic licence. Nobody is perfect. Joe Barry, the director-general, understood this very well. The more I impetuously demanded action on child-targeted commercials, the more he retained his avuncular calm. Only once did he impatiently call me a crank and compare my unrelenting campaigning to that of a previous Authority member, Dr Bill Loftus. This good man, the coroner for County Mayo, daily witnessed the bloody result of alcohol-induced carnage on the roads and incessantly called for the abolition of advertisements for drink. He, too, was ignored.

In a manipulative mediocracy, the standard defence against 'novel' thinking is to call for a report or to invoke oracles called consultants. The advantage of these is that, like royal commissions and Irish tribunals, they enable decisions and retribution to be postponed. Moreover, when their expensive advice proves worthless, they can be blamed. This tactic is a catch-all for indecisiveness. It produces what F.R. Scott has called 'the rain of facts which deepens the drought of the will'. Handling the demands of people like Loftus and myself was easy: the Executive would simply promise a report on the financial implications.

John Horgan of DCU, an experienced broadcaster, wrote about this time: 'If RTÉ stays much the same and tries to muddle through, the chances are it will be overwhelmed. There is not likely to be a second chance.'

Those were my sentiments entirely. I had, therefore, circulated a three-page list of direct questions for the Executive. They were designed to underline for the greenhorns on the Authority the rationalisations behind what appeared to me to be contradictions in RTÉ's financial, programming and scheduling strategies. Ben Barenholtz once said to me that when somebody asks a simple question and somebody gives a simple answer, God is listening. My questions were obviously not simple enough and went unanswered. God developed wax in his ears.

The worst thing I suggested was that the members of the Authority have five minutes on their own after each session: no Executive present, no note-takers, no record, to give the Authority the opportunity to discuss informally its officers' and servants' performances. That suggestion was not even allowed to reach the starting post. Neither did my later proposal that the highly paid senior executives should have temporary contracts similar to those they imposed on producers and directors.

It was high summer in Conamara. In July it was a relief to escape from the sogginess of Dublin to the sweet air of the West. The spiralled yellow cores of ox-eye daisies lined the roadsides, and puffs of bog cotton exploded all over the marshes. On my personal bog, purple was the dominant colour: loosestrife, marsh orchid, spiraea and heather carpeted the place. Meadowsweet was the perfume. Here, like the Prince of Wales, I could resume my dialogue with trees. RTÉ was also getting out of the city, its programmes following staff and management to their holiday hideaways round the country. After August it is assumed that when they return from Kerry, Conamara and Donegal, nobody is left in these desolate places and RTÉ can revert to being Radio Teilifís Dublin again.

To further educate its new Authority into the nature of broadcasting reality, the Executive arranged an informational weekend for September.

Donal McCann – Dark Soul
(Donal McCann Remembered, 2000)

A tribute to the late actor Donal McCann, who had lead roles in Poitín. Budawanny *and* The Bishop's Story, *from a collection edited by Pat Laffan and Faith O'Grady and published by New Island Books.*

Donal McCann's greatness as an actor had relatively little to do with his consummate skills and mastery of the crafts of stage and film acting. Many actors were as skilful. But very few had his power to intimidate and thereby control us. The nearest actor I could think of to match his dangerous presence was Rod Steiger.

In my opinion Donal's secret was a darkness of soul which, like that of most marked people, was based on dissatisfaction both with himself and with the way the world was ordered.

What often struck me was a deep and seething anger at himself and at the world for not taking more care. That may be the reason why he was fastidious to the point of psycho-pathology in his work. It was why his presence on stage and on film was so intimidating. He had seen the abyss in certain formative experiences of early life. What he did was not acting. It was real. It was why we were all privately afraid of him. It was why directors handled him with great care, why actors circled him nervously, why audiences watched, fascinated. This was a man in whose dangerous presence, off and onstage, we spoke deferentially, fearful lest we say the wrong thing.

Yet he could also be the mildest and gentlest person imaginable. Yes, he was frequently seen as a bully. It could be justified on his grounds that everybody should be as fanatic about perfection as he. But when he met his artistic equals on stage, the ensemble playing was electric. Ask John Kavanagh and Joe Dowling about *Juno*.

To meet him in preparation for a role was to be sucked into a single-mindedness that was alarming. Every word in his scenes – including the other characters' lines – was absorbed into his interpretation, which was probably why writers loved him. Ask Friel, Murphy, Barry & Co.

The young McCann I knew was outrageously handsome. His brown eyes and Jack Nicholson smile were fly traps. Thirty years ago I brought a young French woman to see him in the Abbey panto, in which he played James Bond. One pint after the show I had lost her to Donal.

Unlike many male actors, he was liked and admired by intelligent and talented men. Francis Bacon was one of his drinking pals in London. So was Peter O'Toole. Paul Durcan, Pat Laffan and Brian Friel were loyal friends to whom he frequently and fondly referred. He saw them not as 'actors', 'painters', 'poets', 'writers', creatures of an irrelevant demi-monde; to him they were real people who shared that precarious vision from which ordinary mortals escape into the day job. But the ones he seemed closest to were betting men.

McCann had a labyrinthine sense of humour and a sure instinct for comedy. Ask Hugh Leonard.

One of the interesting things about him was that he never became a tabloid star, despite all the necessary attributes. He avoided such a fate like poison though he could easily have done so and made a fortune. He was notorious for his stubborn refusals to let journalists turn him into an icon. Perhaps he had an ambiguity about him which attracted the thinking and deterred the unthinking. 'Why aren't you a Hollywood idol?' I once asked him. He said he never wanted to be a star. But he was human: when he saw signs of his old comrade Stephen Rea becoming a star – twenty years ago – he set alight the newspaper in which Stephen was immersed, in a hotel in Carraroe.

There is no doubt he was a sentimentalist. I know he could never accept the fashionable modern judgement on his father's plays – those that kept the Abbey solvent in the fifties – which says that they were simply light comedies and would fail today. I would guess that one of his greatest and sadly unfulfilled ambitions would have been to act in a revival of one of them.

McCann was a survivor all his short life. In 1978 I asked him why he pushed himself so hard. He replied, 'To see how much I can take'. The characteristic of saints and madmen.

On location on Clare Island in 1986, Donal and the late Freda Gillen, then 76 years of age, would rise at 5am and drink tea together. I don't know what they talked about but Freda developed a great fondness for him, always asked for him, and told me that he was a very religious man.

If you get a reputation for being an early riser you can stay in bed all day. The reverse is also true as far as his drinking reputation was concerned. He acted with the late Broderick Crawford and Niall Tóibín in *The Championship Game*. Niall and Donal used to take Broderick for long drives during the day to keep the American actor sober for that night's performance. They weren't always successful. Tóibín might also recall playing sober games of Scrabble at night with Donal during the filming of *Poitín*. When he arrived in Los Angeles to make *The Dead*, Huston's assistant director took Donal aside and said, 'If you do a [named actor] on John, I'll kill you.' It was a reference to Huston's *Under the Volcano*, in which a main actor was clearly drunk all the time. Donal was exemplary on *The Dead* and worked with his colleagues to produce the best example of ensemble playing by Irish actors ever recorded on film.

It was not always thus. On *The Bishop's Story*, the early-morning taxi that picked him up reported a puncture. A half-hour later there was another puncture. And then another. When he eventually arrived, having toured various hostelries via Blessington, he was in a fairly dishevelled state. As he was being paid, the taxi driver handed over a half-eaten package of mints with the remark, 'He forgot his puncture-repair kit.' Donal always had a siesta in the afternoon. This time he took it on the steps of the Dominican Church in Tallaght.

He was an erudite conversationalist, extremely well-read and a brilliant user and punner of words. The trouble for a media interviewer was that he thought before he spoke. Andy O'Mahony will testify to that. I heard a radio interview between them. The pauses before answering were of Pinter/Beckett duration. Cliff-edge stuff. Nowadays such pauses would be edited out. But you couldn't have a showbiz-type interview with McCann.

His phone calls to me usually coincided with the end or the beginning of a project. They lasted a long time. He reminded me of the definitive Bach player, Glenn Gould, who had a wide circle of telephonic friends and used to ring them at all hours. One friend reported falling asleep during one call with Gould and waking up an hour later to hear the pianist still talking. You could not do that with McCann. His antennae could read your silence. Nevertheless, whatever hell Donal inhabited became a semi-private soirée to which his friends were invited. One Sunday morning he rang me in a clearly distressed state to report the palpable presence of evil, and he was sure that Satan would appear. All I could think of advising him to do was to go to Mass and thus exorcise the feeling, because it seemed to me that religion was the source of his demons in the first place. I never heard more about the subject. Still, one always felt that one was the only confidante.

The only confidante... perhaps that was one of his acting secrets. His performances seemed to touch you and you alone. You were oblivious to the other thousands witnessing the man's sheer energy and effort in the cause of his craft, art, call it what you will. It was certainly more than acting.

It was his own very personal *ars gratia artis*.

Why Desmond Fennell is No. 2
(Desmond Fennell – his life and work, 2001)

From a collection of essays on the late Irish writer, edited by Toner Quinn and published by Veritas.

During the coffee break of an Aosdána meeting in Kilmainham in 1991, I found myself standing adjacent to the poet Seamus Heaney. For want of something profound to say, I inquired: 'How's that row between yourself and Fennell going?' He sharply retorted, 'How would I know; I'm only the subject', turned his back and walked away, leaving me with the realisation that I had become involved in a civil war of ideas.

The trouble was that my friend, Desmond Fennell, had been the sole member of the Irish literary community daring enough to publish a negative critique of his own friend Heaney's body of work. It was entitled *Whatever You Say, Say Nothing – Why Seamus Heaney is No. 1*. My only personal interest in the pamphlet was that Fennell had dedicated it to me as a person 'who never says die'. Willy-nilly, I had been drafted as a foot soldier into the army of one general, Desmond Fennell.

Famous Seamus' snub did not bother me at all; I am accustomed to the prickliness of artists towards any criticism. I would feel the same myself. And the flattery of Fennell's dedication, whether it got me into trouble or not, was adequate recompense. But the incident forced me to do a crash course in Heaney. Precisely because his poetry appeared to be extraordinarily popular, I had only glanced at it since his charming *Death of a Naturalist* made him the hero of southern nationalists in the mid-sixties. His prose, *The Government of the Tongue* for example, I found less opaque and Delphic than his TV utterances, and it was generously argued. His poetry I found pleasant and vaguely nineteenth-century-esque, reminding me of Emily Dickinson. It certainly had not the power of my idols, T.S. Eliot and Philip Larkin, and was not obviously superior to the work of such as Patrick Kavanagh or John Montague. In a public reading that I attended, I found Heaney's persona modest and camera-friendly. I had nothing for or against the poet. I confess that I was surprised when he was awarded the Nobel Prize for literature, which honour I had thought was traditionally reserved for heavyweights. My own personal heavyweight, Larkin, had not acquired the distinction in his lifetime, so maybe it was all the luck of the draw, historical timing or, like many a literary award, a matter of fashion, taste, hustling, commerce and politics.

After the Nobel award, I read the second edition of Fennell's pamphlet, to which samples of verse were added. I found it equally well-argued and at least politically convincing. Fennell's position was consistent. He had expressed a similar attitude in the early 1980s in one of his *Sunday Press* columns. There he also uttered reservations about Heaney's poetry and had even joined the poet Seamus Deane as co-defendant to his, Fennell's, charge of their poetic timidity in the face of the Northern war. However, even I felt that this was already apparent; I had thought Heaney excused his position well in *Station Island* in a sentiment attributed to Joyce's ghost, which went as follows: 'You lose more of yourself than you redeem / doing the decent thing / Keep at a tangent.' There was a war on and Heaney's words were a sensible approximation of every sane soldier's motto in war: never volunteer for anything.

In fact, the only aspect that intrigued me in this dispute was that these three men were, or had been, friends. Fennell once told me that on their way in a car to a Field Day occasion in Derry, Heaney and he stood shoulder to shoulder in a *pissoir*. Fennell took the opportunity to ask Heaney what was the real pursuit of his work and Heaney replied: beauty. Which response made sense, at least to me.

The unusual thing for me, Southerner, was the public nature of the attack that Fennell had mounted on his friend. Such an action is usually unheard of in the South (meaning Dublin), where members of the literary community live in each others' ears. Private assassinations of public writers are the *lingua franca* of artistic conversations throughout the South. Prominent poets fumed privately at Heaney's elevation, but public silence was their order of the day. Unlike them, but like Heaney and Deane, Fennell's roots are in the plain-speaking, confrontational North from which he derives his forthright manner.

Fennell spent a happy infancy and formative childhood in Belfast, until his parents came back from America and transplanted him to Dublin, a culture away from the grandparents who had hitherto reared him. For some reason the expression 'snatched untimely from the womb' comes to mind.

In Fennell's breaching of the Southern code I find a perfect example of why the man, while arousing ire, also demands respect; he is utterly fearless in the expression of his opinions. But in a culture whose essential characteristic is a facility for dissembling, Fennell's desperate approach has been a form of social and professional *felo de se*. And that, it seems to me, has always been his inescapable destiny.

Fennell and I are ships that have bumped in the night over the past forty years. In the sixties, I directed RTÉ programme discussions in which he articulately and bilingually (he is fluent in five languages) participated. He lived in Dundrum, Dublin, with his beautiful wife Mary, a biblical scholar in her own right, in a little gate lodge opposite the cemetery where two of my grandparents are buried. Our social circles – his, intellectual and artistic; mine, hedonist and alcoholic – rarely intersected, although he and the late Paddy Gallagher paid me the compliment of crashing my farewell party (I was leaving for Canada) in 1967. In 1969, when I had finally left RTÉ, Fennell chaired a meeting in Taibhdhearc na Gaillimhe. Never neutral or shy, he pointed out the flaws in Jack Dowling and Lelia Doolan's and my analysis of, and particularly our remedies for, both national broadcasting and the nation in general. Having already dismissed the relevance of Dublin, he was disappointingly unsupportive of our campaign to reform RTÉ. However, it was the first time I heard him spelling out the 'view from the periphery' that had become so central to his vision.

If people have something to say and convincingly argue their personal perspective, I listen as carefully as I read – purely as part of the personal search for insights into the human and social dilemma. The popularity, political correctness or otherwise of ideas rarely bothers me. For instance, since Tehran, 1968, where I first purchased and read *The Thief's Journal*, I have been attracted to the work of the homosexual criminal and writer Jean Genet. Similarly to Francis

Stuart, Brendan Behan and Pádraig Pearse, who each pilloried respectable society in their own ways. The idea of confronting society's assumptions, whether objectively right or wrong, and aligning oneself with the maligned, appears to me to be at least one valid approach to the absurdities and injustices of life. Admittedly, this approach may be a covert expression of psychological inadequacies, insecurities, buried hurts or whatever ills the mind is heir to – so be it; in case evidence is demanded for this sweeping assertion I can only plead the fifth amendment. It remains an intuition, supported by mere literature. Christ was crucified in the lost childhood of Judas.

Consequently, the consistency and defiance of the naysayers' approach, behaviour and especially the conviction with which they say 'nay!' is what touches and attracts the attention of a mental gadfly and agnostic like myself.

Thus, in autumn 1970, when I was living on the dole with a wife and child in a Volkswagen van in Donegal, I wrote to Fennell. He had by then moved to Carna in the Conamara Gaeltacht and I had read about his plan to colonise this Irish-speaking area with thousands of Gaeilgeoirí – an ironic reversal of de Valera's 1930s scheme to colonise County Meath with Conamara people. In my letter I asked Fennell whether it was possible for such as I – a non-Gaeilgeoir – to also survive economically in Conamara and his reply was brief and confident: of course, it simply said. Come! Respecting his opinion – or clutching at a straw – I arrived there on a cold November night and knocked on his door. It was unlatched and unbolted. From inside a bedroom came the sleepy murmur of children saying that both their parents were attending the first Oireachtas na nGael in Ros Muc. We did not know where Ros Muc was located, so we camped for the night in the Fennell household.

Subsequently we lived in various rented houses in the area, including Ros Muc, and maintained a friendly discourse with the Fennell family. Thirty years later I still live in Conamara, like flotsam washed up by an unusual circumstance, happily above the high tide line. Fennell is long gone from here, but he left me with the above-mentioned 'view from the periphery', which has been fundamental to my work.

They lived in Muighinis, which seemed to be as far from Dublin as one could possibly move. It was an island, connected to the mainland village of Carna by a bridge of perilous aspect. Very soon in his writings Fennell was referring to the place as Mao-inis to signify his approval, later withdrawn, for the Chinese communist cultural revolution. At the same time, Israel's revival of the Hebrew language was a matter of great import and admiration for him – it gave him the title '*Iosrael in Iarchonnacht*'. This highlighted for me an apparent, but consistent, paradox in my friend's ideas. He was a staunch defender of Roman Catholicism as the necessary local and national expression of man's innate religious sense. I have no doubt that if he had been reared in China, he would have defended Buddhism. Therefore he took a practical and constructive interest in Church affairs, but at the same time preached radical ideas, which owed little to organised religion and less to international socialism. A friend of mine has recently called him, after a first meeting, a radical conservative.

In the 60s and 70s, possibly stimulated by the other revolution that was the Second Vatican Council, Fennell wanted the self-defined People of God to take an active part in the secular aspects of their religion. He was what the local people in Conamara called a *stróinséir*, a stranger or blow-in, and yet he had the temerity to go to the parish priest of Carna and suggest the formation of a parish council with teeth, one that would be more than a ladies' committee charged with putting fresh flowers on the altar. Knowing Fennell, this may have sounded to the priest more like a demand than a request. However, the latter authorised his young curate to organise a poll among the parishioners as to the value of such an idea. The local Fianna Fáil hierarchy – the real hierarchy in those days – fought bitterly against this possible diminution of their stranglehold on all social affairs in the parish. Fennell was, not for the first or last time, demonised, but a courageous young curate was not deflected from his object and the parish voted for the desired council. It was one of Fennell's rare victories.

In his two-story, rented home in Maoinis I listened often and politely to this man's discourses on anthropology, geography, history and philosophy. His respect for, and knowledge of, classical Roman and Greek civilisation was impressive. Occasionally he would play popular songs from pre-war Germany and enthuse at the enjoyment of life they suggested. 'Celebration' was a constant theme of his, perhaps expressing a keen sense of its absence both locally and nationally. I myself was a fan of melancholy German lieder so there was a loose affinity of taste between us – even though Fennell occasionally trod a daring hairline between admiration for the historic achievements of the German nation and a clinical assessment of the nation-rebuilding techniques of the post-Weimar Nazis. If his ambition was the renewal of the spirit of an Irish nation – and I believe it was – then he was entitled to look for inspiration everywhere, be it Israel or Germany, China or Cuba. The scale of such a grandiose ambition invariably left me as a spectator, *an t-iománai ar an gclaí.*

On the importance of the Irish language and the Gaeltacht in the affairs of Ireland he showed no ambiguity. Being a Dublin gurrier I was then fairly non-committed to this dimension of national life. But Fennell's constant praise for the linguistic felicity as well as the ingenuity and energy of his neighbours was infectious. The irony was that at all times his Gaeltacht neighbours seemed to keep a wary, almost xenophobic, distance from his ideas for the 'improvement' of their lives. This was partly because they may not have received a clear idea of what he was really talking about but, more likely, because of his manner: an unconcealed impatience with what he perceived as slapdash thinking and an intolerance of a fatalistic or servile approach to life. It was very 'un-Irish'.

I must mention that, in mitigation for their less than enthusiastic reception of his ideas, the people of Conamara had long been subjected to a procession of idealists coming from Dublin to 'Save the West'. It was easy to fit Fennell into that category in 1969. He was not providing summer colleges to fill the B&Bs; he was not creating jobs of any kind; he had no political pull. He was a mere writer. All he had was that debased coinage: ideas. It didn't put food on the table.

Indeed, when thirty years later I directed a documentary on the rise of the Gaeltacht Civil Rights Movement in which Fennell played a seminal role – composing most of their first list of demands – it was fascinating to discover that the same wary attitude to him prevailed, especially among some who might have mellowed into a sophisticated appreciation of his motives.

Fennell's *Iosrael in Iarchonnacht* tactic was to challenge the urban Gaeilgeoirí – whose revivalist ambitions he had correctly identified as a failure – to come and settle in the place where Irish was actually the first language. He suggested that the skills they might bring with them – butchers, bakers, perhaps even candlestick makers – were what Conamara needed to build vibrant communities that might reinvigorate what he saw as a depressed, dole-oriented community. The idealism of Fennell is well illustrated in this ambition. The logic of his proposal was impeccable and quite feasible if one was driven by the desperation of, say, post-war Jews, and facilitated by the self-interest of imperial powers. He was aware of, but ignored, the excuse that most urban Irish speakers are civil servants, locked in safe pensionable jobs. To them, the idea of throwing up such security for what they saw as the wilds of Conamara – from which many of them had escaped in the first place – was a non-starter. Fennell certainly roused the ire of his peer group, successful émigré Gaeltacht journalists then prominent in RTÉ – such as Breandán Ó hEithir and Proinnsias Mac Aonghusa. It made for many acerbic public exchanges between them. Fennell's nationalist vocabulary also became a soft target for the Workers' Party members in that same organisation.

On the more important local front, he ignored the implication – which was perceived instantly by his neighbours – that historically they had proven themselves incapable of pulling themselves up by their own bootstraps. Indeed he had no hesitation in saying that they, like the general population of the country, still had 'the landlord in the skull'. This was not likely to make him popular either with his neighbours or with the urban Gaeilgeoirí who proclaimed their love of language, nation and Gaeltacht. Similarly, the idea of thousands of urban people with bad Irish settling on their poor but jealously-held land was not attractive to Conamara people either. In other words, and with hindsight, it may be said that Fennell's idealism confronted and challenged the fact that life in southern Ireland was and is approached as a matter of survival, a progress of small ambitions and negotiations. Without powerful political or financial backing, grandiose homegrown plans for both secular and spiritual salvation have no fruitful soil here. Even with such backing, many a grand plan has foundered in Ireland.

However, Fennell's ideas for Conamara were significantly endorsed when he and his young fellow-conspirator, Seosamh Ó Cuaig, travelled to a meeting of Conradh na Gaeilge in Dublin. Present was the living, patron saint of the Gaelic revival movement, Máirtín Ó Cadhain. This honest man stated publicly that he saw much sense in Fennell's ideas and, further, that he himself might have achieved more for the Irish language had he stayed at home in his Gaeltacht powerbase. After Fennell finally left Conamara twenty years ago, I made a documentary film in which he expressed his considered judgement on the place; the film was called *Laetha Deiridh na Gaeltachta/The Last Days of the Gaeltacht*. It won the premier award at the Celtic Film Festival of 1982. I have a vivid memory of meeting the writer in the Skeffington hotel in Galway when it was clear that Conamara would no longer be his home. In response to my vague comment that he appeared to be leaving all he loved, he cryptically answered: 'too much sacrifice can make a stone of the heart.' I did not pursue the matter.

I appear to have dived in at the deep end in these comments on Fennell. Let me backpaddle to lighter matters. In fact, I realise immediately that such do not spring lightly to my mind. For Fennell, life appears to have been always real, earnest and short. His jokes and laughter have invariably resonated with irony and black humour. I do recall one of his children telling me how their father trained them not to stare at the sun and damage their eyes. He encouraged them to imagine that Mason Island, in the line of the setting sun through their front window, was a possible target for nuclear attack. Therefore they must shield their eyes from the sun as rehearsal for a nuclear attack. It was a grim, wildly unlikely, but effective preventive measure.

It illustrates a Fennell penchant for insisting on the relationship between immediate experience and the larger context, making parables out of apparent trivia, seeing a world in a grain of sand. This may be why he and Mary produced five intelligent, well-travelled and well-read children who, incidentally, do not lack a sense of humour. Long ago at my own dinner table I witnessed his daughter Sorcha, then a teenager, now an indefatigable Third World worker, impressing her contemporaries with her charm and subtle awareness of world affairs. The psychic damage that all parents inadvertently inflict on their children does not appear, in the Fennell case, to be incommensurate with other people's experience, and certainly not with my own. But then, my lifelong motto is: knowledge enters through pain. It is no doubt a relic of the generation to which Fennell and I belong.

Which brings me to puritanism. Fennell once described a puritan as 'correct, self-contained, unsensual, pained by the world and himself, and disdainful of charm and communication because to be right is enough.' Many of his opponents would fasten on that as a crude description of the writer himself. As a friend I have to recognise the approximation, but regard it as quite inadequate to describe his complexity. Then, who knows anybody? Certainly the 'stating of truths' as he sees them, with conviction and passion, and an impatience with those who sit on the fence, is a prominent part of the Fennell make-up. One of his favourite quotations to me was from the Book of the Apocalypse: 'Because you are lukewarm, and neither hot nor cold, I will spit you out of my mouth!'

That conjured up for me an army of *apparatchiks* scurrying fearfully around the thrones of their masters, practising the techniques of forced smiling, networking, speaking prudently in wisps and wraiths of meaning, keeping the lid on things, praising when it is superfluous, condemning when it is safe, exercising invisible sanctions, inhabitants of a grey Kafkaesque world. This bleak image must approximate to what Fennell felt when his career was sabotaged by the Cosgrave government in 1976. I have written of this elsewhere so, briefly, what happened was this:

He was invited by Dr Eoin McKiernan of the Irish American Cultural Institute to participate in a fourteen-city cultural tour of the United States. The IACI had impeccable credentials, was backed by the Irish Government and necessarily had to accept modulations of its tune as suggested by that Government. Thus when the Department of Foreign Affairs, at the instigation of its ambassador in Washington, objected to Fennell's participation in the tour, he was dropped by McKiernan. It was a cruel blow to an Irish writer who was circumscribed by the paper wall of the Dublin media, which itself was hamstrung by the British paper wall around Ireland. There were two additional ironies. Dr McKiernan replaced Fennell with yours truly, this writer, who was totally oblivious to the reason for Fennell's cancellation – until it was divulged to me in Washington at the very end of the tour. I realised that my friend had decided not to spoil my party. The second irony was that the minister for Foreign Affairs who took the advice of his minions and effected the guillotine was none other than Fennell's old schoolmate, Garret FitzGerald.

I assume this left a bitter taste in Fennell's mouth; but I am also certain that his subsequent lashing of FitzGerald in newspaper columns (the *Sunday Press* in particular) was not personal. It was based on the writer's contempt for, as he saw it, successive government policies of placating the loyalists and denigrating the nationalist population in Northern Ireland, i.e. what he saw as the Irish Government slavishly following a British line on the North for peace at any price. Indeed it has always been a revelation to me how Fennell can sit down with friend and foe and discuss their divergent views, forcibly yes, but rarely with rancour. I witnessed this phenomenon early one night in a near-empty Baggot Street club to which Fennell brought me. The first sight that greeted me was a handsome woman pirouetting alone on the dance floor. To my astonishment, Fennell, whom I had rarely seen attempting to tread the light fantastic, went straight up to her and asked her to dance with him – which she did. I studied the odd pair and admired the confidence and unselfconsciousness of this man who, as far as I could see, had two left feet.

The real insight was to come. An unlikely pair, capitalist senator Shane Ross and socialist TD Michael D. Higgins, were communing at a nearby table. Fennell, by general reputation an outspoken Catholic, defender of the Provos, attacker of the political consensus and unashamed Irish nationalist, suggested we join them. These three unlikely bedfellows subsequently exchanged pleasantries for a while. I was the odd man out, feeling exactly as James Plunkett once described, 'the gap in the circle of my friends'. Outside once more, I asked Fennell to explain the warmth between what I would have imagined were deadly ideological enemies. 'Who else have as much in common to talk about as political animals,' he responded.

I learned something about Irish political culture that night.

In preparing this essay I made two lists. The first consisted of who and what Fennell has at one time or another publicly and trenchantly criticised. It included Fianna Fáil, Fine Gael, FitzGerald, Heaney, Hume, Tone and Davis, Trade Unions, divorce, abortion, contraception, the Catholic clergy, Vatican Two, the Church of Ireland, the modern Gaelic revivalists, RTÉ, the *Irish Times*, the British Government, the Irish Government, consumer liberalism, imperialism, conservatism, sexual libertinism, the middle class, feminism, bureaucracy, the colonising device of 'Celticism', incompetent local government, the inertia of central government, Sinn Féin, unionists, the United States and the USSR.

What emerges from this first list is a catholicity of targets. Indeed, it contains a range of subjects that is the staple diet and the target of most working journalists. It does not support the image of a narrowly conservative ideologue, as Fennell is frequently portrayed by those who have never read his more complex works. If anything, it suggests the broad range of interests of any educated, middle-class person. What it might also illustrate is that a speed-reading audience is less moved by the content of an argument than by the body language and tone used to convey it. Form transcends content. Fennell speaks as he writes: with supporting clauses and many emphases, the latter usually signalled by his frequent use of italics in case we should miss one of his more subtle points. This may sometimes appear patronising and can certainly distract from his core arguments.

The second list I made was more difficult to fill in: for whom and for what does Fennell express affection or approval? I once asked the following question of Anne Harris, deputy editor of the *Sunday Independent* and admirer of Conor Cruise O'Brien: knowing as we all do what O'Brien despises, I asked, what does the man love? She smiled her beautiful smile and said: 'That is a very clever question.' A question she did not answer. What a person loves is more revealing than what they hate.

In relation to Fennell I racked my brains and came up with the following list of what he approves, or at least of what he at some stage approved: Francis Stuart, Charles Haughey, Camille Paglia, James Connolly, George Russell, Pádraig Pearse, the film *Odd Man Out*, the working class, Christianity, the creative members of the bourgeoisie, hence Edward Maguire's painting, Mary Kenny, Nuala O'Faolain, Brian Friel's *Translations*, Tom Murphy's *The Gigli Concert*, the Israelis, the Palestinians, the IRA, E. Schumacher's *Small is Beautiful,* his wife and children, Italian art, German philosophy, Heidegger's humanism, Sister Stanislaus, Margaretta D'Arcy, celebration, Olivia O'Leary, local initiative and Tom Barrington.

Any attempt by me to analyse these lists, to systematise them, find a thread, and make a clear unambiguous statement about Fennell would be fruitless. First of all, I am not equipped to find auguries in entrails; secondly, I approach each person as a welcome example of the diversity of our species and the greater the difference the less likely to succumb to the dreaded homogenisation. Let the lists speak for themselves. Let me confine myself to an area about which I am more qualified to give impressions: the realm of the senses.

In 1969 Seosamh Ó Cuaig and Fennell – who despite an age difference had in common their respective attempts to understand, explain and affect social and political reality as it impinged on Conamara – set out in Ó Cuaig's car on the previously mentioned journey to meet Conradh na Gaeilge. It rained all the way and the windscreen wipers were faulty. The two men talked intently, as was their wont, all the way. Ó Cuaig occasionally remembered to hop out to rub a half-potato over the windscreen and thus achieve moderate visibility. When they arrived in Dublin, Fennell noted for the first time the deficiencies in the wiper apparatus and kindly brought the matter to Ó Cuaig's attention. Ó Cuaig patiently responded that it had been malfunctioning since they left Conamara. Why then, demanded Fennell with a puzzled air, did you not repair it before we left? This to a close friend and fellow intellectual who was equally undistinguished in things mechanical and who, when he brought the same car into a garage in Indreabhán, Conamara, accepted the proprietor's gloomy prognosis: '*Ah, a Josie, tá tú ag tempteáil Fate.*'

Fennell reminds me of Archimedes, who, pondering certain geometric problems in the sand before being taken away to be executed, uttered his only concern: do not disturb my circles.

On another occasion he borrowed my rubber boots to walk in the garden. Half-way round he stopped and declared that he would walk no further in such ill-fitting boots. Their removal revealed that he had not noticed my old socks were stuffed in the bottom of them. Fennell's tolerance of the discomfort reminded me of the Irish chieftain who did not flinch when St Patrick's sceptre impaled his foot, imagining that it was part of his baptism ceremony. This might suggest that Fennell is not truly immersed in the 'sensible' world, that his encounter with the scruffy reality of human existence is tangential, secondary to his attempts to make intelligible, to put in words and recommend remedies for, those aspects of existence that we prosaic mortals resignedly accept. All I have to say to that suspicion, even if it were justified, is that it would be a sad society that could not accommodate such a philosophic personality.

And accidentally I appear to have arrived at my main point: the apparent resentment of official Irish society toward the ideas of Fennell. This confuses me because I am aware that, before he abandoned Ireland in disgust for Italy nearly five years ago, Fennell was on friendly terms with many of the formative elements in Dublin society. My natural scepticism suggests the possibility that the very people whom he considered as friends were in fact *apparatchiks*, even carpet-baggers in the new social reality whose deficiencies he endlessly highlighted. For instance, one of his oldest friends was the mistress of one time Taoiseach Charles J. Haughey, with whom he was also on speaking terms. If he had access to such powerful people why did his ideas not impinge on their decisions? Or, at least, why did he never secure what they call 'advancement'? It seems sadly clear that his particular brand of social idealism was not, at that given point in our history, the one chosen pragmatically to sanctify present political and economic actions. I remember once chauffeuring Fennell out to Kinsealy, Dublin seat of Haughey, precise mission unknown, waiting patiently outside the gates and noticing the dissatisfaction of Fennell's demeanour when he finally emerged. I know that Fennell admired the independence of Haughey's stance on the Falklands War and that he expressed considerable disappointment at the man's subsequent stances when in power. On the occasion of this visit, I hardly think that he was asking the Taoiseach to invade the North, and in fact I did not inquire too closely about what had transpired at their meeting. The very fact that he could visit the Boss in his own home is what impressed me. I am easily impressed.

I have only recently begun to suspect why Fennell's ideas may sit so uncomfortably beside our thrusting new 'global' culture: he is a heretic. I understand the term to mean a person who adheres to fundamental beliefs, once held by all to be eternal truths, which are now considered superfluous, even irritating obstacles to progress. I think of the fields and hedgerows that support ecological diversity but which must now be bulldozed to make room for motorways. The idea of a Catholic, nationalist, united and self-reliant Ireland is no longer sustainable, and therefore has had to be hastily jettisoned. All suspected fellow-travellers of such ideas are unsound. It is heresy to oppose this enlightenment. Heretics are not innovators but custodians of ideas. They are essential social brakes, a bit like parents who try to prevent their children from making the same mistakes as themselves. And we know that all children at one stage or another consider their parents to be, however lovable, tyrannical fuddy-duddies. It is no coincidence that one of Fennell's extraordinary output of books, pamphlets, monographs and articles was entitled: *Heresy*.

One of the heresies that he and I share is that the 'periphery' is at least as important as the 'centre' – in a society, in a country, on a planet. Len Murray, Australian poet, put it well: only flat-earthers think that the planet has 'margins'. This viewpoint, which was the cornerstone of Fennell's existence in Conamara, I have happily embraced. It was the fuel that drove me for four years to produce my *Atlantean* trilogy of films in 1984 and which I am happy to be assured still has attractive resonances on this island. I will always remain indebted to Fennell for this insight.

This Ireland – as Conamara poet, playwright and humorist Johnny Chóil Mhaidhc once pointed out to me – may be a small island, but it's a big country. Therefore, members of the same class tend to know each other, at least by reputation. Some years ago I thought it might be possible for Aosdána, the Irish parliament of artists, of which I am a member, to expand its criteria of creativity from the confines of poetry, literary fiction, music and the visual arts to include creative and independent thinkers like Conor Cruise O'Brien and Desmond Fennell. As constituted, neither Edmund Burke nor Tom Paine would have been eligible to join. I was encouraged in this ambition by the successful nomination – on the grounds of his exquisite prose and cartography – of Tim Robinson to Aosdána, a nomination I enthusiastically supported as a member of the Toscaireacht (steering committee).

However, when I privately inquired of a cross section of 37 of the 150 members as to their attitude to a Fennell nomination, only 14 replied. One wrote a huge 'NO' on a postcard; another an equally emphatic 'YES'. Most of the responses were sympathetic and supportive, but many expressed doubt about Fennell's chances of being elected. I was aware that members of Aosdána cannot be intimately familiar with every other artist's work and mainly rely on the recommendation of members whose judgment they respect. I was also aware that a timely exposure in the media of any given nominee can be influential; despite their popular image, artists are keenly aware of and sensitive to what is going on around them. In other words, they are human; therefore a negative media image can also militate against a candidate. The artists who responded, although mainly positive towards the idea, were keenly aware of this dimension and therefore pessimistic.

At almost precisely this time, an article appeared in *Magill* in which Fennell was quoted as having severely critical opinions about Aosdána, the very body that I was hoping to persuade to accept him. I despaired of him then; the man has no concept of the slithering, political necessities of making friends and influencing people. Yet, allied to a substantial body of creative thought, would this quality in a prospective member not be invaluable to a body such as Aosdána? Not wishing to embarrass my friend, I decided not to proceed with the nomination – yet.

I can think of several possible reasons why my fellow-artists – many of whom are as agnostic as myself – shared my fears about his chances. Firstly, Fennell's insistence that a partial step on the way towards Ireland recovering a self-confident identity (as distinct from the trading post status that it enjoys at present) would be through an admission and retrieval of its personality as, de facto, a Catholic nation. In the recent thirty years of revisionism of all things 'Irish', this is not a popular political platform. I am ambivalent on this specific issue; I am of the generation of Irish people whose religion equally damaged and spurred them on. However, any form of social cohesion – social glue, I call it – including Roman Catholicism, would be preferable to the spiritual wasteland we now inhabit. Indeed, most of the recent radical statements about our society have come exclusively from CORI, the Conference of Religious in Ireland. On the other hand, I stoutly believe that the fact of rampant anti-intellectualism – which Fennell considers to have militated against his ideas, although he himself energetically attacks the ideas of fellow intellectuals – can be at least partially traced to a period when the Catholic Church and its gombeen collaborators dominated intellectual discourse in this island. It is hard to revive a worthy version of a discredited intellectual climate. What would, in my opinion, be more worth reviving would be the culture of the dispersed and gradually silenced footsoldiers and footmen whom the Protestant Ascendancy shamelessly abandoned in the southern part of this island. Their quietude left a stultifying intellectual homogeneity in the public culture, only occasionally punctuated by figures such as Hubert Butler. To put it another way, the Irish anti-intellectualism that Fennell properly excoriates may have less to do with the withering of, for instance, hierarchical Irish Catholicism than with the diminution of Protestant free thinking. In this matter alone I tend to agree with, of all people, Eoghan Harris.

My impression simplifies – and possibly distorts – Fennell's perspective. My comments are solely intended to emphasise that he examines problems that many of us sidestep. For instance, his early and repeated suggestion of respect for all the traditions on this island, especially including the Northern British, and the possibility of federal arrangements – a community of communities, as he put it, to assuage the ongoing antagonisms – long anticipated the Good Friday agreement. He is never credited with this foresight.

There is one subject on which it is hard to disagree with him: the eggs that were necessarily broken when the American omelette called 'women's liberation' was adopted by the Irish middle class. He was once kind enough to give me credit for the perception that there was a neo-Victorian dimension to this phenomenon. For instance, the indignation shown towards males who regarded females with desire, i.e. treating them as 'sex objects', tried to deny the most fundamental biological instinct in both male and female. The objections made for evolutionary nonsense. The ideological attempt to discourage men and women from regarding each other lustily belonged in medieval times. The parallel – and successful – attempt to portray men as the sole initiators and perpetrators of domestic violence has recently been shown to be also grotesquely unbalanced. Violence is not the exclusive prerogative of either sex. Fennell has been saying this unfashionable thing for years – as have many of the sane women and men I know, but *sotto voce*. The ideological revolution, necessary though it was, called 'feminisim', may be likened to the opening of Pandora's box, an event from which some unmanageable problems were rashly generated. This apparent liberation, like the consumer culture that facilitated it, is – as is the fate of all revolutions – beginning to be questioned by the common sense of men and women. Fortunately, when by the opening of Pandora's box many blessings took flight, one remained: hope.

And hope may be what has supported Fennell's intransigent posture for the past forty years. He likes to quote my all-time favourite filmmaker, Ingmar Bergman:

> You see, in Sweden we have everything, or rather, we live in the illusion of having everything. But in the midst of this wealth a great emptiness holds sway… In my films I describe this emptiness and everything that people think up in an attempt to fill it, and I believe that in doing this I am tackling the problem of the present time, its most important problem, that is, how to give a purely 'welfare' civilisation a spiritual and human content. At all events this is the problem that I personally am concerned with all the time. Don't ask me to talk of other things – I couldn't.

By contrast, Fennell as thinker is driven to incessantly discuss 'other things'. In recent years he has broadened his palate to an almost apocalyptic view, pronouncing judgement on what he refers to as postwestern civilisation and postmodern chaos. Because his thesis – crudely, that Western, Christian civilisation ceased to be either civilised or Christian at the moment of Hiroshima – perilously undermines the very ground on which we strut, the very basis of our confidence; it is not welcome. We are almost in John the Baptist territory here. This was well illustrated on his last television appearance in Ireland some years ago when he was invited to discuss his latest book on the subject: *Uncertain Dawn*. The normal custom was that writers were accorded, at least initially, a fairly courteous reception from their host, whatever about the audience. On this *Late Late Show* a chosen panel of hand-picked and intellectually lightweight hecklers effectively shouted Fennell down, preventing the writer from calmly explaining the basis of his critique. One of them even had the bad manners to plug his own forthcoming book. Gay Byrne sat idly by. It was a shocking spectacle, not just to his friends but to any fair-minded observer. I half-expected to see Salome grinning in the audience. Part of the tragedy was that Fennell's own son was the producer of the show. I understand that, in a scrupulous attempt to avoid charges of nepotism, he had left the organisation of this particular slot on the show entirely in the hands of, perhaps significantly, a female researcher. This necessary professional decision resulted in a travesty of broadcasting. I think the event may have been, for Fennell, the last straw. He now writes from a village outside Rome where his latest daring has produced an iconoclastic *The Revision of European History*. Whatever one's opinion of Fennell, he can never be accused of absorption in petty matters; his canvas is De Millean.

And at the back of it all, what? Certainly he still retains the sense of wonder glimpsed in the title of his first travel book, *Mainly in Wonder*, and continued years afterwards in the deceptively clear reportage of his *A Connacht Journey*. Sometimes I have detected a personal quality that falls somewhere between naivety and innocence; equipped with this, he seems to wander through a world populated by three-card tricksters.

In case I have given the impression of an impractical dreamer, out of touch with the earthy stuff of life as lived, let me leave you with the following image. The thin soil of my Conamara garden rests on granite, is very soggy and difficult to drain. This requires the cutting of tiny channels through the unyielding stone. The last time Fennell visited Conamara, he borrowed my chisel and lump hammer and exited the house. For the next couple of hours he was to be glimpsed, squatting beside one of these narrow channels, patiently chipping away.

I think it is an appropriate image for his Sisyphean life, which, though the above may have the atmosphere of an obituary, he is still fortunately celebrating.

A Jaundiced Ear
(The Journal of Music, September 2012)

Leonard Cohen is in the middle of another world tour. One can only say: what a man!

Or: how sad.

Two years ago he was in the west of Ireland.

A W.B. Yeats twilight hovered over one of his favourite places, Lissadell, County Sligo. The distant ensemble of musicians, so small onstage they looked like puppets to the outdoor audience, were barely discernible. Two moths caught in a spotlight began to dance. A voice sang:

Oh let me see your beauty when the witnesses are gone
Let me feel you moving like they do in Babylon ...
Dance me to the end of love.

The amplified sound turned the moths into fireflies, boomed at 10,000 ant-like people. Most were rapt, others a continuous parade of pint-bearers to the left and loo-seekers to the right, as the principal puppet sang:

Like a bird on the wire
Like a drunk in a midnight choir.

The irony was ignored, the urgent paraders and queuers only vaguely attentive to the venerable poet/minstrel on the distant stage.

Dusk intensified; the puppets were gradually seen to be playing and singing in perfect synchronism with giant figures on TV screens to left and right. Soon the darkness camouflaged both the dimly lit puppets and also, blessedly, the parade of drinkers obstructing our view. We could transfer our gaze from the stage, relax into savouring the real thing: a live, closed-circuit TV broadcast of Leonard Cohen. Only the huge screens seemed real, the puppets merely miming. One hundred metres separated us from the flesh and blood performers but we were seduced by the greater reality of the images on the screens – as, presumably, intended. But 'Field Commander Cohen' was still holding his own, the self-described 'patron saint of envy and the grocer of despair'.

It was quality music: well-rehearsed playing; outstanding riffs by old and young pros; the solo performer genuflecting like a celebrant, doffing his hat in tribute to his ensemble, to his angelic trio of a backing choir. The audience was enthralled. I could already imagine it on Sky Arts 2.

At which thought I straightened up. There was a disjunction here. Between form and content. What was going on? I could be sitting at home in comfort looking at this on TV instead of wrestling with a bad back in a plastic chair. He sang on:

Everybody knows it's coming apart
Take one last look at this Sacred Heart
Before it blows
And everybody knows.

Why had no print commentator warned me? All I had read was journeymen and women hyperboleying the occasion in their broadcheats – which coincidentally depend on expensive half-page spreads to publicise such commercial ventures as these. The back-story, which they had recycled endlessly, was that the Cohen of our youth, latterday Buddhist, had been robbed of his savings; the hint was that we should help an old friend in trouble. This was his third year collecting, repeating exactly the same programme, the same genuflections, the same hat doffing, from Oslo to Melbourne, from New Zealand to Phnom Penh! Surely he had by now recouped enough at least for a pension? It was journalistic nonsense. Cohen doesn't need us, materially or spiritually; we need him.

Other comments were merely ageist. They all marvelled rightly at the energy of the old man, the phenomenon of the performance, as if Leonard Cohen at seventy-four was akin to a circus dog that could talk. Matteradamn whether it made sense or not; the miracle was that it could still get up on its hindlegs and talk – and sing:

Because of a few songs
Wherein I spoke of their mystery,
Women have been
Exceptionally kind
To my old age.

They always were. They still are and deservedly so.

If only there were a social philosopher at hand to answer my queries.

Why, for instance, would hundreds of thousands of adults pay exorbitant sums to be present at what is really a closed-circuit TV show? (My own alibi? I was the convalescent guest of a generous and beautiful old friend.) From what I could see of my fellows in Lissadell I was possibly the person next oldest to Leonard himself. The next candidate in line was the man in front of me who hadn't the energy to clap, merely to raise both arms in silent adoration at the end of each song.

My mind wandered, as is my geriatric privilege, to a line from his 'Closing Time':

And I just don't care what happens next
Looks like freedom, but it feels like death.

And then, bizarrely, Leni Riefenstahl, filmmaker, came to mind. Perhaps my subconscious nudged me with the fact that in 1964 Cohen, coming from a tiny Montreal Jewish minority, had ironically entitled a collection of his poems *Flowers for Hitler*.

Remember Riefenstahl? She made classic films of the original Nuremberg rallies and the 1936 Olympic Games. Whether they were art or propaganda films, celebratory or warning, is irrelevant. They were overwhelming. She never made another decent film; her Nazi sponsors were vanquished. Why did I think of her? Did the larger-than-life screen images of talented musicians on this Lissadell stage remind me of her Goebbels-scale work?

I fear massed audiences, but how indelicate of me to align such opposite messages, separated by seventy years and sixty million dead. I realise that Kurt Vonnegut was right: old men are obscene and accurate! But consider dispassionately the technology, the very act, the size of the events in question. Both suggested we were tiny, powerless, lost, that our pain could be assuaged if we temporarily lost ourselves, became idolatrous followers. Followers of what?

Another Canadian ghost joined in these musings: Marshall McLuhan. His cliché resonated in my head: the medium is the message. The irony of it! An aged Jewish poet still singing songs of love, anguish and despair (flavoured by wonderful pinches of black humour and a rich invocation of Catholic pieties) separated by seventy years from a raging anti-Semite preaching revenge for the Treaty of Versailles but – and here is the point – both using exactly the same pyrotechnical principles of showbusiness: amplification, gigantism, Goebbels' big lie (repetition), and Barnum's dictum about never going broke underestimating public taste. To me, what Cohen said or sang was becoming blurred in the hugeness of the presentation, despite the fact that, on a personal note, long ago at Christmas 1967 in his hometown Montreal, his just-issued first record, *Songs of Leonard Cohen*, became my soundtrack to a love affair worthy of the maestro himself.

Cohen is a year older than me. I still love many of his original songs, 'Suzanne', 'Sisters of Mercy', 'Who By Fire' *et alia*. Even though this night his voice was reduced to a few rich-as-Robeson bass notes, even though he had no higher register left, even if there was a mantra-like sameness to his melodies, I ached as he sang them again. The poet in him, his lyrics, were what always seduced us. But this was different: the packed amphitheatre mocked the whole point of his persona of intimacy.

Yes you who must leave everything that you cannot control.
It begins with your family, but soon it comes 'round to your soul.

At this point I had to seek real painkillers (as usual, I had lost my prescription and on medical advice must not anaesthesise myself with alcohol). So superb was the military (hmm) precision of this occasion, I had little difficulty excavating the young doctor on duty from the portaloo crowd. No problem, he said, when I mentioned recent surgery, and he agreed to give me the required medicaments.

'I'd say you've been kept busy this weekend, especially with Westlife on Friday night,' I sympathised with him.

'Not at all,' he replied. 'In fact it's this Cohen crowd which has me run off my feet.'

'What!'

'Yes. Elderly people trying to recapture their youth. Drinking amounts that they might have been able to absorb in the past. But no longer.' He spoke kindly.

The beer stalls, burger joints, oyster counter and coffee dispensers still did a roaring trade. Meanwhile the queues for the portaloos raced the shadows. At the interval I met a handsome young woman of my acquaintance. 'I want to bop,' she complained, 'but not on my own.' I realised I had seen nobody dancing.

Another interpretation: the supermarket culture – LIDL, IKEA, M&S, B&Q, the mall experience – has wiped out the old intimacies of the small community. It has closed the corner shops and little post offices, opened drink emporiums, and turned us into domestic alcoholics. But we are social animals, are nothing without social intercourse. The nuclear family is no longer enough. The recording for television of open-air gigs like Riefenstahl's, the Beatles, Live Aid, U2's Zoo TV tour, Yevtushenko's poetry masses in the sixties, Pope John Paul's 1979 hysteria in the Phoenix Park, Dublin, and yes, tonight, Cohen's, have one thing in common: providing a placebo for the human need of communality – the very need that Goebbels cashed in on. The music is secondary, anticipation of the spectacle everything. The Beatles learned this, feared it, retreated from the mob hysteria to the studios. At least Leonard has the grace to spend much of his time going down on one knee, seeming to beg our forgiveness, our absolution for the grossness of the overwhelming technology and commercialism which diminisheth even him.

In peace as much as war, wherever there is money to be made, we become a technologically manipulable outdoor mass, not just of teenagers or soccer fanatics, but of all who are in need of the reassurance of shared human experience, the camaraderie of our species. The condition embraces all classes and ages, has extended to the disappointed middle-aged and old. Lose me in the crowd, take me out of myself, save me from my life. Give me parables. Expense no object. I suppose, in a way, this is preferable to war.

Cohen once put music to a minor piece by my all-time favourite Canadian poet, F.R. Scott. I wish Cohen had set the following Scott poem, 'To Certain Friends':

They make a virtue of having an open mind...
To the rain of facts that deepens the drought of the will...

Till one day, after the world has tired of waiting,
While they are busy arguing about the obvious,
A half-witted demagogue will walk away with their children.

Lissadell made me believe that we are ripe for another despot. Is the rough beast's hour come round at last? If so, it certainly won't be that decent and gentle old minstrel, Leonard Cohen; I can't see him slouching towards Bethlehem to be born, not even in a Popemobile. I hope he confines himself to the acoustic guitar. And no cameras, lights, action, please. Just a couple of fireflies.

Part IV

Final Thoughts
Smaointe Deireanacha

Death
(Cassandra Voices, August 2021)

I'm of an age to be intrigued by death.

My 84-year-old grandmother, widowed, came to live with our family, and took over my bedroom. I was forced to give up the room, to share instead with a sibling.

The old woman was hale and hearty, retained her wits, preserved her down-to-earth assessment of life, referring to her late, much loved husband – my favourite male relation – as 'the old fool'. One day she said to me: 'Ye're just waiting for me to die, aren't ye? Well yiz'll be waiting a long time.' I was taken aback at her frankness. She died a year later.

When my old friend Dinno was on his deathbed, I asked him what he was thinking of. He said: 'Gone-ness. I'm wondering what gone-ness will be like', and did not need to elaborate. We had understood each other well.

My father roared indignantly on his deathbed in the old Mater hospital. His wife and other children had gone home, reassured that he had survived the first heart attack and would survive until morning. I stayed and was the only witness to his last belligerent protest.

My mother spent her last days carefully organising her own funeral and the disposal of her one asset (a house). She waited only for my return from Canada until, in my presence, she removed the oxygen mask from her mouth and stopped gasping for breath.

I am of an age to be intrigued by these quite normal dramas. Love dies. Beauty dies. Everybody and every thing dies. As Woody Allen said: 'I'm not afraid of death. I just don't want to be there when it happens.'

What he might have meant was: better to lose your mind before your body gives up.

Dementia and Alzheimer's are a tragedy for the nearest and dearest but a blessing for the sufferers because they don't suffer at all; they are unaware of the impending disaster. What a way to go!

One of my brothers died in a similar condition. I envied him. One of my sisters died, still worrying about it. Poor thing. Another sister, the eldest in the family, is fortunately still alive. She's lucky too; has no idea what's going on around her, I think.

The phenomenon is an everyday one and still we wonder at it; in what sense are we alive one day and gone the next, vanished without trace? No body. No soul. All disappeared, remembered briefly, forgotten forever. How extraordinary. Even when we breed frantically, seeking immortality, knowing our seed will also die, we still do it, procreating, making stains on life, producing work, writing, building solid bridges and skyscrapers, empires. All made of dust. Even dinosaurs lived a million years and now are merely known as skeletons.

People invented the idea of heavenly immortality: wishful thinking. They even invented god. We are at heart optimists.

There is no sting in death without consciousness; and nobody knows yet of what precisely that consists of. Fortunately death can be simulated under the surgeon's knife until we wake and are reminded by pain of what we have mindlessly endured. Think of that.

Some people choose euthanasia but that's a sin, we're warned. It's a cop out. We should be allowed to enjoy this once in a life experience. It is unique to each of us, just like our birth, to be celebrated as a never-to-be-repeated exercise. We are born astride a grave with, not a silver spoon, but a shovel in our hands.

I once speculated that nobody dies. We are bundles of transformed energy – the frantic impulses of copulation when we are conceived. Food becomes our energy fuel. What happens this energy at the point of death? Energy cannot be destroyed, only transformed like breath into gas, into condensation, into water into ice into steam etc etc. So what happens to us – bundles of energy? My speculation involves the millions and billions of galaxies and further billions of stars in each galaxy. Each of us, I suggest, becomes a twinkling star in the endless infinity of the universe. There is room for everybody out there.

There's a happy thought. Perish our tiny worries. We are immortal. We just leave our egos behind. And good riddance.

So Far, So Good
(Ollscoil na Gaillimhe/University of Galway, 2022)

Bob's speech on being awarded an Honorary Doctor of Arts by Ollscoil na Gaillimhe/University of Galway in April 2022. An English translation follows.

Nuair a bhí mise naoi mbliana d'aois bhí timpiste agam agus briseadh m'uillinn.

Chaith mé sé seachtaine san ospidéal mar gheall ar fhadhb ar a dtugtar morgadh, nó *'gangrene'*. Bhí an baol ann go gcaillfinn mo lámh.

Ach níor chaill.

Nuair a míníodh dom nárbh iad paidreacha mo mháthar ach scil na ndochtúirí a shábháil an lámh thogair mé, nuair a bheinn fásta suas, go mbeinn – ní i mo shagart – ach i mo dhochtúir.

Bhuel, thóg sé breis is ceithre scór bliain orm an teideal sin a ghnóthú. Anois, faoi dheireadh tá sé agam, Dochtúireacht, *by dad!*

Ach faraor, níor éirigh liomsa tada a leigheas ariamh. Agus níl leigheas fós agam ar an saol féin. Mar a dúirt mo sheanchara, an scríbhneoir Kurt Vonnegut, *'Life is no way to treat an animal.'*

Cheapfá, mar gheall ar an gcéim seo, gur saoi de chineál éicint mise.

Ní hea ná baol air. Níl mise cinnte faoi rud ar bith ach aon rud amháin: an t-aon leigheas atá ar an saol ná píosa gáire.

Faoi mar a dúirt an fear a bhí ag titim anuas ón *skyscraper* agus é ag teannadh leis an talamh: *'So far, so good!'*

Is í seo an chéad cháilíocht acadúil a bronnadh ormsa ó fuair mé an Ardteistiméireacht beagnach seachtó bliain ó shin.

Le bheith macánta libh, níor chuir mise mórán suime san oideachas tríú leibhéal seachas gur thuig mé i gcónaí cé chomh haineolach is a bhí mé.

Luaigh mé é sin leis an scríbhneoir Francis Stuart blianta fada ó shin agus is éard a d'fhreagair sé: *'Cherish your ignorance. It is the only unique thing you possess.'*

In ainneoin na comhairle sin, sa mbliain 1967, thóg mé scíth ón scannánaíocht agus ón teilifís agus chaith mé bliain i mo *'auditor'* in ollscoil i gCeanada, ag léamh agus ag éisteacht le léachtaí faoin tsocheolaíocht agus gach ar bhain léi.

Ní raibh mé ag iarraidh céim a bhaint amach. Ba iad na léachtaí sin a d'oscail fuinneoga i m'intinn agus a scaoil isteach solas geal an eolais.

Den chéad uair thuig mé cé chomh ceangailte – nó *'relative'* – is atá chuile rud: chuile chreideamh, chuile idé-eolaíocht, chuile shórt beo. Oscailt súl a bhí ann agus bhronn sé saoirse intinne orm.

Ach mar a dúirt m'athair blianta roimhe sin: *'A little education is a dangerous thing.'*

B'fhíor dó: faoi dheireadh thréig mé creideamh m'athar agus creideamh mo shinsear agus chuaigh mé leis an námhaid: an sóisialachas.

D'fhoghlaim mé rud eile fós, sin a fhlaithiúlaí is atá scoláirí lena gcuid eolais: casadh mórscoláirí orm anuas trí na blianta, leithéidí Heinrich Wagner, Lelia Doolan, John Blacking, Paddy Henry, Alf MacLochlainn, Hilary Richardson, Micheál O'Connell, Deasún Fennell, Françoise Henry, Pádraic de Bhaldraithe, Donncha Ó hÉallaithe agus go leor eile agus roinn chuile dhuine beo acu a saineolas go fial liomsa.

Ba léir go raibh luí acu le filíocht Robert Graves: *'we expect scholars to excavate cleanly, so that their findings can be interpreted by poets and artists.'*

Ar ndóigh, tá filí agus ealaíontóirí ann atá in ann eolas a chur ó mhaith freisin agus mísc a dhéanamh de. Dhiúltaigh mise do bheagnach chuile chreideamh mar gheall go raibh siad, mar a dúirt an té a dúirt, ina *'anathema to creativity'*. Agus faoi mar a dúirt Picasso, *'art is the illusion that illustrates the truth.'*

Saol saor ó chreideamh diongbháilte i rud ar bith a chaithimse ach ag an am céanna tá dóchas agam i chuile rud, 'sé sin le rá, *I can hold six contradictions in my head at the one time.*

Tá réiteach ag Gerard Manley Hopkins, an té a scríobh 'Pied Beauty', ar an gceist seo seo:

Glory be to God for dappled things...
All things counter, original, spare, strange;
Whatever is fickle, freckled (who knows how?)

Nach mé atá sásta go bhfuil intinn '*pied*' agus '*dappled*' nó bhreac agam. Is cruthúnas é nach bhfuil mé fásta suas go fóill agus go bhfuil mé chomh hóg agus chomh sean libhse, a dhaoine uaisle. *All our brains are dappled.*

Ach tá bealach timpeall air sin freisin, sin samhlaíocht agus fiosracht. Bígí i gcónaí fiosrach.

A bhuíochas leis an onóir seo, agus, dar ndóigh, le mo sheisear clainne agus le mo bhean chéile fhoighneach, faoi dheireadh tá mé in ann a rá gur mór an sásamh a bhain mé as an saol.

Tuigim gur gradam onórach an dochtúireacht seo sna dána.

Bhí ar mo laoch, Dean Jonathan Swift, a cheann féin a cheannach ach d'úsáid sé an teideal i gcónaí ina chuid filíochta.

I ndáiríre, mar gheall go bhfuil a fhios agam go maith nach bhfuil an onóir seo tuillte agam, tá mé fíorbhuíoch d'Uachtarán na hOllscoile seo agus den institiúid féin.

Go raibh maith agaibh uilig.

***

When I was nine years old, I had an accident and broke my elbow. I spent six weeks in the hospital because of gangrene. The danger was that my arm would be lost.

But it wasn't.

When it was explained to me that it was not the prayers of my mother but the skill of the doctors that saved my arm, I decided, when I was older, that I would be – not a priest – but a doctor.

Well, it took almost 80 years to get that title, but at last, a doctorate, by dad!

But alas, I have never healed anything in my life. And I still don't have a remedy for life. As my old friend, the writer Kurt Vonnegut, said: 'Life is no way to treat an animal.'

You would think, because of this degree, that I am a wise man. That is far from the truth. I am sure of nothing but this: the only medicine for life is a sense of humour. As the man who was falling from a skyscraper and getting nearer to the ground said: 'So far, so good!'

This is the first educational qualification that has been bestowed on me since I did the Leaving Cert almost seventy years ago. To tell you the truth, I have not had much connection with third-level education except for one thing: I always understood how ignorant I was.

I said this to the writer Francis Stuart years ago and he answered: 'Cherish your ignorance. It is the only unique thing you possess.'

Despite this advice, in 1967, I took a break from filming and television and spent a year as an 'auditor' at a university in Canada, reading and listening to lectures on sociology and everything associated with it. I did not want a degree however. These lectures opened the windows of my mind and let in light in the form of knowledge. For the first time, I understood how connected, or relative, everything is: every belief, every ideology, everything alive. It gave me mental freedom.

But as my father said years before that: 'A little education is a dangerous thing'. He was absolutely right: in the end, I left the faith of my father, that of my ancestors, and I went with the enemy: socialism.

But I also learnt just how generous scholars are with their knowledge: over the years, I have met with scholars such as Heinrich Wagner, Lelia Doolan, John Blacking, Paddy Henry, Deasún Fennell, Alf MacLochlainn, Hilary Richardson, Micheál O'Connell, Françoise Henry, Pádraic de Bhaldraithe, Donncha Ó hÉallaithe and many more. They shared their knowledge with me. They understood what the poet Robert Graves said: 'we expect scholars to excavate cleanly, so that their findings can be interpreted by poets and artists.'

It should be said that poets and artists can make a mess of those findings. I threw out almost every belief because they were, as another person said, 'anathema to creativity'. And as Picasso said, 'art is the illusion that illustrates the truth.'

Now I can live without a strict belief in anything, but with faith in everything, at the same time. That is to say: I can hold six contradictions in my head at the one time.

There is a solution to this sickness in Gerard Manley Hopkins. As he wrote in 'Pied Beauty':

Glory be to God for dappled things...
All things counter, original, spare, strange;
Whatever is fickle, freckled (who knows how?)

I am happy that I have a 'pied' and 'dappled' mind. That is the proof that I have not grown up yet, that I am as young and as old as you, ladies and gentlemen. All our brains are dappled. But there is a solution to that too: imagination and curiosity. Always be curious.

Because of this honour, if I include six wonderful children and a patient wife, at last I can say: I have enjoyed life.

I understand that this is an honorary doctorate in arts. My hero, Dean Jonathan Swift, had to buy his doctorate, and he used the title constantly in his poetry.

In truth, because I know well that I do not deserve this honour, I am very grateful to the President of the university and to the institution.

Thank you very much everyone.

Acknowledgements

The publication of *Count Me Out: Selected Writings of Filmmaker Bob Quinn* would not have been possible without the generous support of the following: Acadamh na hOllscolaíochta Gaeilge, Ollscoil na Gaillimhe, An Cheathrú Rua, in particular Treasa Uí Lorcáin and Aodh Ó Coileáin; Grattan Healy; Paul Cummins and Telegael; Alan Esslemont and TG4; and Bill Whelan. Sincere gratitude to these friends and colleagues.

Thank you to the publishers who kindly granted permission to reproduce the essays: Lilliput Press for the chapter from *The Atlantean Irish*; O'Brien Press for extracts from *Smokey Hollow* and *Maverick* (the latter originally published by Brandon Books); New Island Books for 'Imagining Conamara' and 'Dark Soul'; Goldsmith Press for 'James McKenna and *Cloch*'; Veritas for 'Why Desmond Fennell is No. 2'; *New Hibernia Review* for 'Conamara Revolution', and *Comhar* for 'Raidió Pobail'. Thank you also to *Hot Press*; *The Irish Times*; Gemma Creagh of *Film Ireland*; Conor Murphy of the Dublin Business School, which holds the archive of *Film Ireland*; the staff of Ardán, which holds the archive of *Film West*; and Frank Armstrong of *Cassandra Voices*.

Thank you as always to colleagues at the *Journal of Music* and Boluisce Press for their dedicated work on this title, in particular Assistant Editor Shannon McNamee and Editorial and Marketing Assistant Oliver Quinn.

Many people provided welcome advice, information and assistance including Donncha Ó hÉallaithe, Seosamh Ó Cuaig, Helen Quinn, Miriam Allen, Joe Comerford, Lelia Doolan, Norbert Payne, Hannah Quinn, Tim Fleming, Dominic Quinn, Odí Ní Chéilleachair, Jerry White, Rónán Mac Con Iomaire and Vinny Browne. Thank you also to Robert, Bairbre and Marcus Quinn, Colm and Kay Quinn, and Pat and Mairin Quinn.

For their support of my father's work, thank you to Galway City of Film, Sunniva O'Flynn and the Irish Film Institute, Professor Ciarán Ó hÓgartaigh, former President of Ollscoil na Gaillimhe/University of Galway, and President Michael D. Higgins and Sabina Higgins.

Finally, thank you to Liz, Ruby and Saise Quinn for all of their support and enthusiasm for this project. *Mo bhuíochas libh go léir.*

Filmography

RTÉ

Kindergarten (1964)

Love Song of J. Alfred Prufrock (1964)

This Place, These Shapes, These Human Beings (1965)

Discovery series

- *Puck Fair* (1965)
- *The Jews in Ireland* (1965)
- *Many Hands Make Life Work* (1965)
- *The Nurse* (1965)

Horizon series

- *Cheshire Homes* (1966)
- *Why Don't They Shoot People?* (1966)
- *Inside the Outsider* (1966)
- *The Silent World* (1966)
- *The Island* (1966)
- *Missing, Believed Dead* (1966)
- *The Flower Pot Society* (1967)

Cinegael

Fág an Bealach (1973)

Oireachtas na nGael (1973)

Caoineadh Airt Uí Laoire (1974)

Cloch (1975)

A Film Board for Ireland (1976)

Self-Portrait with Red Car (1976)

Vet on the Rocks (1976)

Poitín (1978)

Listen (1978)

An Bealach Eile (1978)

The Family (1978)

Aisling Gheal series

- *Ceol na Húicéar*: Stockton's Wing (1979)
- *Ceol na Húicéar*: De Danann, Áine Uí Fhátharta, Pádraig Bradley and Brian Bourke. (1979)

- *Ceol na Húicéar*: Mary Bergin, Bruce du Ve, Éilín Ní Ríordán, Prionsias Mac Donncha, Seosamh Mac Con Iomaire, Máirtín Ó Gríofa and Jay Murphy. (1979)
- *Ceol na Húicéar*: Noel Hill, Tony Linnane, Liam O'Hara, Tommy Mannion and Brian Bourke. (1979)
- *Cruinniú na mBád*: Johnny Jimmy Mac Donncha and the crew of *An Mhaighdean Mhara*. (1979)
- *Master Musicians of Jajouka* (1980)
- *A Jehovah in Galway* (1980)
- *Oileán Mhanann* (1980)
- *Na hAncairí* (1980)
- *Peadar Lamb* (1980)
- *Ballymun School* (1980)

Gaillimh De Danann (1980)

Laetha Deiridh na Gaeltachta/The Last Days of the Gaeltacht (1980): presented by Desmond Fennell.

I M'Aonar Seal series
- *Lillipup* (1980): Brian Bourke, Jay Murphy, Pádraic Ó Carra and Malachy Bourke.
- *Josie Sheáin Jack Mac Donncha* (1981)
- *Edward Delaney* (1981)
- *Tony MacMahon* (1981)
- *Flann Ó Riain* (1981)
- *Pearse Hutchinson* (1981)

Seimineár ar an Sean-nós sa Spidéal (1981): Mícheál Ó Súilleabháin, Máire Áine Ní Dhonnchadha, Seán Mac Réamoinn, Breandán Ó Madagáin, Pat Phádraic Tom Ó Conghaile, Nioclás Tóibín, Caitlín Maude, Tomás Mac Eoin, Liam Ó Conchúir, Máirtín Ó Conghaile, Tadhg Ó Riagáin, Peadar Mac Donncha, Seosamh Mac an Iomaire and Treasa Ní Mhiolláin.

Atlantean (1984)

Budawanny (1987)

Pobal i London series (1988)
- *Taxi*
- *South and O'Hanlon's*
- *Busking*

217

- *Union Tavern*
- *Fly Tippers*

Pobal i mBoston series (1989)

- *Máire*
- *Illegal*
- *Clann*
- *The Archivist*
- *Scoil Sailearna*
- *Transplanted*

Pobal in Deutschland series (1990)

- *Morris Minor*
- *Mná na hÉireann*
- *Gael Force 8*
- *Celts in Bonn*
- *Ceol in Deutschland*

Muintearas (1990)

The Bishop's Story (1994)

Graceville: Na Connemaras i Minnesota (1996): presented by Seosamh Ó Cuaig

Atlantean 2: Navigatio (1998)

It Must Be Done Right (1999): Donal McCann

Damhsa an Deoraí/The Emigrant Dance (2004)

An Chéad Laoch (2003): James Brendan Connolly; presented by Seosamh Ó Cuaig.

Splanc Deireadh na Gaeltachta (2004): Gluaiseacht Cearta Sibhialta na Gaeltachta; research and script by Donncha Ó hÉallaithe.

Con Tempo Goes West (2005)

They'll Never Show That (2006): Joe McAnthony

Vox Humana (2008)

Bog Graffiti (2019)

Bibliography

Sit Down and Be Counted: The Cultural Evolution of a Television Station, Jack Dowling, Lelia Doolan and Bob Quinn (1969)
Atlantean: Ireland's North African and Maritime Heritage (1986)
Smokey Hollow (1991)
Conamara: An Tír Aneoil – The Unknown Country, photographs by Bob Quinn; text by Liam Mac Con Iomaire (1996)
Maverick: A Dissident View of Broadcasting Today (2001)
The Atlantean Irish: Ireland's Oriental and Maritime Heritage (2005)
The Accompanist (2006)
Aristophane's Apple (2020)
Darwin on the Shannon: A Story of Survival (2021)
The Specific Gravity of Water (2022)

For more on Bob Quinn's work, visit www.cinegael.ie.

Index